THE POEMS OF MICHAEL WIGGLESWORTH

Edited by
Ronald A. Bosco

UNIVERSITY
PRESS OF
AMERICA

Lanham • New York • London

Copyright © 1989 by

University Press of America,® Inc.

4720 Boston Way
Lanham, MD 20706

3 Henrietta Street
London WC2E 8LU England

All rights reserved

Printed in the United States of America

British Cataloging in Publication Information Available

Library of Congress Cataloging-in-Publication Data

Wigglesworth, Michael, 1631–1705.
[Poems]
The poems of Michael Wigglesworth / edited by Ronald A. Bosco.
p. cm.
Bibliography: p.
I. Bosco, Ronald A. II. Title.
PS871.A4   1989   88–34214 CIP
821'.4– –dc19
ISBN 0–8191–7345–2 (alk. paper)

All University Press of America books are produced on acid-free paper.
The paper used in this publication meets the minimum requirements of American
National Standard for Information Sciences—Permanence of Paper for Printed Library
Materials, ANSI Z39.48–1984.   ∞

FOREWORD

The Poems of Michael Wigglesworth had its inception in the requests of my undergraduate and graduate students, who, having been introduced in my classes to occasional anthologized snippets of Wigglesworth's verse, wished directions to greater access to his poems and more detailed information about the man. Typically, the directions I was able to give them only increased their frustration, for despite the phenomenal currency Wigglesworth's poetry enjoyed in pre-Revolutionary America and the influence he personally exerted on Puritan New England during the politically troublesome years between 1685 and 1705, both his poetry and his reputation have languished in a virtual limbo for nearly two centuries as a result of the negative, revisionist attitudes advanced against Puritans and their art by nineteenth- and twentieth-century American literary critics. Tangible evidence of Wigglesworth's fall from critical respectability can be found in the fact that over the past century only one substantive biography of the man memorialized as *Maldonatus Orthodoxus* and few substantial critical assessments of his merit as a poet have appeared. Similarly, although there have been a few attempts in this century to put Wigglesworth's known publications into some kind of bibliographic perspective, attempts to prepare editions of the poetry have been frustrated by the sheer mass of Wigglesworth's poetic achievement, by the difficulty of deciding on the authority of the many editions of *The Day of Doom* and *Meat Out of the Eater* published during and immediately after his life, and by the complexity associated with reconstruction of the compositional history of and occasion for the poetry.

I have conceived of the present edition of Michael Wigglesworth's poems, which is the first complete collection of all his known poems, not as an end, but as a beginning. In effect, I intend the edition to serve a dual purpose: first, to provide students and scholars with accessible texts of the poems, a necessary first step toward their consideration of Wigglesworth's merit as a poet and of his place in American letters, and, second, to invite textual scholars, particularly those following the theory articulated in this century by W.W. Greg and Fredson Bowers, to take up and resolve the ultimately tortuous history of Wigglesworth's publications.

I am indebted to the officers and staffs of several libraries and learned societies for courtesies extended to me during my preparation of texts included in this volume, particularly, those of the American Antiquarian Society, the Boston Public Library, the Houghton Library of Harvard University, the Library of Congress, the Massachusetts Historical Society, and the New England Historic Genealogical Society. Additionally, librarians at the State University of New York at Albany, the Lilly Library at Indiana

University, the Widener Library at Harvard University, and the Yale University libraries were thorough, prompt, and gracious in responding to my inquiries during the research phase of this volume.

Over the years, a number of professional colleagues have shared with me their critical insight and wisdom. In connection with the present volume, I am grateful for the advice and encouragement of Professors Eugene K. Garber, John C. Gerber, and Perry D. Westbrook of the State University of New York at Albany; O.M. Brack, Jr., of the Arizona State University at Tempe; Andrew Delbanco of Columbia University; Everett Emerson of the University of North Carolina at Chapel Hill; and Arlin Turner, late of Duke University.

Preparation of this volume has been facilitated by grants from the American Philosophical Society and the Research Foundation of the State University of New York.

Finally, it is only fitting that *The Poems of Michael Wigglesworth* be dedicated to those many students of early-American life and letters it has been my privilege to teach over the past fifteen years. This dedication is a modest acknowledgment of the pleasure I have taken in their company and of the excitement and challenge they have created for me through their expressive and deft exercise of intellect and imagination.

R.A.B.

CONTENTS

FOREWORD	iii
INTRODUCTION	vii
Reputation and Criticism: A Reading of Inherited Opinion on Michael Wigglesworth	ix
Reading the Poems of Michael Wigglesworth	xviii
Significant Events in the Life of Michael Wigglesworth	xxix
A Note on the Present Text of the Poems	xliv
THE POEMS OF MICHAEL WIGGLESWORTH	1
THE DAY OF DOOM	3
"To the Christian Reader"	5
"A Prayer unto Christ"	9
"The Day of Doom"	11
"A Short Discourse on Eternity"	67
"A Postscript unto the Reader"	73
"A Song of Emptiness"	83
GOD'S CONTROVERSY WITH NEW-ENGLAND	87
"The Authors request unto the Reader"	89
"New-England planted, prospered, declining, threatned, punished"	90
MEAT OUT OF THE EATER	103
"Tolle Crucem" and 10 Meditations	105
"A conclusion Hortatory"	138
RIDDLES UNRIDDLED, or Christian Paradoxes	143
"Light in Darkness" and 10 Songs	145
"Sick mens Health" and 4 Meditations	177
"Strength in Weakness" and 4 Songs	189
"Poor mens Wealth" and 5 Meditations	201
"In Confinement Liberty" and 3 Songs	215
"In Solitude Good Company" and 3 Songs	223
"Joy in Sorrow" and 5 Songs	235

"Life in Deaths" and 3 Songs	251
"Heavenly Crowns for Thorny Wreaths" and 5 Songs	259
OCCASIONAL VERSE	277
Latin and English Verses Composed about 1660	279
"When as the wayes of Jesus Christ"	280
"Upon the much Lamented Death of that Precious servant of Christ . . . Benjamin Buncker"	282
"Upon ye return of my dear friend Mr Foster"	286
"Death *Expected* and *Welcomed*"	289
"A Farewel to the World"	290
APPENDICES	293
I. "I *Walk'd and did a little* Mole-hill *view*"	295
II. Jonathan Mitchell's "On the following Work, and It's Author"	299
NOTES ON SOURCES, EDITIONS, AND TEXTS	301
The Day of Doom	305
God's Controversy with New-England	310
Meat Out of the Eater	312
Occasional Verse and *Appendices*	320
NOTES TO INTRODUCTION	325

INTRODUCTION

Reputation and Criticism:
A Reading of Inherited Opinion on Michael Wigglesworth

On June 24, 1705, Cotton Mather traveled from Boston to Malden, Massachusetts, to preach *A Faithful Man, Described and Rewarded*. His audience for the sermon was the congregation then mourning the passing of Michael Wigglesworth, Malden's pastor, teacher, poet, and physician for more than fifty years. By 1705, Mather was an unquestioned master of the Puritan sermon form, regularly preaching sermons and preparing them for the press at a rate that had made him by then New England's foremost published preacher. Yet a comparative reading between Mather's sermon on Wigglesworth and others that he preached on the death of ministers discloses that it possesses an unexpected degree of authorial sympathy for its subject and of careful, detailed preparation. These qualities suggest that Mather was not only conscious of but also had a personal stake in the rank and reputation of the man whose life he memorialized as a pattern of piety and long-suffering for the edification and consolation of Malden's people, indeed, for the edification and consolation of all New England's saints.

Memories of Wigglesworth's personal and private relation to Mather's family and details of this preacher-poet-physician's public life obviously filled Mather's mind for the two weeks between Wigglesworth's death and his own visit to Malden, for all achieve fair expression in *A Faithful Man*. On the personal side, there were, to be sure, stories from Mather's father, Increase, who remembered Wigglesworth as his tutor at Harvard College during the early 1650s and numbered him among his principal friends and counselors during the half-century that followed. Also, Mather must have recalled how, as a child, he might leave off his study of Scripture and the writings of the church fathers to receive more than adequate doctrinal and moral instruction by reciting the ballad stanzas of Wigglesworth's "The Day of Doom."

On the public side, evidence of Wigglesworth's career and contributions to colonial New England culture must have appeared to the literary-minded Mather to be both overwhelming and filled with pathos sufficient to move even the hardest Puritan heart. It is on Wigglesworth's public life that Mather decided to concentrate in his sermon, with details such as these humanizing the character of the man soon to be called *Maldonatus Orthodoxus*: Wigglesworth's rise to a position of influence and prestige from the unlikely beginnings typical of many early-New Englanders; his profound conversion experience at Harvard College, which led him to postpone his study of medicine in order to prepare for the ministry; his deeply-felt confusion, doubt, and anxiety over his fitness to do God's work;

his thirty-year period of physical and psychological distress, which, brought on by the death of those close to him as well as by his own spiritual depression and doubt, forced him to relinquish his ministry to the whims of others; his exercise of poetical and medical talents as partial means to compensate the public during his years of ministerial inactivity; his precarious existence among townspeople who for thirty years had no qualms about letting him know that he was living off their generosity or about libeling him when he married one whom they considered far below his station; his miraculous physical and psychological recovery, which enabled him to move to the forefront of New England's political and ecclesiastical affairs during the last twenty years of his life and to resume a fruitful ministry among those who had once reviled him; and, finally, his position as an eminent standard-bearer for and vigorous poetic defender of the *old* "New England Way" -- one of the last of that breed.[1] When *A Faithful Man* was printed in Boston several months after its delivery, Mather inserted an epitaph of his own design, "*The Excellent* Wigglesworth, *Remembred by some Good Tokens.*" In its multiple allusions to Wigglesworth's public, private, and poetic concerns, Mather's poem provided an apt summary of the life and contributions of its subject:

> His Pen did once Meat from the Eater fetch;
> And now he's gone beyond the *Eaters* reach.
> His *Body*, once so *Thin*, was next to *None*;
> From Thence, he's to *Unbodied Spirits flown*.
> Once his rare skill did all *Diseases* heal;
> And he does nothing now *uneasy* feel.
> He to his *Paradise* is Joyful come;
> And waits with Joy to see his Day of Doom.[2]

Various testimonies survive to indicate that in *A Faithful Man* Mather had not exaggerated either Wigglesworth's character or the impact of his poetry on colonial society. As a measure of the esteem in which Wigglesworth was held by the people of Malden, Malden historical and church records reveal that immediately following his death the town voted in favor of a stipend to support his widow and family, while for a half-century after his death, answers to the question "What would Mr. Wigglesworth say?" frequently decided the outcome of debates on doctrinal and disciplinary issues among members of his former congregation. Among religious literature, the Bible and the *Bay Psalm Book* were the only serious rivals to Wigglesworth's *The Day of Doom*, which during the poet's life went through three known American editions (in 1662, 1666, and 1701), two supposed but unverified American editions (in 1663 or 1664 and in 1683), and three known but unauthorized English editions (in 1666, 1673, and 1687). Though not as popular as *The Day of Doom*, *Meat Out of the Eater* also enjoyed considerable success between 1670, the year of its first publication, and 1689, the year it was printed in a fourth edition, the last during Wigglesworth's life.

For decades after Wigglesworth's death, editions of his poems continued to exert an impressive and documented hold on the imagination of American audiences and to represent profitable investments for American publishers. For instance, in 1717, *Meat Out of the Eater* was printed in Boston in an edition marked for five different booksellers, while in 1770, another edition was published in New London, Connecticut. Complete editions of *The Day of Doom* were reprinted in America in 1715 and 1751, and abridged editions appeared in 1774 and 1777. Of course, by the nineteenth century interest in Puritan writers had diminished appreciably among American readers, with readers variously repulsed by the theology of America's early-New-England settlers or charmed by the quaint, antiquarian flavor of their language and by their curious assumptions about their share in the human condition. Nevertheless, demand for *The Day of Doom* persisted into the nineteenth century, for editions of the complete volume appeared in Newburyport in 1811, in Boston in 1828, and in New York City in 1867.[3]

Despite the impressive show represented by the publication of his works well into the nineteenth century, Wigglesworth, along with most other major Puritan writers, suffered a sharp decline in popularity among general readers and in esteem among literary and social historians as the century wore on. Though many Puritan writers have been rescued from the slights and caustic comments of nineteenth-century reviewers and though Puritan literature generally has been redeemed as an area appropriate for serious scholarship and investigation by twentieth-century literary historians and others, Wigglesworth's poetry and his reputation as a figure of significance during the colonial period have not been rescued. In fact, except for the edition of *The Day of Doom* prepared by Kenneth B. Murdock in 1929, Wigglesworth's poetry has remained in a virtual limbo since the last popular editions of the early-nineteenth century; *Meat Out of the Eater* is now one of the most inaccessible items for study of colonial poetry. Wigglesworth's reputation has fared no better, as the review that follows shows.

In the nineteenth century, Wigglesworth's literary fortune was tied invariably to that of other Puritan writers in that Wigglesworth, like Cotton Mather, was then among the best known and most accessible writers and so could be singled out easily to substantiate any assertion (positive or negative, but usually negative) about Puritan culture generally, Puritan literature specifically. For instance, critics in the early-nineteenth century who might wish to express disdain for Puritan theology had to go no further than "The Day of Doom" to find ample evidence of what were then defined as the "grotesque" doctrinal inclinations of the early settlers. Those inclinations were then said to have affected not only the public policy of the Puritan era but also the aesthetic competency of those who engaged in *belles lettres* during the era. With examples such as innocent babes cast into the easiest room in hell or society's most upright, public citizens cast into the eternal flames along with obvious sinners (as happens in "The Day of Doom"), a nineteenth-century critic could immediately rest (and win) his case against America's Puritan past. In their effort to debunk Puritanism, writers such as Nathaniel Hawthorne and Ralph Waldo Emerson, who had a more than ordinary personal investment in the Puritan past, made that past a subject for personal and national humiliation.[4] When discussions turned to the specifics of Puritan literature, the best critics could do was to apologize for early-American letters; the worst they could do was to libel them.

Such extremes in criticism are represented especially in the writings of literary historians from this period. In 1829, when Samuel Kettell prepared an introduction for his three-volume *Specimens of American Poetry*, he assessed the contributions of seventeenth-century Puritan writers in terms that made little distinction between appreciating a Puritan poet for his charm and ridiculing him for his theology. Though he kept to generalizations and refrained from making attacks on individuals, what Kettell wrote applied to Wigglesworth as much as to any others he might have had in mind. Of "the earliest attempts in the department of polite literature" in America, Kettell thought that while they "possess[ed] an interest arising from the curiosity we naturally feel to view the most ancient memorials of literary effort on record among us," nevertheless they "must certainly be considered rude and feeble."[5]

During the decades following the appearance of Kettell's work, critics sharpened their attack against Puritanism and Puritan writers and supplied names to support their generalizations. Rufus Griswold, introducing his *The Poets and Poetry of America* in 1842, asserted that "the poetry of the colonies was without originality, energy, feeling or correctness of diction." In his anthology, Griswold excluded all American poets who wrote before Philip Freneau, and he justified their exclusion, saying that the best one might find in Mather or Wigglesworth is a collection of "quaint and grotesque absurdities."[6] Griswold's anthology, which went through sixteen editions in thirteen years, unquestionably influenced the tone and range of much of the criticism to come.

After Griswold's time, Wigglesworth increasingly became the example of what was wrong with both the Puritan temperament and Puritan poetry. Though it is filled with judgments that twentieth-century critics have revised extensively, Moses Coit Tyler's *A History of American Literature, 1607-1765*, made, from the nineteenth-century point of view, a sound and lasting case against Puritans, Puritan literature, and Wigglesworth. Summarizing the relation between Puritan faith and Puritan art, Tyler wrote:

> It will hardly be said that any typical Puritan of [the seventeenth] century was a poetic personage. In proportion to his devotion to the ideas that won for him the derisive honor of his name, was he at war with nearly every form of the beautiful. He himself believed that there was an inappeasable feud between religion and art; and hence, the duty of suppressing art was bound up in his soul with the master-purpose of promoting religion. He cultivated the grim and the ugly. He was afraid of the approaches of Satan through the avenues of what is graceful and joyous.... [His] theology drove poetry out of many forms in which it had been used to reside.... [He] stamped his foot in horror and scorn upon many exquisite and delicious types of literary art.... [His] prayers were often a snuffle, his hymns a dolorous whine, his extemporized liturgy a bleak ritual of

ungainly postures and of harsh monotonous howls.... [In seventeenth-century] New England, we may perhaps imagine [the Puritan] as solemnly declining the visits of the Muses of poetry, sending out to them the blunt but honest message -- 'Otherwise engaged.'[7]

In Tyler's opinion, then, Puritanism was a villainous influence on the poetic imagination of any who subscribed to its tenets. The "grim and the ugly," "a snuffle ... a dolorous whine," and "harsh monotonous howls": these were the principal expressions of an imagination tainted by a "horror and scorn" of things "graceful and joyous," and they survived in print to insult the good taste and sense of polite nineteenth-century readers and critics. No Puritan writer, whether or not respected today, escaped Tyler's harsh judgment. Anne Bradstreet, for example, was "grossly misled" by the imaginative restraints Puritanism placed on her reading of "ample precedents in English literature for [her] form of poetry." "The fatal taint in all her poetical life was that, badly instructed ... [she] drew her materials from books rather than from nature"; acceding to the demands of her faith and the expectations of her audience, Bradstreet wrote poetry that "is nothing" -- "nothing more than rhymed historical teaching." For this, Tyler sarcastically observed, Bradstreet's contemporaries likely "gave to her their choicest praise, and called her, for [her] work, a painful poet; in which compliment every modern reader will most cordially join."[8]

Actually, Tyler's judgments about Bradstreet are mild in comparison to those he reserved for his real literary target: Wigglesworth. In Wigglesworth, "the explicit and unshrinking rhymer of the Five Points of Calvinism; a poet who ... perfectly uttered in verse the religious faith and emotion of Puritan New England," Tyler found evidence to support all the negative and uncomplimentary assumptions he had advanced concerning Puritanism and the Puritan poetic imagination. Only by "exercising the utmost intellectual catholicity," Tyler said, could he (or could his readers) escape "disgust and detestation for ... this poet's message." Tyler's attack on Wigglesworth was both personal and literary. On the literary side, he asserted that Wigglesworth's "blazing and sulphurous" verse was "quite lacking in art; its ordinary form being a crude, swinging ballad measure, with a sort of cheap melody, a shrill, reverberating clatter, that would instantly catch and please the popular ear, at that time deaf to daintier and more subtle effects in poetry." On the personal side, Tyler systematically assaulted every claim upon which Wigglesworth's public and poetic reputation had been based for the previous two centuries. Allowing that "[there] was in him the genius of a true poet" and that "his imagination had an epic strength," Tyler contended that a fatal flaw in Wigglesworth's character, his faith, forever stifled his genius and perverted the natural ends of his imagination. Wigglesworth, Tyler concluded, "had given up to a narrow and a ferocious creed what was meant for mankind; in his intense pursuit of what he believed to be the good and the true, he forgot the very existence of the beautiful ... [and thus was] forever incapable of giving utterance to his genius."[9]

Of course, there is no way that the comprehension of beauty, truth, and good by Puritan writers could ever coincide with the values attached to those terms by America's

Romantic and post-Romantic critics. Yet the opinions of critics like Griswold and Tyler were lasting and influential, and for some time they established not only the tone of criticism directed at Puritan writers but also Wigglesworth as the terminus in the range of all criticism that dealt negatively with Puritan subjects. Matters for Puritan writers generally or Wigglesworth specifically hardly improved in the early decades of the twentieth century. One school of criticism, best represented by Vernon Louis Parrington, elected to omit entirely reference to Puritan poetry in evaluations of the broad sweep of American literary culture or in comments on the relation between letters and American intellectual history. Those critics who did include reference to colonial writers and poets were not always kindly disposed toward their subjects.

The career and opinions of Kenneth B. Murdock, who prepared the aforementioned 1929 edition of *The Day of Doom* and whose contributions to the study of colonial culture cannot be minimized, offer a fine case in point. In 1927, Murdock published *Handkerchiefs from Paul*, a collection of previously inaccessible Puritan poems, with some poems taken from manuscripts, some from previously published texts. Though *Handkerchiefs from Paul* certainly improved critics' access to the works of selected Puritan poets, Murdock's comments in his lengthy introduction show that neither he nor his fellows had advanced very far from the judgments rendered fifty years earlier by Tyler. Speaking of the contents of his book, Murdock said, "[The] world's great poetry is no whit increased by bringing these forgotten works ... to light. They deserve printing not for any appeal which they can make to sophisticated students of *belles lettres*, but for their historical implications, for the sidelights they shed upon Puritan character and taste." In other words, Puritan poetry was worth studying not for whatever measure of art or conscious artistry might be found therein, not for the unique application of the imaginative, poetic process revealed therein, but for the revelations it made about "Puritan character and taste." Well, Tyler had already scoured those "sidelights" exhaustively, and what he found reversed two centuries' worth of claims for a culture and its poets. Approaching his own conclusion, Murdock told his readers what they might expect from their own scouring of such sidelights. For a mere price charged "in harshness and lack of music," readers would have "a glimpse of the deep emotion which demanded expression of writers unequal to their task"; for the same price, readers would also find themselves charmed by "[the] stark crudeness of the colonial verse-writers [which] has, after all, an effect, if not a completely developed one."[10] To be sure, Murdock had sympathy for his subject; however, his tone in expressing that sympathy does little to make others eager to share it.

Wigglesworth received no mention by Murdock in *Handkerchiefs from Paul*. In the introduction to his edition of *The Day of Doom*, however, Murdock developed the character of the poet and evaluated the worth of his art in terms identical to those he had used earlier to discuss Puritan poetry in general. "It is ... as a historical document that *The Day of Doom* [referring to the title poem, not the volume] is most precious,"[11] he wrote. Though its chief distinctions are "its sulphurousness, the cruelty of its doctrine, and its harping on the horrors of Hell," Murdock allowed that the volume as a whole "smells no more strongly of brimstone than the utterances or writings of hundreds of others, in New

England and out of it, during Wigglesworth's life, and before and after it."[12] Like the poems collected in *Handkerchiefs from Paul*, the poems of *The Day of Doom* deserved to be "[denied] the title of great poetry," but they did not deserve to be forgotten. In all, the volume had much to offer, for as "a supreme example of theologic fire-breathing," it represented explicitly the form of Puritan aesthetics and logic, and it provided a reliable measure of the character and competency of Puritan New England's foremost poet. What did *The Day of Doom* reveal of Wigglesworth's character and competency? Of character, it revealed a man "sick, sensitive, gentle-natured, beset day and night by fears and hopes as to his future estate, and haunted by an image of a just God condemning with cold logic myriad souls to a living death of torment."[13] Of competency, it revealed "the artist at work and waging his battle against the handicaps [of faith and environment] which warp and distort his expression."[14]

By the end of his introduction, Murdock found himself in a bind. Realizing, perhaps, that what he had just written might do more to condemn Wigglesworth to infamy or obscurity than to rescue him from either, Murdock added that, in fact, "*The Day of Doom* ... can be read quite without concern for its historical or theological suggestiveness." In a tone reminiscent of his advice to "sophisticated students" in *Handkerchiefs from Paul*, he suggested that the volume and its title poem might help us "in our more relaxed moments to glow with a pleasant sense of our own virtue [by proving to us that] we are not as other men were." That failing, one might nevertheless find Wigglesworth's poetry appealing "simply because it is -- or seems -- comic."[15]

Rather than leave us with the uncritical and, finally, unsubstantiated opinions of Murdock and earlier critics, scholars of recent decades have given us many sound and viable suggestions as to how we should view Puritan culture and the Puritan imagination. Over the years the writings of social and literary historians and of feminist critics and the efforts of textual editors have brought new life and meaning to the body of writings that early critics were content to let charm or repulse us. Especially favored among scholars writing since 1930 have been sermonic, historical, and personal or autobiographical literature from the Puritan period. But Puritan poetry has also received extensive attention and comment, particularly since the discovery of Edward Taylor during the late-1930s. Today, old opinions on Puritan poetry have been reviewed and revised, with the result that colonials Taylor and Bradstreet are now ranked among America's finest and most competent poets. Both Taylor and Bradstreet have earned our respect as conscious artists *and* as Puritans; in their writings critics have discovered an apparently full and verifiable measure of the aesthetic concerns and literary competency of the Puritan artist. What of Wigglesworth?

Despite the volumes of scholarship produced over recent decades, inherited opinions on Wigglesworth have not been systematically reviewed. Since 1929, when Murdock had his ultimately devastating say about Wigglesworth's character and his competency as a poet, Edmund S. Morgan, the editor of Wigglesworth's diary for the years 1653-1657, and Richard Crowder, Wigglesworth's sympathetic biographer, have alone come forward to rescue the poet's character. No one, however, has attempted to revise or, even, to prove the *critical* acceptability of opinions that Murdock and others once expressed about Wigglesworth's competency as a poet.

Writing in the same year that Murdock was preparing his edition of *The Day of Doom*, F.O. Matthiessen added his voice to what by then had become a familiar chant: Wigglesworth "was a conscious artist ... [who had an] interest in art ... [and] an instinctive sense of what the art of poetry should be." Like other Puritans who expressed themselves in verse and song, Wigglesworth "did not exclude the arts [from his life; however, his] sin was in wholly subordinating them with everything else to a narrow creed." Thus, for Matthiessen, Wigglesworth's poetry fails, and "Wigglesworth, a little feeble shadow of a man, stands as a symbol of [all Puritans'] parched sterility."[16] When in 1943 Harold S. Jantz devoted a few paragraphs to Wigglesworth in *The First Century of New England Verse*, he concentrated on Wigglesworth's versatility as a rhymer and dramatist. Jantz claimed that "[the] most amazing phenomenon ... Wigglesworth shows throughout his poetic career is the range of his literary expression from the most utterly shallow and diffuse drivel to truly concentrated and impressive verse." Unfortunate for Wigglesworth's reputation, Jantz was not able to cite evidence of the latter. Instead, he disposed of Wigglesworth altogether, saying, "just as his fine gallant soul shone forth through a poor sickly body, so in his lyrics the sincere and noble spirit is generally clothed in inadequate dress."[17] In his monumental *American Poets: From the Puritans to the Present* (1968), Hyatt H. Waggoner delivered Wigglesworth the ultimate insult: he simply ignored him.[18] A few years later, Donald Barlow Stauffer, writing a brief version of Waggoner's effort, redressed his predecessor's apparent bias, but not to Wigglesworth's advantage. In *A Short History of American Poetry* (1974), Stauffer compared Wigglesworth's achievement to that of Taylor and Bradstreet, and on all counts, he found Wigglesworth lacking. Though "Wigglesworth's poetry is well known," he said, "it is not representative of the quality of Colonial verse." For too long Wigglesworth's verse was the measure of colonial poetic talent; that measure, Stauffer argued, "too often led us to judge the poetry of New England on the basis of *The Day of Doom*." "Fortunately," he concluded, with access to the writings of other poets "we have now been able to revise many [early] opinions [on the quality of New England poetry] and in doing so place Wigglesworth several rungs down the ladder."[19]

The positions on Wigglesworth taken by Matthiessen, Jantz, Waggoner, and Stauffer fairly represent the state of Wigglesworth scholarship today. To their opinion, however, must be added that of Robert Daly, whose *God's Altar: The World and the Flesh in Puritan Poetry* (1978) is the most substantial account of Puritan poetry that we have. Writing in an era in which colonial scholars have devoted most of their energy to revising inherited theories on Puritan culture and the Puritan imagination, Daly provides insightful and fair readings of Bradstreet and Taylor; on Wigglesworth, however, he is remarkably short in patience and brief in comment. Limiting his comment principally to *The Day of Doom* (though he does briefly address one stanza out of the whole of *Meat Out of the Eater*, and more extensively addresses "I *Walk'd and did a little* Mole-hill *view*," a poem that some, including the present writer, seriously doubt is Wigglesworth's creation) he accepts the inherited wisdom of Wigglesworth's early commentators, though he dresses up his subject in more popular jargon than earlier critics would indulge. For Daly, Wigglesworth is "the Gnostic, the Neoplatonic Puritan of the popular stereotype. For him, the sensible world is meaningless and corrupt; the body is merely a prison for the soul. Separation of the body and soul is not ... misery ... but a longed-for joy."[20] According to Daly, Wigglesworth made this "longed-for joy," which, of course, translates into union with God, the subject of his poetry. Within individual poems, the affairs of the world at large as well as the individual's inner corruption are repeatedly singled out as obstacles that must be surmounted in order for one to win the joy so anxiously sought after. But except for Puritans who in their collective temper found merit in poetry directed at such concerns, poetry like Wigglesworth's has very little to offer: "Its popularity among contemporary readers derived ... from its good moral tendency, from the orthodoxy of its doctrine, and from its simplicity. It had the theological directness of Billy Graham, the universal availability of Norman Vincent Peale, and a theme comparable in its universal importance to that of Erich Segal." Thus, though like the works of Graham, Peale, and Segal, Wigglesworth's works were quite popular in their day and apparently had something valuable to say to individuals in their large Puritan audience, Daly, taking on a tone reminiscent of Murdock's, states, "we need conclude neither that Puritan taste was any more demented than our own ... nor that [Wigglesworth's poems] had some great merit lost on modern readers."[21]

If Wigglesworth is ever to escape from critical obscurity and if his poems are ever to be regarded as more than disposable representations proving that "Puritan taste was [or was not] any more demented than our own," a liberated generation of readers and critics will have to appear, which, rising above critical prejudices of the past and present, is willing to re-examine Wigglesworth's aesthetics and re-read his art in their original context. To their credit, Harrison T. Meserole and Kenneth Silverman have made significant contributions toward the possibility of such an enterprise in their respective anthologies of early-American poetry.[22] Their sensible commentary on and judicious selections from Wigglesworth's work do much to offset the burden of inherited opinion, which typically treats Wigglesworth as a minor, one-poem poet, and a not particularly capable one at that. Both Meserole and Silverman treat him as a major poet, not only in terms of the phenomenal popularity he enjoyed in his own time but also in terms of the aesthetic and social qualities an objective reading of his poems may reveal for readers today. Both, further, place him squarely in the company of Anne Bradstreet and Edward Taylor as an equal, rightly differentiating between their individual accomplishments on the basis of their individual purposes for poetry, not on the basis of a critical position foreign to the time and place in which they wrote. Addressing the reputation of "The Day of Doom," Meserole makes the following observation, which may serve not only to characterize the reputation of that poem but also to summarize the flaw inherent in most inherited opinion on Wigglesworth's character and the value of his art: "Perhaps no poem in American literature has been so maligned.... It has been repeatedly denounced as inexorably stern doggerel by those who would have it be what it is not."[23]

Reading the Poems of Michael Wigglesworth

As artist and as devout Puritan, Wigglesworth, to be sure, is a figure not without qualities that tax the critical sensibility as well as the good will of the modern reader. It may be, as Donald Barlow Stauffer has said, that Wigglesworth deserves to be ranked "several rungs down the ladder" of Puritan poets. It may be too that the poetry of, say, Anne Bradstreet and Edward Taylor reveals a better sort of Puritanism, more humane and more aesthetically and intellectually complete and acceptable to us, than does Wigglesworth's poetry, in which event Wigglesworth and his poetry might be justly ignored. In the same vein, it may be that the Puritan instinct represented by Wigglesworth is so personal or idiosyncratic that in order to find any merit in Puritan culture we must reject that instinct on whatever evidence we have of it. But such judgments, if they are ever to be persuasive and if they are ever to contribute to the ongoing, necessary revision of inherited opinion on Puritanism generally and Wigglesworth specifically, must be made *critically*, and made *anew*. Such judgments must be based on reviews of Wigglesworth's entire poetic achievement, not on reviews of individual items such as "The Day of Doom," regardless of the currency which that poem once enjoyed. There should be no fear involved in approaching Wigglesworth this way, for even if in the end readers decide that opinions on Wigglesworth advanced by earlier critics were indeed on the mark, they can be assured that their own more recent investigation and judgment will possess an intellectual integrity and completeness heretofore missing.[24]

An open-minded reading of Wigglesworth definitely has its rewards. Contrary to inherited opinion, he is not a one-poem poet. During the decades of his primary poetic activity, he composed more than seventy poems, which should impress those whose attitude toward him has been shaped by a reading of only "The Day of Doom." In these poems Wigglesworth frequently departed from the often-cited "stampeding fourteeners" of ballad verse and wrote in a number of different poetic forms, which offer variety that should sustain a reader's interest. For instance in Song IX of the "Light in Darkness" sequence of *Meat Out of the Eater* and in his "Song of Praise" on the return of William Foster, he experimented with the lyric form. As stanzas in "The Day of Doom," *God's Controversy with New-England*, Song X of "Light in Darkness," Song IV of "Sick mens Health," and Song III of "In Solitude Good Company" (all from *Meat Out of the Eater*) show, he dealt with both dramatic monologue and dramatic debate. "The Day of Doom," *God's Controversy with New-England*, the elegy on Benjamin Bunker, and "A Farewel to the World" reveal him seriously engaged in the devices of narrative and descriptive writing. Finally, as might be expected, a didactic and hortatory pulpit style is in evidence throughout the span of Wigglesworth's career and is especially noticeable in "A Postscript unto the Reader" (from *The Day of Doom*), the closing lines of both *God's Controversy with New-England* and the elegy on Bunker, "When as the wayes of Jesus Christ," and Song V of "Heavenly Crowns for Thorny Wreaths" (from *Meat Out of the Eater*).

Apart from noticing the progressive development of his talent and the development of his various poetic subjects and forms, how else might one read Wigglesworth? What attitude should one have when he first approaches this collection of Wigglesworth's verse? It seems only reasonable and fair that one approach Wigglesworth fresh, that is, that one approach him without many of the assumptions and claims passed down from previous generations of critics. In many ways Wigglesworth was himself aware of what scholars today uncritically accept as the limitations of his poetry; the difference between Wigglesworth and today's scholars is, however, that Wigglesworth never regarded the aesthetic and moral "limits" he placed on his poetry as "limitations." From Wigglesworth's point of view and from that of several generations of colonials raised on his verse, the intentional didactic or sermonic aspect, orthodox content, and plain style of his poetry were its very strengths. These were, for the seventeenth-century New England Puritan, a measure of the quality of verse, just as they were a measure of the quality of historical and theological writing. So it might be illuminating to read with Wigglesworth's limits in mind, to allow him his aesthetic and moral bias, which was fashioned out of an appreciation of the Puritan plain style and a conviction of the rightness of New England's brand of Calvinism. Once a serious reading is completed, one will be in a position to stand back from the bias and assess for himself Wigglesworth's "limits" or "limitations."

Of course, some early assumptions and claims about Wigglesworth have merit and are worth preserving. The comments that follow are intended to put several inherited commonplaces and some original assumptions into a perspective that will help readers to understand the occasion for Wigglesworth's poetry as well as Wigglesworth's position on the role of the poet in society, his sense of poetic style and of the purpose of poetry, and his treatment of important native New England topics. In this connection, one point is indisputable: the principal occasion for Wigglesworth's poetry, New England's apparent decline from the piety and ideals of the first Puritan settlers, coincided with his own physical and periodic psychological distress. That distress rendered the preacher incapable of performing those duties for which the Malden congregation had ordained him and forced him to seek out somewhat unconventional means to fulfill his ministerial charge.

Ill, depressed, lonely, and subject to fits of doubt and anxiety over his own spiritual condition, Wigglesworth was unable to discharge the principal responsibilities of his ministry between the late 1650s and the mid-1680s. Yet as he and most other Puritan ministers believed, this was a period in which New England desperately needed powerful and persuasive voices in her pulpits. The years 1660 to 1690 encompass a period commonly referred to today as the time of New England's great "declension." (Declension is usually defined as the loss among New Englanders of the original purpose for which the colonies had been established in the 1620s and 1630s.) Evidence was then everywhere to be found that the "plantation religious" contracted for by God in his Covenant with New England's founders was on the verge of collapse. Helped by the observations of Puritan historians and preachers, scholars have produced a near-endless checklist of the signs and presumed effects of declension. However, to appreciate fully the occasion for Wigglesworth's poetry, only a few of the signs and effects need be mentioned. For instance, by the early 1660s, New England's civil and ecclesiastic leaders were shocked to find that "inordinate worldliness," self-serving pride, "carnal security," and hypocrisy had taken hold among the people who were entrusted by the founders to preserve a strong sense of communal piety at all cost. For many, the heritage of the founders was further insulted by the Half-Way Covenant, which, in 1662, relaxed old standards governing church membership and discipline. To make matters worse, day-by-day the few remaining original saints were passing away, leaving their children as well as newcomers to assume to civil and ecclesiastic power that the strict founders once held. As the Half-Way Covenant seemed to prove, the generation coming to power was either disinterested in or unequal to the challenge of preserving and promoting the old ways.[25]

Believing that God spoke to his people through events, believing that God's will or disposition toward his people was discernable in everything from the weather to the state of New England's economy, New England's orthodox leaders put their symbolic imaginations to work. They were horrified by what they discovered. Droughts, storms, pestilence, a high mortality rate, political tensions between the authorities of old England and New, a rising crime rate, and, by the end of the century, the presence of witches all suggested to them that God was not ignorant of New England's backsliding. Something of a vicious cycle ensued, for phenomena such as these were seen variously as warnings from God against any further backsliding by his people and as judgments or punishments from God for his people's neglect of the Covenant. To remedy the situation, preachers took to their pulpits, and through jeremiads, a then newly fashioned sermonic form, they told the people that God's patience with them was at an end. Indeed, the time to repent and reform had come. With the cooperation of civil leaders, who were as distressed as the preachers by New England's decline in piety, the churches of New England called one-hundred-seventy-one days of fast and humiliation between 1660 and 1679. Though the process of fast and humiliation did not originate in New England (it originated in the practices outlined in Deuteronomy, Samuel, Kings, Chronicles, Jeremiah, and Micah -- books of the Old Testament in which a sinful and falling Israel was instructed in the means to win restoration of God's favor), the New English Israelites put the process to extensive use, hoping that humiliation for sin and a return to the ideals of the founders would be sufficient to achieve the restoration of God's favor toward them.[26]

At his ordination in 1657, Wigglesworth was named Malden's teacher. "Pastor" and "teacher" were the technical terms used in seventeenth-century New England to define a minister's position in his church. According to the *Platform* adopted in Cambridge in 1648 by the Congregational churches of New England, the pastor's "special work [was] to attend to exhortation, and therein to administer a word of wisdom." The teacher was "to attend to doctrine, and therein to administer a word of knowledge." Beyond these distinctions, both were expected to "administer the seals of [their] covenant," "execute censures," and preach.[27] Large congregations usually could afford both a pastor and a teacher; small congregations, like the one in Malden, usually had to settle for one or the other. In making their choice between pastor and teacher, small congregations often called ministers to their pulpit according to the talent the congregation felt was most needed. Thus, from the time Wigglesworth began his formal association with the Malden congregation, all parties understood that he was to provide instruction in morals and church discipline, direction and advice in matters of doctrine, and practical motivation for his people to pursue the right and good. During the period of declension the work of teachers was crucial to the successful outcome of any campaign waged by the clergy against New England's backsliding. Wigglesworth's ministerial colleagues understood this; the people of Malden understood this; Wigglesworth too understood this.

That he was not serving the purpose for which his congregation had called him undoubtedly added to Wigglesworth's psychological distress in the early 1660s. This was the time that his congregation needed him most. No longer able to preach and too weak, apparently, to lend even his presence before the congregation as a sign of support for their effort to rid themselves of declension's taint, Wigglesworth turned to poetry. Lest this scenario be misread, the Wigglesworth who turned to poetry was not exactly the "little feeble shadow of a man" that critics like Matthiessen would have us see. Poetry demands intellectual and spiritual vigor; didactic poetry, particularly the sort Wigglesworth frequently wrote, demands, additionally, conviction, a firm control of ideas, an understanding of the power of language, an appreciation of the dimensions and value of emotion, and a talent for persuasion. In the early 1660s, when he first turned to poetry, Wigglesworth possessed all these traits. Whatever figure he cut in the neighborhoods of Malden, the figure he cut in his study was charged with a Puritan teacher's brand of energy and power.

This positive view of the occasion for Wigglesworth's poetry and of the origins of Wigglesworth's poetic career is supported by two contemporary accounts as well as by comments by Wigglesworth in several poems. In *A Faithful Man*, Cotton Mather observed, "that he might ... *Faithfully* set himself to Do Good, when he could not *Preach*, [Wigglesworth] *Wrote* several Composures, wherein he proposed the edification of such Readers as are for plain Truths, dressed up in a *Plain Meeter*. These Composures have had their Acceptance and Advantage ... and one of them, the *Day of Doom* ... may find our Children till the *Day* itself arrive."[28] It is in the same vein that Jonathan Mitchell, who as his spiritual mentor for more than ten years knew and understood Wigglesworth better than most, treated Wigglesworth's character and the value of his poetry in "On the following Work, and It's Author." Although Mitchell portrayed him as one " ... with many griefs afflicted sore, / Shut up from speaking much in sickly Cave" (11. 19-20), he did not believe that in his "sickly Cave" Wigglesworth wallowed in self-pity or neglected the charge of his ministry. Instead, Wigglesworth accepted the cave as a "happy Cave" and was transformed thereby into a "happy Pris'ner that's at liberty" through "painful leisure ... to write the more" (11. 25-26; 21). From his cave, Mitchell told readers, the poet-teacher "sends thee Counsels" and shares with all the fires that have freed him to write from the soul. Those fires, as reported in Wigglesworth's verse, deserved notice by readers, for they provided practical instruction in how at least one saint pursued the right and good despite all personal adversity. As far as Mitchell was concerned, in writing poetry, Wigglesworth more than satisfactorily fulfilled his ministerial obligation:

> A Verse may find him who a Sermon flies,
> ... Great Truths to dress in Meeter;
> Becomes a Preacher; who mens Souls doth prize,
> That Truth in Sugar roll'd may taste the sweeter.
> No Cost too great, no Care too curious is
> To set forth Truth, and win mens Souls to bliss. (11. 1-6)

From 1661 to 1669, the years of his most intense literary activity, Wigglesworth viewed his writing of poetry as a useful, valid, and honorable means of service as Malden's, indeed, as all New England's, teacher. Like his fellow Puritan poets Bradstreet and Taylor, he understood the purpose of poetry to be instruction and the role of the poet to be illustrator and interpreter of man's relation to the right and good. Unlike them, however, Wigglesworth saw the poet as principally a public figure, and he believed that the poet's creations belonged to the public, regardless of the personal motives that inspired them or the insights into the poet's private character and belief that they might reveal. In fact, Wigglesworth was quite open about his poetry and himself. For instance, in lines such as these from his address "To the Christian Reader" in *The Day of Doom*, he acknowledged that he intended his poetry to serve a dual purpose: to compensate those for whom he had no pulpit messages and to relieve himself of personal "grief" for not being able otherwise to serve Christ and Christ's people:

> *Thou wonderest perhaps*
> *That I in Print appear,*
> *Who in the Pulpit dwell so nigh,*
> *Yet come so seldome there:*
> *The God of Heaven knows*
> *What grief to me it is,*
> *To be with-held from Serving Christ:*
> *No sorrow like to this. . . .*
>
> *For his dear sake have I*
> *This service undertaken,*
> *For I am bound to honour Him,*
> *Who hath not me forsaken.*
> *I am a Debtor too,*
> *Unto the sons of men;*
> *Whom wanting other means, I would*
> *Advantage with my Pen.* (11. 9-16; 89-96)

As the remarkable public response to Wigglesworth's poetic activity suggests, colonial readers fully accepted the public and private motives out of which Wigglesworth had turned to poetry. Certainly, they must have appreciated the honesty with which he exposed himself as subject or example in his verse, for by the time he began to write and collect pieces for *Meat Out of the Eater*, he had no qualms about admitting that the content of the volume had its origin in personal experience:

> It is my daily Prayer,
> Lord let me never teach,
> That unto others which my self
> Have little care to reach.
> I have not told thee Tales,
> Of things unseen, unfelt,
> But speak them from Experience:
> Believe it how thou wilt.
> ("A Conclusion Hortatory," 11. 33-40)

Later in *Meat Out of the Eater*, Wigglesworth returned to personal experience as a means to edify his audience. Alluding to the period when he first turned to poetry, he advised all who have had public careers cut short to acquiesce cheerfully to the will of God and not harbor anger or indulge in self-pity:

> If Christ hath call'd thee off,
> After a short assay,
> From Publick Service; cease dispute,
> And cheerfully obey.
> ("Strength in Weakness," Song III, 11. 25-28)

Acquiescence to the will of God, Wigglesworth argued, is not a sign of weakness or ineffectuality. Despite the loss of talent, friends, position, or health, man, who cannot always fathom God's final intentions, must nevertheless strive to serve God and the good of his people through whatever means God leaves to him. Out of his own experience this poet had learned that one can always turn weakness to advantage, find strength in apparent ineffectuality. As the following lines reveal, Wigglesworth believed that as poet he was serving the will of God and advancing the good of God's people more effectively than if he had remained in the pulpit. Further, they reveal that he believed he was garnering more than adequate compensation for his poetic effort in this world, a prelude to the final compensation he would receive in the next.

> If Christ disable thee
> From doing as before,
> He calls thee to some other work
> That he approveth more.
> Passive Obedience

> More hard then Active is:
> And Christ will own and honour that,
> Who owns and crowneth this.
> ("Strength in Weakness," Song III, 11. 9-16)

A misconception that some entertain today about the Puritan preacher in general may influence adversely their reading of Wigglesworth's poetry. Some would see the Puritan preacher as the original "pulpit thumper." Despite considerable recent scholarship which proves that the image results from a misreading of the style, tone, and content of popular Puritan preaching, the image, largely a holdover from uncomplimentary reviews of Puritan preachers by nineteenth-century critics, has persisted. Today it is found in media representations of the Puritan preacher, and it receives support from the bias created out of imbalanced representations of "typical" Puritan sermonic prose in popular anthologies of American literature. Yet there is no primary evidence to support this exclusive view of the Puritan preacher. As the record of their published sermons shows, New England preachers of the late-seventeenth and eighteenth centuries often spoke to their people out of the voice of the sympathetic spiritual father or the voice of the calm mediator between God's expressed will toward man and man's own expressed desires and needs. Only when one of these voices proved inadequate to move sinful, backsliding people to repent and reform would preachers resort to another voice. This third voice is, indeed, the haranguing, vitriolic voice of the Puritan conscience. A highly effective voice, it received its fullest expression in Puritan jeremiads. The model for this voice was that of the Old Testament prophet Jeremiah: the prophet and priest warning God's people for the last time that their backsliding, transgressions, and defilement of the "plantation religious" had to be checked and reformed.

This correction of the way some view the typical Puritan preacher has significant implications for the way one ought to view Wigglesworth. As poet-preacher, Wigglesworth believed that the end of his poetry was instruction. He knew that in order to instruct effectively he had to appear sincere and be persuasive and his messages, dressed in whatever aesthetic trappings they might be, had to be both practical and sympathetically delivered. Thus, in a majority of his poems Wigglesworth adopted variously the voice of the spiritual father and the voice of the mediator between God and man. These voices were no less suited to the verse he wrote than they were to the pulpit he would otherwise have occupied. In the calm, understanding voice of the spiritual father, for instance, he could move his audience to a sense of their failure or support and advise them in their effort to check, say, declension in their own lives. Similarly, the voice of mediator allowed Wigglesworth to suggest practical means to reconcile one's personal desires and needs to the larger purpose for which God had set man on earth.

Of these two voices, Wigglesworth used the second more extensively and effectively, perhaps because the instruction he often conveyed in his verse was personally tested before it went into print. As the examples from *Meat Out of the Eater* which were cited above suggest, Wigglesworth's own anguish was the starting point for many meditations and songs in that volume, yet the volume as a whole reveals that Wigglesworth was able to transform his anguish and his sense of failure into resolutions to improve himself, through his art, for the good of God's people. That in mind, it should be apparent that at least as mediator, Wigglesworth was confident that his messages were practical and useful and that the verse in which he expressed them could offer to others some therapeutic benefit which he had himself once enjoyed. Further, with the subject for much of his poetry obviously drawn from personal experience and with the tensions which that experience once held resolved, as mediator and as spiritual father Wigglesworth knew that he had the distinct advantage of speaking to his people under the authority of having been through it all himself. The sheer volume of personal reference in his poetry and Wigglesworth's frequent pauses to speak in his own voice indicate that he never lost sight of that advantage. He believed (and the popular reception of his poetry in colonial times shows that he was correct) that the authority of having been through it all was sufficient to persuade people to consider seriously whatever observations or suggestions he might make concerning their own condition. Also, with a preacher's talent for understanding audience psychology, Wigglesworth knew that as he spoke under such authority no one could doubt either his sincerity or the sympathy he extended to all in comparable circumstances.

Examples of Wigglesworth speaking as spiritual father and as mediator abound in his verse and offer fair illustrations of his tone, language, and imagery. Whether as spiritual father or as mediator, Wigglesworth, like most seventeenth-century New England authors, always followed the prescriptions of Puritan plain style in his compositions. Typically, he related his personal experience or advice through homely language and commonplace events; he alluded to accessible biblical figures and stories for authority higher than his own to underscore both the universality of his experience and the value of such advice as he might offer; and he appealed directly to the common sense and faith of his audience for final verification of his point of view. In "A Postscript unto the Reader" from *The Day of Doom*, for instance, he used the spiritual father voice on several occasions in order to ameliorate the harsh emotive impact of events elaborated on in the title poem of that volume. Justifying the shock that he knew readers probably still felt from their reading of "The Day of Doom," Wigglesworth wrote:

> Nor speak I this, good Reader to torment thee
> Before the time, but rather to prevent thee
> From running head-long to thine own decay,
> In such a perillous and deadly way.
> We, who have known and felt Jehovah's terrours,
> Perswade men to repent them of their errours,
> And turn to God in time, e're his Decree
> Bring forth, and then there be no Remedee!
> If in the night, when thou art fast asleep,
> Some friend of thine, that better watch doth keep,
> Should see thy house all on a burning flame,

And thee almost inclosed with the same:
If such a friend should break thy door & wake thee,
Or else by force out of the peril take thee:
What? wouldst thou take his kindness in ill part?
Or frown upon him for his good desert? (11. 199-216)

Many important, typical elements of Wigglesworth's style and tone are represented in this passage. Concerning style, for instance, it is suggestive that here the terror of burning for eternity in hell, which earlier in *The Day of Doom* is documented through elaborate biblical evidence, is related to the imagined but commonplace terror of burning to death while asleep in one's own house. That image is not at all inappropriate, for in colonial times fire (along with storm or pestilence) was a common experience, with whole settlements reduced to ashes over night. Of course, Wigglesworth's readers would know this and so now would naturally relate the spiritual peril that Wigglesworth develops here and earlier to the physical peril they realized always threatened them. In this particular passage, he uses both the spiritual father pose and the mediator pose. Neither takes precedence over the other here; instead, they are developed as literary and psychological complements. On the one hand, the poet as spiritual father is a friend, who seeing his friend's house on fire, wakes the friend and so saves his life. In this instance, the spiritual father-friend is especially noteworthy for his interest and kindness, for the fires that threaten the spiritual lives of those in his flock are infinitely more destructive than the fires that someday may threaten their houses and bodies. On the other hand, the poet as mediator is a friend, but with the important difference that as mediator the poet has known "Jehovah's terrours" and writes in order to spare his friends from having to know them too. Finally, there is a purposeful consistency between the language of this passage and the language of poems that appear earlier in the volume. Words such as "torment," "decay," "perillous," "Remedee," and "desert" were quite familiar to readers at this juncture and may, in fact, have revived in some the terror and fear conveyed by their former use. However, here such words are significantly less threatening than before and serve the speaker's purpose by expressing his ultimate sincerity and concern. Whereas, for example, "desert" took on a distinctly negative tone whenever Christ or the narrator used it in "The Day of Doom" (as in, hell is the "just desert" of the wicked), here "desert" has a distinctly positive connotation, for it represents a gesture of kindness from a friend.

But perhaps the best examples of Wigglesworth speaking as spiritual father and mediator are to be found in *God's Controversy with New-England* and *Meat Out of the Eater*. In both works he uses the voices to great advantage as means to motivate people to follow his suggestions for reviving religion in both their communities and their individual lives. *God's Controversy with New-England* is a poetic jeremiad. For much of the poem Wigglesworth's voice is that of an angry Jehovah, who is on the verge of returning New England ("a fruitfull paradeis") to its original state ("an howling wildernes," possessed only by "bruits and salvage wights" [11. 191-192; 176]). Jehovah reminds Puritan readers that they come from godly stock ("folk ... from the brittish Iles," who "prized libertee" and wished "To serve and worship ... with all their might" [11. 169; 163; 166]), a stock which he has personally nourished and preserved in times of adversity. However, Jehovah is now angry because New Englanders have squandered their inheritance, and the litany of complaints he raises against his people more than sufficiently shows that his patience is at an end. Wigglesworth allows Jehovah 185 lines (11. 157-342) in which to elaborate his case against this "stiff-neckt race" (1. 313), and then has the narrator, "*a lover of New-England's Prosperity*," who opens the poem, return and, as mediator, report on the warnings and judgments Jehovah has displayed to prove New England's situation is desperate and summarize New England's options. Then, Wigglesworth steps in. In his own voice, a voice filled with sentiments such as sincerity and love, a voice that underscores the affirmative, positive tone that this particular poet-teacher wishes to convey, Wigglesworth speaks to a falling New England. There is no rancor, sulphur, or spleen here, only the genuine concern of the spiritual father for his flock. Rancor, sulphur, and spleen may move some people, but as far as Wigglesworth is personally concerned, positive shows of affection finally outweigh all negative shows as means to edify an audience and, in this case, move them to reform.

> Ah dear New England! dearest land to me:
> Which unto God hast hitherto been dear,
> And mayst be still more dear than formerlie,
> If to his voice thou wilt incline thine ear.
>
> Consider wel & wisely what the rod,
> Wherewith thou art from yeer to yeer chastized,
> Instructeth thee: Repent, and turn to God,
> Who wil not have his nurture be despized. . . .
>
> Cheer on, sweet souls, my heart is with you all,
> And shall be with you, maugre Sathan's might:
> And whereso'ere this body be a Thrall,
> Still in New-England shall be my delight.
> (11. 431-438, 443-446)

These are among the most genuinely personal expressions that Wigglesworth ever wrote. As such, they reveal a depth of character and concern that most previous critics have elected to ignore. Various songs and meditations in *Meat Out of the Eater* produce a comparable effect. There, however, as in the sample provided above from "A Postscript unto the Reader," Wigglesworth relies on homely details to support his observations, substantiate his advice, and convey his sincerity. Speaking from personal experience in the meditation that opens the volume, he had this to say to Christians who thought they could evade the "Cross":

>The Christian that expects
>An Earthly Paradise
>When Christ bids him take up the cross
>And bear it, is unwise.
>We must not on the knee
>Be alway dandled,
>Nor must we think to ride to Heaven
>Upon a Feather-bed.
>>("*Tolle Crucem*," Meditation I, 11. 17-24)

On another occasion he likened bodily and spiritual affliction to a ship's ballast and man's sins and lust to weeds that must be plowed under. For seventeenth-century readers of Wigglesworth's poems, such imagery was immediately comprehensible, and they likely found that they did not have to stretch their imagination too far in order to appreciate the implications that lines such as these held for them:

>Afflictions are like Ballast
>I'th' Bottom of a Ship;
>For tho perhaps without the same
>We might more lightly Skip:
>Yet every little puff
>Would quickly set us over,
>And sink us in the Ocean Sea
>No more for to Recover.
>
>Our hearts are over-run
>Much like a Fallow-field.
>Which must be broke and plowed up
>Before it Fruit can yeild:
>Afflictions are God's Plough
>Where-with He breaketh us,
>Tears up our *lusts* those noisome *weeds*
>And fitteth us for Use.
>>("*Tolle Crucem*," Meditation III, 11. 65-80)

Featherbeds, ballast, and weeds typify the level of homely images that Wigglesworth often developed in *Meat Out of the Eater*. Not only would they be immediately knowable to the reader, but as with their frequent appearance in sermons from this period, such images would also remind the reader that the poet (in this case, poet-teacher) was one of them, that he understood and appreciated their daily cares and concerns, and that no matter how abstract the concept, he wished to make religion relevant to their lives. In effect, such images reduced the distance between preachers or poets and their audience, and as

Wigglesworth's success suggests, they made a poet-teacher's message more appealing and convincing than it might otherwise have been. In a volume like *Meat Out of the Eater*, where man's necessary acceptance of adversity or affliction as a fact of life is a primary theme, such images could make palatable even the most distasteful observations on the human condition. For instance, one problem that Wigglesworth had to deal with in *Meat Out of the Eater* was the problem often represented by the plight of the biblical Job: God's faithful servant, suffering adversity and affliction, wondering why, and wondering too whether continued service to an ideal was worth the effort. Job's was not, of course, a unique experience, and as numerous diaries, autobiographies, and histories written in colonial New England show, in the New England wilderness there were many Puritan Jobs who too painfully understood and sympathized with that Old Testament figure's plight. In order to appeal to them and show he understood the emotional and spiritual turmoil of their lives, Wigglesworth produced passages such as these as preludes to statements about the final rewards all true, enduring saints eventually might enjoy. Speaking of those who despite their outward wickedness prosper, sometimes at the unfortunate expense of saints, he wrote:

> They flourish like a tree,
> They have the word at will:
> Their Breasts are flowing-full of Milk,
> Marrow their bones doth fill.
> They have no sorrows great
> Their vigour to decay:
> Nor is their moisture radical
> Consum'd and sweal'd away.
>
> While better men are sick,
> Their bodies are in health,
> Whil'st others are distrest with wants,
> They flow in worldly wealth.
> They have their time of peace,
> While others are in trouble.
> If other men have plenty too,
> They have it more then double.
> (*"Tolle Crucem,"* Meditation VII, 11. 25-40)

The voices of the spiritual father and the mediator are, then, the voices that Wigglesworth extensively and effectively developed in his verse. However, when neither voice seemed appropriate to his subject or when New England's people seemed to require harsher language to awaken them to the truth, he could effectively use another voice: the haranguing, vitriolic voice of the Puritan conscience. In the majority of Wigglesworth scholarship to date, this voice has been emphasized at the expense of his other poetic voices, and this fact alone may be responsible for the generally unflattering view today's readers and critics hold of Wigglesworth and his art.

Along with preachers Increase Mather, William Stoughton, and Thomas Shepard (the younger), Wigglesworth wrote just at the time that this voice achieved currency in New England in the sermonic form known as the jeremiad. "The Day of Doom," contrary to inherited opinion, does not develop as a jeremiad. However, in poems such as *God's Controversy with New-England* Wigglesworth wrote within the emerging jeremiad tradition and in Jehovah's speech in that poem expressed his position through a distinctly vitriolic voice. (In fact, in *God's Controversy with New-England* Wigglesworth anticipates many of the features of the jeremiad which did not achieve wide currency until the 1670s, but because the poem was not published at the time, he cannot be claimed to have influenced the jeremiad's rise to respectability.) In jeremiads the voice gave credibility to the invariably long lists of punishments for and warnings against the backsliding of New England's people, and it accentuated a preacher's dire predictions about the plantation's eventual fall lest God's latest chosen people repent and reform.

When necessary, Wigglesworth could use this voice with great facility. Sometimes he developed it subtly, as in this brief, sarcastic allusion to the Half-Way Covenant in "When as the wayes of Jesus Christ":

> When some within, and some without,
> Kick down the Churches wall
> Because the doore is found to be
> Too strait to let in all:
> The best can then nought else expect
> But to be turned out,
> Or to be trampled under foot
> By the unruly rout. (11. 9-16)

More often, however, he was quite open about his use of the voice and the effect he intended it to elicit. In *God's Controversy with New-England* Jehovah has the primary responsibility for unleashing invective upon New England. After specifying his complaints against New England in terms that leave nothing to the reader's imagination, Jehovah concludes his speech with this dread-inspiring, tightly-worded statement:

> Now therefore hearken and encline your ear,
> In judgement I will henceforth with you plead;
> And if by that you will not learn to fear,
> But still go on a sensuall life to lead:
> I'le strike at once an All-Consuming stroke;
> Nor cries nor tears shall then my fierce intent revoke.
> (11. 337-342)

And just in case Jehovah's point has been missed, Wigglesworth has his narrator, that lover of New England's prosperity, conclude his review of New England's options with this straight-forward restatement of Jehovah's position:

> Beware, O sinful-Land, beware;
> And do not think it strange
> That sorer judgements are at hand,
> Unless thou quickly change.
> Or God, or thou, must quickly change;
> Or else thou art undon:
> Wrath cannot cease, if sin remain,
> Where judgement is begun. (11. 423-430)

At times, Wigglesworth developed the vitriolic voice as his own, expressing thereby the poet-teacher's personal conviction of the extremity of New England's situation. He found room for the voice in *Meat Out of the Eater*, where one might least expect to find it. In "A Conclusion Hortatory," which completes the opening "*Tolle Crucem*" sequence of the volume, Wigglesworth predicted this result for people who did not properly improve upon affliction and adversity as God's gentle warnings against sin:

> Oh let *New-England* turn,
> When gentler Warning's given:
> Lest by our sins the Lord to use
> Severity be driven. (11. 97-100)

When Benjamin Bunker, his associate in the Malden church, died in 1670, Wigglesworth read Malden's loss as yet another "stroke" from God for his people's decline and decay. In itself, this was not an extreme gesture on Wigglesworth's part, for in the popular election, execution, and humiliation jeremiads of the 1670s and 1680s the loss of godly men was a familiar item in the long lists of God's warnings and judgments. What was unusual in this case, however, was Wigglesworth's method of elaborating on that stroke in an elegy.

Realizing, perhaps, that a vitriolic voice was inappropriate to an elegy, Wigglesworth devoted the first fifty-six lines of "Upon the much Lamented Death of that Precious servant ... Benjamin Buncker" to a sympathetic, consolatory description of Bunker's character. Bunker, he wrote, was "another Timothie," "a true Nathaniel," "A down-right honest Teacher," "A zealous, painfull Preacher" (11. 1, 9, 18, 20). Such language and description was, of course, appropriate to this particular poetic form and would have been expected by the audience. But the audience would not expect Wigglesworth's sudden shift in line 57 to the vitriolic voice and to what became, in effect, a fifty-five line poetic jeremiad. Wigglesworth opened the second section of the poem thus:

> O Maldon, Maldon thou hast long
> Enjoy'd a day of Grace;
> Thou hast a precious man of God
> Possessed in this place:

>But for thy sin, thou art bereft
>Of what thou did'st possess;
>Oh let thy sins afflict thee more
>Then do thy wants thee press. (11. 57-64)

In the six stanzas that follow this, Wigglesworth assumed the posture of Jeremiah. For the first three of those stanzas he reminded the people of Malden that "Great strokes, Great Anger do proclaime, / Great Anger, Greater sins" (11. 65-66), and he counseled them, "Awake, awake," "Repent, Repent" (11. 73, 81). For the last three stanzas he advanced several dire predictions about the future of God's latest chosen people and said that all would come to pass unless those people repent and reform. Speaking in terms that all could understand, he surmised,

>If that the founder melts in vain
>(Thy lusts do not decay)
>God will account thee worthless Dross,
>Fit to be cast away. (11. 89-92)

Finally, in a tone reminiscent of that expressed by Jehovah and the narrator in *God's Controversy with New-England*, Wigglesworth, in his own voice, concluded the elegy with this, the worst prediction of all for a "plantation religious":

>If this, and such like awfull strokes
>Do not our hearts awaken,
>Doubtless the Gospel will ere long
>Be wholly from us taken. (11. 105-108)

With the occasion, motivation, compensation, style, and voice of his poems supplied by a combination of external and personal influences on his life, the principal challenge remaining for poet Wigglesworth was to supply appropriate and readable topics for his verse. Except for the few Latin and English lines that he wrote sometime between 1659 and 1661, there is no evidence that he faced this challenge before mid-to-late-1661, when he began to compose poems for *The Day of Doom*. At that time he appears to have had little difficulty in finding specific topics to illustrate the message that as teacher he wanted to deliver. In the case of *The Day of Doom*, the title poem was likely composed first, its subject evolving out of an experience he recorded in his diary for 1653: "in my sleep I dream'd of the approach of the great and dreadful day of judgment; and was thereby exceedingly awakned in spirit ... to follow god with teares and crys until he gave me some hopes of his gracious good wil toward me."[29] The other poems that comprise the volume were likely composed in no particular order, save for the last in the volume, "A Song of Emptiness," which, according to its subtitle (*"To fill up the Empty Pages following"*), may have been composed as late as when the volume was in press. As a sign of Wigglesworth's artistic competency at this early stage of his career, it is important to notice that all poems in *The Day of Doom* serve as topical and thematic complements to "The Day of Doom," elaborating and clarifying for the edification of the reader concepts such as "judgment," "eternity," and "emptiness," which are first introduced in the volume's title poem.

As suggested above, principal topics for the songs and meditations collected in *Meat Out of the Eater* evolved exclusively out of Wigglesworth's personal experience with affliction and adversity. In that, the volume offers a unique measure of his character, a feature of the volume which only biographers have appreciated. Wigglesworth's intention for the volume was obviously that it console and edify all "enduring" saints by providing them with meaningful, universal lessons tested by the poet himself. Except for Song III of the "In Solitude Good Company" sequence, which Wigglesworth acknowledged in the volume was written about eight years before the other songs and meditations, the volume was composed in a rush of intense poetic activity in 1669. In his manuscript commonplace-book, now preserved at the New England Historic Genealogical Society, Wigglesworth recorded some details of the volume's composition. Without stating exactly how far along he was, on September 17, 1669, he wrote, "I have been long imployed in a great work composing poems about the cross." Though what Wigglesworth meant by "long imployed" is anyone's guess, in some entries he indicated that on a good day he could compose as many as twenty stanzas. During the last weeks of September and the first week of October he worked steadily on the volume, pausing only to address this brief supplication to his "muse": "[October 4,] And now do I seriously & honestly begg thy help & assistance for I am deeply sensible that without thee I can do nothing, & for thee I desire to do all. Oh guide my head, heart, hand, & all my might this day for thy sake & for the honour of thy name Amen." On October 15, he reported, "I am now upon the last Head (Heav'ly Crowns &c)." Finally, on October 18, 1669, he celebrated his birthday and "the birthday of this Book it being finished this morning," and he offered this prayer of thanks: "And now through thy grace & daily assistance, I have done composing. *Laus Deo*."

Topics for the remainder of his poems clearly evolved out of events in a world that Wigglesworth scrutinized with a poet-teacher's eye. Unlike the poems collected in *Meat Out of the Eater*, the poems in *The Day of Doom* as well as *God's Controversy with New-England* and the eight pieces collected in this edition as "occasional verse" all possess topical immediacy. Of these last pieces, the three sets of Latin and English verse composed about 1660 are highly personal and anticipate the personal content of *Meat Out of the Eater*. Wigglesworth wrote them as personal expressions of loneliness (brought on by the death of his first wife) and of depression and guilt (produced by his inability to fulfill the requirements of his ministry). In them, he achieved a level of consolation comparable to that which he eventually offered his public in *Meat Out of the Eater*. These verses were not published during Wigglesworth's life, and because of their highly personal content, there may be reason to believe he never intended for them to appear in print.

The remaining five pieces of occasional verse are essentially public statements. Though none were published during his life, there is no reason to suspect that Wigglesworth purposely suppressed any of them. Each addressed events that his audience would have been aware of and interested in and concerning which they might have appreciated a word from their poet-teacher. The elegy on Benjamin Bunker, for instance, addressed an event very close to the heart of the Malden community, while the "Song of Praise," composed on William Foster's return from captivity in 1673, spoke to an issue in which many New Englanders had an emotional, personal investment. In "When as the wayes of Jesus Christ" (about 1665), Wigglesworth provided a report on the status of New England's effort to check declension, and as his comments in that poem on the Half-Way Covenant, which are cited above, suggest, he, along with the popular preachers of the day, thought the effort had not gone far enough.

Finally, even "Death *Expected* and *Welcomed*" and "A Farewel to the World" are public statements. As the record of sermons published in New England between 1660 and 1750 indicates, a preacher traditionally presented his congregation with some final sermonic testimony concerning their association with each other. Such sermons typically addressed the close relation that had been established between the minister and his congregation, provided a first-hand assessment of both what the minister thought he had accomplished and what he thought the congregation had to improve on after he was gone, and offered the congregation this consolation: despite the pleasure he and the congregation had taken in each other's company, the minister advised that, finally, he was about to enter that world for which he was destined from the start. In "Death *Expected* and *Welcomed*" and "A Farewel to the World," Wigglesworth, the poet-teacher, presented his audience with a minister's "swan song," using the medium in which he had addressed them during so much of his career.

Chronology:
Significant Events in the Life of Michael Wigglesworth[30]

1631 The son of Edward and Esther (or Hester) Wigglesworth, Michael is born on October 18 in Yorkshire, England, which many years later he describes as "an ungodly Place, where the generality of the people rather derided then imitated . . . piety, . . . a place where . . . children had Learnt wickedness betimes."

1638 Before Michael is seven, the Wigglesworths, "meeting with opposition & persecution for Religion," decide "to pluck up their stakes . . . [and] expose themselves to the hazzard of the seas, and to the Distressing difficulties of a howling wilderness, that they might enjoy Liberty of Conscience & Christ in his ordinances"; after a treacherous voyage, they arrive in Charlestown, in New England, sometime between August 7 and September 15, remaining there for only a few weeks; in October, probably in the company of followers of the Rev. Ezekiel Rogers, they travel to New Haven, Connecticut, aboard a ship that is nearly lost in a storm; the Wigglesworths pass the winter of 1638-39 in a damp cellar in New Haven, where Michael falls ill.

1639-41 Before his eighth birthday, Michael is sent to study with Ezekiel Cheever, New England's famous schoolmaster and within two years he is writing Latin compositions; while working in his fields during the winter of 1640-41, the elder Wigglesworth strains himself, which results in a debilitating lameness that lasts until his death; probably in the spring of 1641, Michael is removed from school to assist with household and farm responsibilities.

1644 Having lost his competency in Latin and having "no disposition" to resume his studies, Michael is forced to return to school by his father; he later gives this account of his father's decision: "not judging me fit for husbandry," he "was not wel satisfied in keeping me from Learning whereto I had been designed from my infancy."

1647 After three years of diligent effort and with "the benefit of Religion & strict education," Michael enters Harvard College.

1647-51 At Harvard, by reason of social position or intellectual competency (probably the latter), Wigglesworth ranks first among classmates Thomas Dudley (grandson of Gov. Thomas Dudley and Gov. John Winthrop), Seaborn Cotton (son of the Rev. John Cotton), and Isaac and Ichabod Chauncy (sons of the Rev. Charles Chauncy); he initially decides to pursue studies in medicine, but under the influence of the Rev. Jonathan Mitchell, his tutor and, later, author of a recommendatory poem for *The Day of Doom*, he undergoes a profound conversion experience in late 1650 or early 1651 and decides to study for another career, which he subsequently explains thus: "I had my Ends and God had his Ends far differing from mine, yet it pleased him to Bless my studies, & to make me grow in Knowledge both in the Tongues & Inferior Arts & also in Divinity. But when I had been there about 3 yeers and a half; God in his Love & Pitty to my soul wrought a great change in me, both in heart & Life and from that Time forward I learnt to study with God & for God ... and did chuse to serve Christ in the work of the ministry if he would please to fit me for it."

1652-53   After graduation, Wigglesworth remains at Harvard as a tutor and is elected a Fellow of the college by the Harvard Corporation; Shubael Dummer, John Eliot, Eleazer Mather, and Increase Mather are among his pupils at this time; now begins a life-long friendship with Increase Mather, based upon mutual respect and a sympathy of religious attitudes; in 1653, Wigglesworth composes two orations on "eloquence" for delivery at the college; throughout this period he prepares himself for the ministry, preaching occasionally around Boston and on Martha's Vineyard in 1653; Edward Wigglesworth dies in New Haven on October 1, 1653, leaving in addition to his widow and son a daughter, Abigail, who is about thirteen at the time.

1654   Wigglesworth preaches at Malden, Massachusetts, where in the early fall he is invited to settle permanently; unsure of his future prospects in Malden and uncertain of his calling, he declines to be ordained, although he remains in Malden and preaches there regularly until spring, 1655; in a spiritual diary kept during the mid-1650s he records numerous instances of religious self-doubt, frets over his apparently declining physical condition, and anguishes over feelings of guilt and shame brought on by an inability to control his sexual urges -- personal concerns that dominate this period and surface throughout his lie.

1655   After a courtship marred by his own questions as to whether his love constituted incest, on May 18, Wigglesworth marries Mary Reyner, his cousin, in Rowley, Massachusetts; throughout the summer, plagued by a cough and sore throat, he remains with his wife's family in Rowley, leaving on occasion to preach several sermons before an increasingly impatient Malden congregation; in September, the people of Malden press him to decide on their invitation, and Esther Wigglesworth writes to say that within the month she and her daughter will be coming from New Haven to live with Wigglesworth and his new wife; pressured by familial responsibilities, on October 4, Wigglesworth finally decides to settle in Malden, and with Mary (then pregnant), Esther, and Abigail, he moves into the Malden parsonage about October 20.

1656   Wigglesworth's daughter, Mercy, is born on February 20; on August 25, Wigglesworth receives a "letter of dismission" from the Cambridge church, which he had joined during his college years, and with letter in hand, he informs the Malden congregation that he is prepared to become one of their members, a necessary prelude to ordination; the Malden congregation accepts him into full communion on September 7, though he is not immediately ordained.

1657 Wigglesworth is ordained in Malden, probably in May; despite his general physical debility, which in fact would last almost without interruption until 1685 or 1686, he settles into the arduous routine of being both teacher and pastor (he was ordained only the former) to the small congregation and appears to have discharged his responsibilities satisfactorily for most of the year; in a minor capacity, he puts the smattering of medical knowledge he gained at Harvard to use among the Malden people.

1658 Increasingly weak and bothered by a recurrent sore throat, Wigglesworth is unable any longer to preach the usual two Sunday sermons and to fulfill other public responsibilities associated with his position; Malden followers of Marmaduke Matthews, Wigglesworth's liberal and unorthodox predecessor in the Malden church, surface to challenge several of their new teacher's conservative opinions on church membership and doctrine, while other members of the congregation, noticing Wigglesworth's lack of vigor and wondering whether his illness might be psychosomatic, begin to question openly the wisdom of their call; on June 19, Wigglesworth responds to what he considers a decline of piety in Malden and answers questions about his health in an open letter to his congregation; eventually happy with Wigglesworth once again, on November 11, the Malden congregation votes to build a new and larger meeting-house.

1659 Despondent and ill throughout the year, Wigglesworth worries about signs of declension and political contention within his congregation; ill for most of the year, Mary Reyner Wigglesworth dies on December 21, leaving her ailing husband to care for his aged mother and his four-year old daughter (his sister, Abigail, is by this time married to Benjamin Sweetser).

1660-61 Wigglesworth increasingly reduces his ministry to the point of scandal, and though he is allowed to live in the Malden parsonage, he receives no financial compensation from his parish; disconsolate over the loss of his wife and his lack of energy for pastoral labor, he composes three sets of verse, two in Latin, one in English, which reveal the depth of his depression, self-doubt, and loneliness; with all devout New England Puritans, he is devastated by the news, which reaches the colony in November, 1660, that Charles II has assumed the throne; in 1661, no longer able to address his people from the pulpit, Wigglesworth decides on another medium -- poetry -- to convey his overdue instructional messages, and he begins to compose "The Day of Doom" and related poems; in December, 1661, the Malden congregation considers the possibility of hiring a pastoral assistant to serve with Wigglesworth.

1662 Wigglesworth continues to work on poems for *The Day of Doom*, and by the end of January he enters into an agreement with printers Samuel Green and Marmaduke Johnson of Cambridge for publication of the volume upon its completion; with *The Day of Doom* completed and in press, in late summer Wigglesworth begins to compose a long piece, *God's Controversy with New-England*, in which he lashes out against New England's declension and interprets evidence of God's wrath toward and judgments against his latest chosen people; he completes *God's Controversy with New-England* before the end of the year, but the poem is destined to remain in manuscript for the next two centuries.

1663 When it appears, probably in summer, 1662, *The Day of Doom* is a success, with all 1,800 copies of the first printing selling out within a year; on September 23, Wigglesworth embarks with John Younglove, a friend, on a voyage to Bermuda, hoping to find a cure there for his lingering sickness, but during the month-long voyage, he catches a severe cold and is further weakened by the rolling and pitching of the ship; after he leaves Malden, the congregation calls Benjamin Bunker to serve as pastor.

1664 A second printing of *The Day of Doom* probably appears during Wigglesworth's absence; his health somewhat restored but still suffering the psychological burden of depression, doubt, and loneliness which marked his earlier years, Wigglesworth returns to New England in May; leaving all ministerial duties to Bunker, he enlarges his medical practice, having studied recent advances in remedial medicine during his Bermuda sojourn, and he begins to tutor local boys for admission to Harvard; with forty-seven of the colony's ministers, he signs (as "pastour") a letter protesting any imposition of articles associated with the Church of England on Congregational churches of Massachusetts Bay.

1665-68 Moderately active in his medical practice, but with his own health yet unrestored, Wigglesworth continues to leave the Malden ministry to Bunker and has minimal dealings with the affairs of the larger Massachusetts Bay ministry; about 1665, he composes "When as the wayes of Jesus Christ," a poem in which he predicts that a day of reckoning for its backsliding and its relaxation of rules governing church membership is about to befall New England; he prepares a new edition of *The Day of Doom*, which, enlarged with notes and *marginalia*, is published at the Cambridge press under his supervision in 1666, the same year that the unauthorized edition appears in London; Wigglesworth likely composes some additional occasional verse during the period, but no concrete evidence of it survives.

1669 Still suffering from a variety of physical ailments, in the spring Wigglesworth consults a number of local physicians on a cure, but without positive results; in late summer and early fall he composes several new poems "about the cross," which, with "Riddles Unriddled or, Christian Paradoxes," composed between September and October, he collects under the title *Meat Out of the Eater*.

1670-78 Enduring the most dreary, unproductive, and lonely period of his life, Wigglesworth becomes a sort of living proof of "the necessity of afflictions" theme that unifies *Meat Out of the Eater*; his associate, Benjamin Bunker, dies on February 3, 1670, on which occasion Wigglesworth composes an elegy that remains in manuscript for two centuries, and though the exact date is unknown, Esther Wigglesworth is presumed to have died early in this period; Mercy, Wigglesworth's daughter, marries Samuel Brackenbury, a physician, in 1672, and eventually moves to Boston; maintaining a modest medical practice, Wigglesworth has no energy for pastoral responsibilities, so in 1674 a distressed congregation calls Benjamin Blakeman (or Blackman) to serve as his assistant, but Blakeman finds the Malden ministry (and, possibly, Wigglesworth) disagreeable and moves to Maine in 1678; throughout this time Wigglesworth is at odds with leaders of his congregation who subscribe to many of the liberal innovations then sweeping through New England's churches, and his occasional appeals on behalf of the old-style orthodoxy are largely ignored by a rebellious and, with good reason, disaffected congregation; *Meat Out of the Eater* appears from Green's and Johnson's Cambridge press early in 1670, but the volume falls far short of the success enjoyed by *The Day of Doom*; in addition to his elegy on Bunker, Wigglesworth composes only one other known poem during the period, a "Song of Praise" in 1673 in celebration of William Foster's return from captivity under the Turks.

1679 After twenty years of "widowhood" and of almost constant physical, psychological, and sexual distress, Wigglesworth shocks his Malden congregation and scandalizes his ministerial colleagues throughout the colony by falling in love with Martha Mudge, a woman at least twenty-five years his junior, who had been employed as his housekeeper; an outraged Boston clergy tries to reason with him against his apparent intention to marry Martha, and on May 8, Increase Mather, voicing the concern of all, writes to his friend and former tutor, denouncing Martha as "your servant mayd . . . of obscure parentage . . . & of no church, nor so much as Baptised," and cautioning him, "The like never was in New-England. Nay, I question whether the like hath bin known in the Christian world;" unimpressed by public opinion and, for one in a precarious financial position, unconcerned that he might lose both his parsonage and whatever meager compensation he was receiving from his congregation and patients, Wigglesworth marries Martha at an undisclosed location sometime before the end of the year; in September, the ministers of the colony hold a synod in Boston, and in *The Necessity of Reformation* (Boston, 1679), penned by Increase Mather, they outline the causes of New England's fall from God's grace and prescribe cures for the same not unlike the causes and cures specified years earlier by Wigglesworth in "The Day of Doom" and *God's Controversy with New-England*; sometime late in the year, Wigglesworth, still unable to serve the spiritual needs of his congregation and insulted by public displays of disrespect toward Martha, draws up "Some Grounds & Reasons for Laying Down My Office Relation," thereby offering his resignation to the people of Malden.

1680-81 The Malden church ignores Wigglesworth's offer to resign and in February, 1680, hires Thomas Cheever, the son of Wigglesworth's first schoolmaster, to serve as his assistant; though physically weak, Wigglesworth maintains his medical practice and on May 19, 1680, is named one of the four freemen from Malden; now, as a member of the colony's political élite and as a continuing member of the colony's ecclesiastic hierarchy (though in a diminished capacity), he joins with his colleagues in noticing various practical demonstrations of God's wrath toward New England (numerous fires, the harshness of the 1680-81 winter, and the dissolution of Parliament by Charles II in March, 1861); twenty-five years after the birth of his first child, Wigglesworth's second child, Abigail, is born in

March, 1681; Thomas Cheever is formally ordained as Wigglesworth's assistant on July 27, 1681.

1682-83 Wigglesworth's family continues to expand, with daughter Mary born in September or October, 1682, and daughter Martha born on December 21, 1683; his health yet impaired, Wigglesworth devotes most of his time to his medical practice and may well have been at work on revisions of *Meat Out of the Eater*, which presumably appeared in two editions between the first edition in 1670 and the fourth in 1689; though there is no evidence to support the assumption, an American edition of *The Day of Doom* is thought to have been published in Cambridge in 1683.

1684-85 Whether because his home was alive again with the activities of a young wife and three young daughters, or because under Cheever the administration of his Malden congregation seemed to be deteriorating rather than improving, or because, as some said, he was touched by divine Providence, Wigglesworth begins to regain his long-lost strength, and by the end of 1685 he is increasingly in the public's view and conversation throughout the Boston-Malden area; after the death of John Rogers in July, 1684, he is approached by Increase Mather to succeed Rogers as president of Harvard, an offer which he declines; with dire implications for Puritan New England, James II assumes the throne in February, 1685, and eventually revokes the colony's right to representative self-government; Wigglesworth's fifth daughter, Esther, is born in April, 1685; making his first major public appearance in almost thirty years, on September 14, 1685, Wigglesworth travels to Cambridge to preach the annual artillery election sermon; preaching after Wigglesworth's funeral in 1705, Cotton Mather offers the following summary of the amazing change that occurs in Wigglesworth during these two years: "It pleased God ... wondrously to restore his *Faithful Servant*. He that had been for ... years almost *Buried Alive*, comes abroad again."

1686-88 Virtually recovered from his physical and psychological distresses, Wigglesworth begins to assume primary responsibility for his Malden congregation; early in 1686 the congregation publicly denounces Thomas Cheever for using profanity in a Salem tavern and for exhibiting a lack of seriousness during Sabbath observances; at Wigglesworth's request, a council of churchmen, which includes Increase and Cotton Mather, Judge Samuel Sewall, and Samuel Willard, convenes in Malden in April to discuss Cheever's conduct and eventually votes to dismiss him from the pulpit; with his personal and public affairs newly ordered, and for the first time in a long time enjoying the open esteem of many of his fellows, Wigglesworth becomes Malden's sole pastor-teacher, restoring a relation that had existed primarily on paper since 1655; on May 12, 1686, he rides to Boston to preach the annual election sermon before the governor and other officials; despite his new-found favor in Malden, Wigglesworth remains at odds with a powerful liberal faction in his congregation, which prevents him from receiving adequate compensation for his duties for several years; on December 20, 1686, Sir Edmund Andros arrives in Boston as Royal Governor of New England, and over the next several months he introduces numerous religious and political reforms, all of which outrage the Puritan populace; Wigglesworth's sixth daughter, Dorothy, is born on February 22, 1687; throughout the remainder of 1687-88, Wigglesworth, like many Puritan colonists, chafes under restrictions imposed by Andros and is hopeful about the mission of his friend and former pupil, Increase Mather, who under the cover of darkness escapes from Boston to England in 1688 to plead the colony's case before the throne.

1689-90 Wigglesworth's seventh child, a son, Samuel, is born on February 4, 1689; in April, 1689, the colonists rejoice at the news that James II is deposed and that New England is once again under Protestant rule; unfortunately, William and Mary show no inclination toward returning New England to the terms of the original charter; a new edition of *Meat Out of the Eater* appears in 1689; on September 4, 1690, Martha Mudge Wigglesworth dies, leaving Wigglesworth, now almost sixty, to care for their six young children; fully engaged in his multiple domestic, pastoral, and administrative responsibilities, Wigglesworth mourns the passing of his wife, but without any of the signs of depression and loneliness that marked the death of his first wife in 1659; on October 13, 1690, he meets in Charlestown with fellow ministers from the Boston area, and with them he forms the "Cambridge Association" and agrees to meet monthly to discuss means to improve the quality of Christian life in New England; sometime in October, 1690, he meets Sybil Sparhawk Avery, the widow of physician Jonathan Avery, in Dedham, Massachusetts.

1691-92 After a pleasant but brief courtship, Wigglesworth marries Sybil Avery in Dedham on June 23, 1691; the people of Malden and Wigglesworth are quite pleased with his new domestic arrangement, though Wigglesworth worries about how he will support his own six children, his new wife, and the three young daughters of her previous marriage; as a sign that he is comfortable with and respected in his public role, on November 10, 1691, Wigglesworth is selected moderator of the council of churches meeting at Lynn, Massachusetts, for the purpose of resolving difficulties within the Lynn congregation; on May 14, 1692, Increase Mather returns from England with a new charter, which, despite its shortcomings, brings a sense of political and religious stability to the colony; for much of 1692 New England is racked by the specter of witchcraft in Salem, and though Wigglesworth does not comment publicly on the Salem trials and executions, on October 3, 1692, he joins with members of the Cambridge Association, who vote unanimously to approve Increase Mather's *Cases of Conscience Concerning Evil Spirits* . . . (Boston, 1692).

1693-1700 Along with his years of domestic happiness with Martha Mudge, this period represents another high-point in Wigglesworth's private and public life; while the power of New England's Puritan clergymen gradually diminishes over these years in consequence of the witchcraft scandal, political reform, and the appearance of an increasingly cosmopolitan, secular temper among New England's people, Wigglesworth stands out for his continual rise in influence and prestige throughout the colony; with the minister's reputation as preacher, poet, and vigorous defender of the old "New England Way" thoroughly established, the Wigglesworths entertain and, in turn, are entertained by members of the colony's political and ministerial élite; members of the Malden congregation are now genuinely concerned about the practical comfort of their minister and his family, voting repeatedly to increase Wigglesworth's fire-wood supply and salary; early in 1693, Wigglesworth's second son, Edward, is born, a boy destined to become Harvard's first Hollis Professor of Divinity; on June 1, 1696, Wigglesworth preaches his second election sermon before the Ancient and Honorable Artillery Company; in 1697, he is appointed a Fellow of Harvard College; probably in 1699, he begins his last revision of *The Day of Doom*.

1700-1705 Now in his seventies, Wigglesworth continues to exert influence on the ecclestiastic affairs of the colony and is a subject of singular praise and admiration throughout New England; continuing his service as Malden's pastor-teacher and physician, he readies a final version of *The Day of Doom* for press; enlarged over previous editions with scriptural notes and *marginalia*, the fifth American edition of *The Day of Doom* appears in Boston in 1701; according to the title page of the 1717 edition of *Meat Out of the Eater*, Wigglesworth undertakes some modest revisions of the volume in 1703, but the extent to which the revisions as found are his own work is open to question; his domestic and social life continuing in the satisfying vein of the period 1693-1700, he spends much time in the company of Increase Mather and Judge Sewall, his closest friends; on July 22, 1704, he writes to Mather to express his personal conviction of guilt and shame over the witchcraft episode; sometime between 1704 and 1705, he writes his last two poems: "Death Expected and Welcomed" and "A Farewel to the World"; on May 27, 1705, he officiates before his Malden congregation for the last time, falling ill with a fever during the following week; after Increase Mather and others visit his bedside, Wigglesworth dies on Sunday, June 10, 1705, and is buried in Malden's Sandy Bank (now Bell Rock) Cemetery; on June 24, 1705, Cotton Mather preaches *A Faithful Man, Described and Rewarded* before Wigglesworth's former congregation; on July 4, 1705, Edward Holyoke, in his Latin oration presented during the Harvard College commencement exercises, memorializes Wigglesworth as *Maldonatus Orthodoxus*; eventually, a carved slate stone is placed over Wigglesworth's grave, which, still standing, reads:

>   Here Lyes Buried ye Body of
>   That Faithfull Servant of
>   Jesus Christ ye Reverend
>   Mr Michael Wigglesworth
>   Pastour of ye Church of Christ
>   At Maulden [50] Years: Who
>   Finished His Work and Entred
>   Apon an Eternal Sabbath
>   Of Rest on ye Lords Day June
>   ye 10th 1705 in ye 74th Year of His Age

He Lies In'erd in Silent Grave
Below   Mauldens Physician
For Soul and Body Two.

A Note on the Present Text of the Poems

In selecting sources for the texts that follow, the editor has consistently chosen manuscript versions over previously published versions of Wigglesworth's poems. However, for *The Day of Doom*, *Meat Out of the Eater*, and several items collected under "Occasional Verse," no manuscripts appear to survive. For *The Day of Doom* and *Meat Out of the Eater*, which together incorporate the overwhelming majority of Wigglesworth's poems, the last *American* editions printed during Wigglesworth's life have been used as sources, their authority predicated on the evidence, albeit slight, that since Wigglesworth is said to have supervised their publication, they may be regarded as representative of his final intentions toward his work. For those occasional poems that survive only in texts provided by someone other than Wigglesworth, versions printed closest to Wigglesworth's own time have been used as sources. Complete publication histories for all poems, for whole volumes as well as for occasional verse, have been provided in headnotes in "Notes on Sources, Editions, and Texts," below.

In the edition that follows, every effort has been made to be complete and to be faithful to what appear to be Wigglesworth's final intentions toward his work. To that end, all stylistic peculiarities and irregularities found in texts used as sources have been preserved. This rule applies to spelling, capitalization, italicization, line indentation, and punctuation -- as long as the way they appear in the source does not impede clear reading and understanding of the poems. Whenever one or the other stylistic feature as found compromised clarity or meaning, the feature was altered in a manner consistent with Wigglesworth's typical usage. All such alterations and other details of editorial method have been documented in "Notes on Sources, Editions, and Texts."

Finally, in the interest of completeness, "I *Walk'd and did a little* Mole-hill *view*" and Jonathan Mitchell's recommendatory poem for *The Day of Doom*, "On the following Work, and It's Author," have been included in appendices to this edition. The first poem has often been attributed to Wigglesworth, although it does not appear in any collection of poems which he is know to have authorized. As explained in "Notes on Sources, Editions, and Texts," the present editor concurs in the judgment of those who reject the poem as Wigglesworth's.

THE POEMS OF
MICHAEL WIGGLESWORTH

THE DAY OF DOOM:
Or,
A Poetical Description of
The Great and Last Judgement.

To the Christian Reader

Reader, I am a fool,
And have adventured
To play the fool this once for Christ,
The more his fame to spread.
If this my foolishness 5
Help thee to be more wise,
I have attained what I seek,
And what I onely prize.

Thou wonderest perhaps,
That I in Print appear, 10
Who in the Pulpit dwell so nigh,
Yet come so seldome there:
The God of Heaven knows
What grief to me it is,
To be with-held from Serving Christ: 15
No sorrow like to this.

This is the sorest pain
That I have felt or feel:
Yet have I stood some shocks that might
Make stronger Men to reel. 20
I find more true delight
In serving of my Lord,
Than all the good things upon Earth,
Without it, can afford.

And could my strength endure, 25
That work I count so dear;
Not all the Riches of Peru
Should hire me to forbear;
But I'm a Prisoner,
Under a heavy Chain: 30
Almighty God's afflicting hand,
Doth me perforce restrain.

>   *Yet some* (I know) *do judge,*
>   *Mine inability,*
>   *To come abroad and do Christ's Work,* 35
>   *To be Melancholly;*
>   *And that I'm not so weak,*
>   *As I my self conceit,*
>   *But who, in other things have found*
>   *Me so conceited yet?* 40
>
>   *Of who of all my friends,*
>   *That have my tryals seen,*
>   *Can tell the time in seven years,*
>   *When I have dumpish been?*
>   *Some think my voice is strong,* 45
>   *Most times when I do Preach:*
>   *But ten days after what I feel*
>   *And suffer, few can reach.*
>
>   *My prisoned thoughts break forth,*
>   *When open'd is the door,* 50
>   *With greater force and violence,*
>   *And strain my voice the more.*
>   *But vainly do they tell,*
>   *That I am growing stronger,*
>   *Who hear me speak in half an hour,* 55
>   *Till I can speak no longer.*
>
>   *Some for, because they see not*
>   *My chearfulness to fail,*
>   *Nor that I am disconsolate,*
>   *Do think I nothing ail.*
>   *If they had born my griefs,* 60
>   *Their courage might have fail'd them,*
>   *And all the Town* (perhaps) *have known*
>   (Once and again) *what ail'd them.*
>
>   *But why should I complain* 65
>   *That have so good a God,*
>   *That doth mine heart with comfort fill,*
>   *Ev'n whilst I feel his Rod?*
>   *In God I have been strong,*
>   *When wearied and worn out;* 70
>   *And joy'd in him, when twenty woes*
>   *Assail'd me round about.*

Nor speak I this to boast;
But make Apology
For mine own self, and answer those 75
That fail in Charity.
I am (alas) *as frail,*
Impatient a Creature,
As most that tread upon the ground,
And have as bad a nature. 80

Let God be magnify'd,
Whose everlasting strength
Upholds me under sufferings
Of more than ten years length.
Through whose Almighty pow'r 85
Although I am surrounded
With sorrows more than can be told,
Yet am I not confounded.

For his dear sake have I
This service undertaken, 90
For I am bound to honour Him,
Who hath not me forsaken.
I am a Debtor too,
Unto the sons of Men;
Whom wanting other means, I would 95
Advantage with my Pen.

I would, But (ah!) *my strength,*
When tried, proves so small,
That to the ground without effect,
My wishes often fall. 100
Weak heads, and hands, and states,
Great things cannot produce:
And therefore I this little Piece
Have publish'd for thine use.

Although the thing be small, 105
Yet my good will therein,
Is nothing less than if it had
A larger Volumn been.
Accept it then in Love,
And read it for thy good: 110
There's nothing in't can do thee hurt,
If rightly understood.

*The God of Heaven grant
These Lines so well to speed,
That thou the things of thine own peace,* 115
*Through them may'st better heed,
And may'st be stirred up
To stand upon thy guard,
That Death and Judgment may not come,
And find thee unprepar'd.* 120

*Oh get a part of Christ,
And make the Judge thy Friend:
So shalt thou be assured of
A happy, glorious end.
Thus prayes thy real Friend,* 125
*And Servant for Christ's Sake,
Who had he strength would not refuse,
More pains for thee to take.*

                    Michael Wigglesworth.

A Prayer unto Christ
The Judge of the World

O Dearest Dread, most glorious King,
I'le of thy justest Judgments sing:
Do thou my head and heart inspire,
To Sing aright, as I desire.
Thee, thee alone I'le invocate, 5
For I do much abominate
To call the Muses *to mine aid:*
Which is th' Unchristian use, and trade
Of some that Christians would be thought,
And yet they worship worse then nought. 10
Oh! what a deal of Blasphemy,
And Heathenish Impiety,
In Christian Poets may be found,
Where Heathen gods with praise are Crown'd,
They make Jehovah *to stand by* 15
Till Juno, Venus, Mercury,
With frowning Mars, *and thundering* Jove
Rule Earth below, and Heaven above.
But I have learnt to pray to none,
Save unto God in Christ alone. 20
Nor will I laud, no, not in jest,
That which I know God doth detest.
I reckon it a damning evil
To give Gods Praises to the Devil.
Thou, Christ, *art he to whom I pray,* 25
Thy Glory fain I would display.
Oh, guide me by thy sacred Sprite
So to indite, and so to write,
That I thine holy Name may praise,
And teach the Sons of men thy wayes. 30

The Day of Doom

1

The security of the
World before Christs
coming to Judgment.
Luke 12:19.

Still was the night, Serene and Bright,
    When all Men sleeping lay;
Calm was the season, and carnal reason
    Thought so 'twould last for ay.
Soul, take thine ease, let sorrow cease,
    much good thou has in store:
This was their Song, their Cups among,
    the Evening before.

2

Matt. 25:5.

Wallowing in all kind of sin,
    vile wretches lay secure:
The best of men had scarcely then
    their Lamps kept in good ure.
Virgins unwise, who through disguise
    amongst the best were number'd,
Had clos'd their eyes; yea, and the wise
    through sloth and frailty slumber'd.

3

Matt. 24:37, 38.

Like as of old, when Men grow bold
    God's threatnings to contemn,
Who stopt their Ear, and would not hear,
    when Mercy warned them:
But took their course, without remorse,
    till God began to powre
Destruction the World upon
    in a tempestuous showre.

4

1 *Thess.* 5:3.

They put away the evil day,
    And drown'd their care and fears,
Till drown'd were they, and swept away
    by vengeance unawares:
So at the last, whilst Men sleep fast
    in their security,
Surpriz'd they are in such a snare
    as cometh suddenly.

	5	
The Suddenness,	For at midnight brake forth a Light,	
Majesty, & Terrour of	which turn'd the night to day,	
Christ's appearing.	And speedily an hideous cry	35
Matt. 25:6.	did all the world dismay.	
2 Pet. 3:10.	Sinners awake, their hearts do ake,	
	trembling their loynes surprizeth;	
	Amaz'd with fear, by what they hear,	
	each one of them ariseth.	40

6

They rush from Beds with giddy heads,
    and to their windows run,
Viewing this light, which shines more bright
Matt. 24:29, 30.   then doth the Noon-day Sun.
Straightway appears (they see't with tears)   45
    the Son of God most dread;
Who with his Train comes on amain
    To Judge both Quick and Dead.

7

Before his face the Heav'ns gave place,
2 Pet. 3:10.   and Skies are rent asunder,   50
With mighty voice, and hideous noise,
    more terrible than Thunder.
His brightness damps heav'ns glorious lamps
    and makes them hide their heads,
As if afraid and quite dismay'd,   55
    they quit their wonted steads.

8

Ye sons of men that durst contemn
    the Threatnings of Gods Word,
How cheer you now? your hearts, I trow,
    are thrill'd as with a sword.   60
Now Atheist blind, whose brutish mind
    a God could never see,
Dost thou perceive, dost now believe,
    that Christ thy Judge shall be?

9

Stout Courages, (whose hardiness
    could Death and Hell out-face)
Are you as bold now you behold
    your Judge draw near apace?
They cry, no, no: Alas! and wo!
    our Courage all is gone:
Our hardiness (fool hardiness)
    hath us undone, undone.

10

No heart so bold, but now grows cold
    and almost dead with fear:
Rev. 6:16.   No eye so dry, but now can cry,
    and pour out many a tear.
Earths Potentates and pow'rful States,
    Captains and Men of Might
Are quite abasht, their courage dasht
    at this most dreadful sight.

11

Mean men lament, great men do rent
    their Robes, and tear their hair:
Matt. 24:30.   They do not spare their flesh to tear
    through horrible despair.
All Kindreds wail: all hearts do fail:
    horror the world doth fill
With weeping eyes, and loud out-cries,
    yet knows not how to kill.

12

Rev. 6:15, 16.   Some hide themselves in Caves and Delves,
    in places under ground:
Some rashly leap into the Deap,
    to scape by being drown'd:
Some to the Rocks (O sensless blocks!)
    and woody Mountains run,
That there they might this fearful sight,
    and dreaded Presence shun.

13

In vain do they to Mountains say,
    Fall on us, and us hide
From Judges ire, more hot than fire,
    for who may it abide? 100
No hiding place can from his Face,
    sinners at all conceal,
Whose flaming Eyes hid things doth 'spy,
    and darkest things reveal.

14

The Judge draws nigh, exalted high 105
    upon a lofty Throne,
Matt. 25:31.   Amidst the throng of Angels strong,
    lo, Israel's Holy One!
The excellence of whose presence
    and awful Majesty 110
Amazeth nature, and every Creature,
    doth more than terrify.

15

Rev. 6:14.   The Mountains smoak, the Hills are shook,
    the Earth is rent and torn,
As if she should be clean dissolv'd, 115
    or from the center born.
The Sea doth roar, forsakes the shore,
    and shrinks away for fear;
The wild Beasts flee into the Sea,
    so soon as he draws near. 120

16

Whose Glory bright, whose wondrous might,
    whose Power Imperial,
So far surpass whatever was
    in Realms Terrestrial;
That tongues of men (nor Angels pen) 125
    cannot the same express,
And therefore I must pass it by,
    lest speaking should transgress.

17

1 *Thess.* 4:16.	Before his Throne a Trump is blown,
Resurrection of the	Proclaiming th' Day of Doom: 130
Dead.	Forthwith he cries, Ye Dead arise,
John 5:28, 29.	and unto Judgment come.

No sooner said, but 'tis obey'd;
    Sepulchers open'd are:
Dead Bodies all rise at his call,   135
    and's mighty power declare.

18

Both Sea and Land, at his Command,
    their Dead at once surrender:
The Fire and Air constrained are
    also their dead to tender.   140
The mighty word of this great Lord
    links Body and Soul together
Both of the Just, and the unjust,
    to part no more for ever.

19

The living Changed.   The same translates, from Mortal states   145
    to Immortality,
All that survive, and be alive,
    i'th' twinkling of an eye:

Luke 20:36.   That so they may abide for ay
1 *Cor.* 15:52.   to endless weal or woe;   150
Both the Renate and Reprobate
    are made to dy no more.

20

All brought to   His winged Hosts flie through all Coasts,
Judgment.   together gathering
Matt. 24:31.   Both good and bad, both quick and dead,   155
    and all to Judgment bring.
Out of their holes those creeping Moles,
    that hid themselves for fear,
By force they take, and quickly make
    before the Judge appear.   160

21

2 Cor. 5:10.	Thus every one before the Throne
The Sheep separated	of Christ the Judge is brought,
from the Goats.	Both righteous and impious
Matt. 25:32.	that good or ill had wrought.

    A separation, and diff'ring station   165
        by Christ appointed is
(To sinners sad) 'twixt good and bad,
        'twixt Heirs of woe and bliss.

22

Who are Christ's Sheep.	At Christ's right hand the Sheep do stand,
Matt. 5:10, 11.	his holy Martyrs, who 170

For his dear Name suffering shame,
    calamity and woe,
Like Champions stood, & with their Blood
    their testimony sealed;
Whose innocence without offence,   175
    to Christ their Judge appealed.

23

Next unto whom there find a room

Heb. 12:5, 6, 7.   all Christ's afflicted ones,
Who being chastised, neither despised
    nor sank amidst their groans: 180
Who by the Rod were turn'd to God,
    and loved him the more,
Not murmuring nor quarrelling
    when they were chast'ned sore.

24

Luke 7:41, 47.   Moreover, such as loved much,   185
    that had not such a tryal,
As might constrain to so great pain,
    and such deep self denyal:
Yet ready were the Cross to bear,
    when Christ them call'd thereto,   190
And did rejoyce to hear his voice,
    they're counted Sheep also.

25

John 21:15.
Matt. 19:14.
John 3:3.

Christ's Flock of Lambs there also stands,
whose Faith was weak, yet true;
All sound Believers (Gospel receivers)
whose Grace was small, but grew:
And them among an Infant throng
of Babes, for whom Christ dy'd;
Whom for his own, by wayes unknown
to men, he sanctify'd.

26

Rev. 6:11.
Phil. 3:21.

All stand before their Saviour
in long white Robes yclad,
Their countenance full of pleasance,
appearing wondrous glad.
O glorious sight! Behold how bright
dust heaps are made to shine,
Conformed so their Lord unto,
whose Glory is Divine.

27

The Goats described or the several sorts of Reprobates on the left hand.
Matt. 24:51.

At Christ's left hand the Goats do stand,
all whining hypocrites,
Who for self-ends did seem Christ's friends,
but foster'd guileful sprites:
Who Sheep resembled, but they dissembled
(their hearts were non sincere);
Who once did throng Christ's Lambs among,
but now must not come near.

28

Luke 11:24, 26.
Heb. 6:4, 5, 6.
Heb. 10:29.

Apostates and Run-awayes,
such as have Christ forsaken,
Of whom the devil, with seven more evil,
hath fresh possession taken:
Sinners in grain, reserv'd to pain
and torments more severe:
Because 'gainst light they sinn'd with spight,
are also placed there.

29

	There also stand a num'rous band,	225
Luke 12:47.	that no Profession made	
Prov. 1:24, 26.	Of Godliness, nor to redress	
John 3:19.	their wayes at all essay'd:	
	Who better knew, but (sinful Crew)	
	Gospel and Law despised;	230
	Who all Christ's knocks withstood like blocks	
	and would not be advised.	

30

Moreover, there with them appear
    a number, numberless
Gal. 3:10.   Of great and small, vile wretches all,   235
1 *Cor.* 6:9.   that did Gods Law transgress:
Rev. 21:8.   Idolaters, false worshippers,
    Prophaners of Gods Name,
Who not at all thereon did call,
    or took in vain the same.   240

31

Blasphemers lewd, and Swearers shrewd,
    Scoffers at Purity
Exod. 20:7, 8.   That hated God, contemn'd his Rod,
    and lov'd Security;
Sabbath-polluters, Saints persecuters,   245
    Presumptuous men and Proud,
2 *Thess.* 1:6, 8, 9.   Who never lov'd those that reprov'd;
    all stand amongst this Crowd.

32

Heb. 13:4.   Adulterers and Whoremongers
1 *Cor.* 6:10.   were there, with all unchast: 250
There Covetous, and Ravenous,
    that Riches got too fast:
Who us'd vile ways themselves to raise
    t'Estates and worldly wealth,
Oppression by, or Knavery   255
    by force, or fraud, or stealth.

33

    Moreover, there together were
        Children flagitious,
Zech. 5:3, 4.   And Parents who did them undo
Gal. 5:19, 20, 21.   by Nurture vicious.   260
    False-witness-bearers, and self-forswearers
        Murd'rers, and Men of blood,
    Witches, Inchanters, & Ale-house-haunters,
        beyond account there stood.

34

    Their place there find all Heathen blind,   265
        that Natures light abused,
Rom. 2:13.   Although they had no tydings glad
        of Gospel-grace refused.
    There stands all Nations and Generations
        of *Adam's* Progeny,   270
    Whom Christ redeem'd not, who Christ esteem'd not,
        through Infidelity.

35

Acts. 4:12.   Who no Peace-maker, no Undertaker,
        to shrow'd them from Gods ire
    Ever obtain'd; they must be pained   275
        with everlasting fire.
    These num'rous bands, wringing their hands,
        and weeping, all stand there,
    Filled with anguish, whose hearts do languish
        through self-tormenting fear.   280

36

    Fast by them stand at Christ's left hand
        the Lion fierce and fell,
    The Dragon bold, that Serpent old,
        that hurried Souls to Hell.
1 *Cor.* 6:3.   There also stand, under command,   285
        Legions of Sprights unclean,
    And hellish Fiends, that are no friends
        to God, nor unto Men.

37

	With dismal chains, and strongest reins,
	like Prisoners of Hell, 290
Jude 6.	They're held in place before Christ's face,
	till He their Doom shall tell.

Jude 6.

    With dismal chains, and strongest reins,
        like Prisoners of Hell,   290
    They're held in place before Christ's face,
        till He their Doom shall tell.
    These void of tears, but fill'd with fears,
        and dreadful expectation
    Of endless pains, and scalding flames,   295
        stand waiting for Damnation.

38

The Saints cleared & justified.

    All silence keep, both Goats and Sheep,
        before the Judge's Throne;
    With mild aspect to his Elect
        then spake the Holy One;   300
    My Sheep draw near, your Sentence hear,
        which is to you no dread,
    Who clearly now discern, and know
        your sins are pardoned.

39

2 Cor. 5:10.
Eccles. 3:17.
John 3:18.

    'Twas meet that ye should judged be,   305
        that so the world may spy
    No cause of grudge, when as I Judge
        and deal impartially.
    Know therefore all, both great and small,
        the ground and reason why   310
    These Men do stand at my right hand,
        and look so chearfully.

40

John 17:6.
Eph. 1:4.

    These Men be those my Father chose
        before the worlds foundation,
    And to me gave, that I should save   315
        from Death and Condemnation.
    For whose dear sake I flesh did take,
        was of a Woman born,
    And did inure my self t'indure,
        unjust reproach and scorn.   320

41

    For them it was that I did pass
        through sorrows many one:
    That I drank up that bitter Cup,
Rev. 1:5.   which made me sigh and groan.
    The Cross his pain I did sustain;   325
        yea more, my Fathers ire
    I underwent, my Blood I spent
        to save them from Hell fire.

42

Thus I esteem'd, thus I redeem'd
    all these from every Nation,   330
That they may be (as now you see)
    a chosen Generation.
What if ere-while they were as vile,
Eph. 2:1, 3.   and bad as any be,
And yet from all their guilt and thrall   335
    at once I set them free?

43

My grace to one is wrong to none:
Matt. 20:13, 15.   none can Election claim,
Rom. 9:20, 21. Amongst all those their souls that lose,
    none can Rejection blame.   340
He that may chuse, or else refuse,
    all men to save or spill,
May this Man chuse, and that refuse,
    redeeming whom he will.

44

Isa. 53:4, 5, 11. But as for those whom I have chose   345
    Salvations heirs to be,
I underwent their punishment,
    and therefore set them free;
I bore their grief, and their relief
    by suffering procur'd,   350
That they of bliss and happiness
    might firmly be assur'd.

                                    45
Acts. 13:48.   And this my grace they did imbrace,
James 2:18.   believing on my Name;
Heb. 12:7.   Which Faith was true, the fruits do shew   355
Matt. 19:29.   proceeding from the same:
                        Their Penitence, their Patience,
                           their Love and Self-denial
                        In suffering losses, and bearing Crosses,
                           when put upon the tryal.   360

                                    46
                        Their sin forsaking, their chearful taking
                           my yoke, their Charity
1 John 3:3.   Unto the Saints in all their wants,
Matt. 25:39, 40.   and in them unto me,
                        These things do clear, and make appear   365
                           their Faith to be unfaigned,
                        And that a part in my desert
                           and purchase they have gained.

                                    47
                        Their debts are paid, their peace is made,
Isa. 53:11, 12.   their sins remitted are;   370
Rom. 8:16, 17, 33, 34. Therefore at once I do pronounce,
                           and openly declare:
John. 3:18   That Heav'n is theirs, that they be Heirs
                           of Life and of Salvation!
                        Nor ever shall they come at all   375
                           to Death or to Damnation.

                                    48
Luke 22:29, 30.   Come, Blessed Ones, and sit on Thrones,
Matt. 19:28.   Judging the World with me:
                        Come, and possess your happiness,
                           and bought felicitie.   380
                        Henceforth no fears, no care, no tears,
                           no sin shall you annoy,
                        Nor any thing that grief doth bring:
                           Eternal Rest enjoy.

49

Matt. 25:34.
They are placed on
Thrones to joyn with
Christ in judging the
wicked.

You bore the Cross, you suffered loss 385
    of all for my Names sake:
Receive the Crown that's now your own;
    come, and a Kingdom take.
Thus spake the Judge; the wicked grudge,
    and grind their teeth in vain; 390
They see with groans these plac't on Thrones
    which addeth to their pain:

50

That those whom they did wrong & slay,
    must now their judgment see!
Such whom they slighted, & once despighted, 395
    must now their Judges be!
Thus 'tis decreed, such is their meed,
1 Cor. 6:2.   and guerdon glorious!
With Christ they sit, Judging is fit
    to plague the Impious. 400

51

The wicked brought to   The wicked are brought to the Bar,
the Bar.   like guilty Malefactors,
Rom. 2:3, 6, 11.   That oftentimes of bloody Crimes
    and Treasons have been Actors.
Of wicked Men, none are so mean 405
    as there to be neglected:
Nor none so high in dignity,
    as there to be respected.

52

Rev. 6:15, 16.   The glorious Judge will priviledge
Isa. 30:33.   nor Emperour, nor King: 410
But every one that hath mis-done
    doth unto Judgment bring.
And every one that hath mis-done,
    the Judge impartially
Comdemneth to eternal wo, 415
    and endless misery.

53

Thus one and all, thus great and small,
    the Rich as well as Poor,
And those of place as the most base,
    do stand the Judge before.
They are arraign'd, and there detain'd,
    before Christ's Judgement-seat
With trembling fear, their Doom to hear
    and feel his angers heat.

54

Eccles. 11:9; 12:14.

There Christ demands at all their hands
    a strict and strait account
Of all things done under the Sun,
    whose number far surmount
Man's wit & thought: yet all are brought
    unto this solemn Tryal;
And each offence with evidence,
    so that there's no denial.

55

There's no excuses for their abuses,
    since their own Consciences
More proof give in of each Man's sin,
    than thousand Witnesses,
Though formerly this faculty
    had grosly been abused,
Men could it stifle, or with it trifle,
    when as it them accused.

56

Now it comes in, and every sin
    unto Mens charge doth lay:
It judgeth them, and doth condemn,
    though all the world say nay.
It so stingeth and tortureth,
    it worketh such distress,
That each Man's self against himself,
    is forced to confess.

57

Secret sins and works of darkness brought to light.
Ps. 139:2, 4, 12.
Rom. 2:16.

It's vain, moreover, for Men to cover
    the least iniquity: 450
The Judge hath seen, and privy been
    to all their villany.
He unto light, and open sight
    the works of darkness brings:
He doth unfold both new and old, 455
    both known and hidden things.

58

Eccles. 12:14.

All filthy facts, and secret acts,
    however closely done,
And long concel'd, are there reveal'd
    before the mid-day Sun. 460
Deeds of the night shunning the light,
    which darkest corners sought,
To fearful blame, and endless shame,
    are there most justly brought.

59

Matt. 12:36.
Rom. 7:7.

And as all facts and grosser acts, 465
    so every word and thought,
Erroneous notion, and lustful motion,
    are unto judgment brought,
No sin so small and trivial
    but hither it must come: 470
Nor so long past, but now at last
    it must receive a doom.

60

An account demanded of all their actions.
John 5:40; 3:19.
Matt. 25:19, 27.

At this sad season, Christ asks a Reason
    (with just Austerity)
Of Grace refused, of light abus'd 475
    so oft, so wilfully:
Of Talents lent by them mispent,
    and on their Lust bestown;
Which if improv'd, as it behov'd,
    Heav'n might have been their own! 480

61

      Of times neglected, of means rejected,
          of God's long-suffering,
Rom. 2:4, 5.   And Patience, to Penitence
          that sought hard hearts to bring.
      Why Cords of love did nothing move   485
          to shame or to remorse?
      Why warnings grave, and counsels, have
          nought chang'd their sinful course?

62

      Why chastenings, and evil things,
          why judgments so severe   490
Isa. 1:5.   Prevailed not with them a jot,
          nor wrought an awful fear?
Jer. 2:20.   Why Promises of Holiness,
          and new Obedience,
      They oft did make, but always brake   495
          the same, to God's offence?

63

      Why still Hell-ward, without regard,
John. 3:19, 20.   they boldly ventured,
Prov. 8:36.   And chose Damnation before Salvation,
Luke 12:20, 21.   when it was offered: 500
      Why sinful pleasures, & earthly treasures,
          like fools, they prized more
      Than heav'nly wealth, Eternal health,
          and all Christ's Royal store.

64

Luke 13:34.   Why, when he stood off'ring his Blood   505
John 5:40; 15:22. to wash them from their sin,
      They would embrace no saving Grace,
          but liv'd and dy'd therein?
      Such aggravations, where no evasions,
          nor false pretences hold,   510
      Exaggerate and cumulate
          guilt more than can be told.

65

They multiply and magnify
    mens gross iniquities,
They draw down wrath (as Scripture saith)   515
    out of Gods treasuries.
Thus all their ways Christ opens lays
    to men and Angels view,
And, as they were, makes them appear
    in their own proper hew.   520

66

Rom. 3:10, 12.

Thus he doth find all of Mankind,
    that stand at his left hand,
No Mothers Son, but hath mis-done,
    and broken God's Command.
All have transgrest, even the best,   525
    and merited God's wrath
Unto their own perdition,
    and everlasting scath.

67

Rom. 6:23.

Earths dwellers all, both great and small,
    have wrought iniquity,   530
And suffer must, for it is just,
    Eternal misery.
Amongst the many there come not any,
    before the Judge's face,
That able are themselves to clear,   535
    of all this cursed race.

68

Nevertheless, they all express,
    Christ granting liberty,
What for their way they have to say
    how they have liv'd, and why.   540

Hypocrites plead for themselves.

They all draw near, and seek to clear
    themselves by making pleas.
There Hypocrites, false-hearted wights,
    do make such pleas as these:

69

	Lord, in they Name, and by the same,	545
	we Devils dispossest,	
Matt. 7:21, 22, 23.	We rais'd the dead, and ministred	
	succour to the distrest.	
	Our painful teaching, & pow'rful preaching	
	by thine own wondrous might,	550
	Did throughly win to God from sin	
	many a wretched wight.	

70

The judge replyeth.	All this, quoth he, may granted be,	
John 6:70.	and your case little better'd,	
1 *Cor.* 9:27.	Who still remain under a chain,	555
	and many irons fetter'd.	
	You that the dead have quickened,	
	and rescu'd from the grave,	
	Your selves were dead, yet never ned,	
	a Christ your Souls to save.	560

71

	You that could preach, and others teach	
	what way to life doth lead;	
Rom. 2:19, 21, 22, 23.	Why were you slack to find that track	
	and in that way to tread?	
	How could you bear to see or hear	565
	of others freed at last,	
	From Satan's pawes, whilst in his jawes	
	your selves were held more fast?	

72

John 9:41.	Who though you knew Repentance true,	
	and Faith in my great Name,	570
	The only mean to quit you clean,	
	from punishment and blame,	
Rev. 2:21, 22.	Yet took no pain true Faith to gain,	
	such as might not deceive,	
	Nor would repent, with true intent,	575
	your evil deeds to leave.	

73

	His Masters will how to fulfill	
	the servant that well knew,	
Luke 12:47.	Yet left undone his duty known,	
Matt. 11:21, 22, 24.	more plagues to him are due.	580
	You against light perverted right;	
	wherefore it shall be now	
	For Sidon and for Sodoms Land	
	more easie than for you.	

74

	But we have in thy presence been,	585
Another plea of	say some, and eaten there.	
hypocrites.	Did we not eat thy Flesh for meat,	
Luke 13:26.	and feed on heavenly Cheer?	
	Whereon who feed shall never need,	
	as thou thy self dost say,	590
	Nor shall they dy eternally,	
	but live with Christ for ay.	

75

We may alledge, thou gav'st a pledge
   of thy dear love to us
In Wine and Bread, which figured   595
   thy Grace bestowed thus.
Of strengthning Seals, of sweetest Meals,
   have we so oft partaken;
And shall we be cast off by thee,
   and utterly forsaken?   600

76

	To whom the Lord thus in a word	
Is Answered.	returns a short reply,	
Luke 13:27.	I never knew any of you	
Matt. 22:12.	that wrought iniquity.	
	You say y'have been my Presence in;	605
	but friends, how came you there	
	With Raiment vile that did defile	
	and quite disgrace my Cheer?	

77

  Durst you draw near without due fear
   unto my holy Table?   610
  Durst you prophane, and render vain
   so far as you were able,
  Those Mysteries? which whoso prize
   and carefully improve,
  Shall saved be undoubtedly,   615
   and nothing shall them move.

78

  How durst you venture, bold guests, to enter
   in such a sordid hew,

1 Cor. 11:27, 29. Amongst my guests, unto those Feasts
   that were not made for you?   620
  How durst you eat for spiritual meat
   your bane, and drink damnation,
  Whilst by your guile you rendred vile
   so rare and great Salvation?

79

  Your fancies fed on heav'nly Bread,   625
   your hearts fed on some Lust:
  You lov'd the Creature more than th' Creator,

Matt. 6:21, 24.   your Souls clave to the dust.
Rom. 1:25. And think you by Hypocrisie,
   and cloaked Wickedness,   630
  To enter in, laden with sin,
   to lasting happiness?

80

1 Cor. 11:27, 29. This your excuse shews your abuse
   of things ordain'd for good;
  And doth declare you guilty are   635
   of my dear Flesh and Blood.
  Wherefore those Seals and precious Meals
   you put so much upon
  As things divine, they seal and sign
   you to Perdition.   640

81

Another sort of hypocrites make their pleas.

Then forth issue another Crew
   (those being silenced)
Who drawing high to the most High
   adventure thus to plead:
We sinners were, say they, it's clear,
   deserving Condemnation:
But did not we rely on thee,
   O Christ, for whole Salvation?

645

82

Acts. 8:13.
Isa. 58:2, 3.
Heb. 64:5.

We did believe and oft receive
   thy gracious promises:
We took great care to get a share
   in endless happiness.
We pray'd & wept, we Fast-dayes kept,
   lewd ways we did eschew:
We joyful were thy Word to hear;
   we form'd our lives anew.

650

655

83

2 Pet. 2:20.

We thought our sin had pard'ned been;
   that our Estate was good,
Our debts all paid, our peace well made,
   our Souls wash'd with thy Blood.
Lord, why dost thou reject us now,
   who have not thee rejected,
Nor utterly true sanctity
   and holy life neglected.

660

84

The Judge uncaseth them.

John 2:24, 25.

The Judge incensed at their pretenced
   self-vanting Piety,
With such a look as trembling strook
   into them, made reply;
O impudent, impenitent,
   and guileful generation!
Think you that I cannot descry
   your hearts abomination?

665

670

85

	You nor receiv'd, nor yet believ'd	
	my Promises of Grace;	
John 6:64.	Nor were you wise enough to prize	675
	my reconciled Face:	
Ps. 50:16.	But did presume that to assume	
Matt. 15:26.	which was not your to take,	
	And challenged the Children's bread,	
	yet would not sin forsake.	680

86

Rev. 3:17.	Being too bold you laid fast hold,	
	where int'rest you had none,	
	Your selves deceiving by your believing,	
	all which you might have known.	
Matt. 13:20.	You ran away, but ran astray,	685
	with Gospel-promises,	
	And perished, being still dead	
	in sins and trespasses.	

87

	How oft did I Hypocrisie	
	and Hearts deceit unmask	690
Matt. 6:2, 4, 24.	Before your sight, giving you light	
Jer. 8:5, 6, 7, 8.	to know a Christians task?	
	But you held fast unto the last	
	your own Conceits so vain:	
	No warning could prevail, you would	695
	your own Deceits retain.	

88

	As for your care to get a share	
	in bliss; the fear of Hell,	
Ps. 78:34, 35, 36, 37.	And of a part in endless smart,	
	did thereunto compel.	700
	Your holiness and ways redress,	
	such as it was, did spring	
	From no true love to things above,	
	but from some other thing.	

89

Zech. 7:5, 6.	You pray'd & wept, you Fast-days kept;
Isa. 58:3, 4.	but did you this to me?
1 *Sam.* 15:13, 21.	No, but for sin, you sought to win,
Isa. 1:11, 15.	the greater libertie.

For all your vaunts, you had vile haunts,
    for which your Consciences
Did you alarm, whose voice to charm
    you us'd these practices.

90

Your Penitence, your diligence
Matt. 6:2, 5.   to Read, to Pray, to Hear,
John 5:44.   Were but to drown'd the clamorous sound
    of Conscience in your ear.
If light you lov'd, vain glory mov'd
    your selves therewith to store,
That seeming wise, men might you prize,
    and honour you the more.

91

Thus from your selves unto your selves,
Zech. 7:5, 6.   your duties all do tend;
Hos. 10:1.   And as self-love the wheels doth move,
    so in self-love they end.
Thus Christ detects their vain projects,
    and close Impiety,
And plainly shews that all their shows
    were but Hypocrisy.

92

Civil honest mens pleas.   Then were brought nigh a Company
Luke 18:11.   of Civil honest Men,
That lov'd true dealing, and hated stealing,
    ne'r wrong'd their Bretheren;
Who pleaded thus, Thou knowest us
    that we were blameless livers;
No Whoremongers, no Murderers,
    no quarrelers nor strivers.

93

Idolaters, Adulterers,
    Church-robbers we were none,
Nor false-dealers, no couzeners,
    but paid each man his own.   740
Our way was fair, our dealing square,
    we were no wastful spenders,
No lewd toss-pots, no drunken sots,
    no scandalous offenders.

94

We hated vice, and set great price,   745
    by vertuous conversation:
And by the same we got a name,
    and no small commendation.

1 Sam. 15:22.   Gods Laws express that righteousness,
    is that which he doth prize;   750
And to obey, as he doth say,
    is more than sacrifice.

95

Thus to obey, hath been our way,
    let our good deeds, we pray,
Find some regard and some reward   755
    with thee, O Lord, this day.

Eccles. 7:20.   And whereas we transgressors be,
    of *Adam's* Race were none,
No not the best, but have confest
    themselves to have mis-done.   760

96

Are taken off & rendred   Then answered unto their dread,
invalid.   the Judge: True Piety
Deut. 10:12.   God doth desire and eke require
Titus 2:12.   no less than honesty.
James 2:10.   Justice demands at all your hands   765
    perfect Obedience:
If but in part you have come short,
    that is just offence.

97

On Earth below, where men did ow
    a thousand pounds and more,   770
Could twenty pence it recompence?
    could that have clear'd the score?
Think you to buy felicity
    with part of what's due debt?
Or for desert of one small part,   775
    the whole should off be set?

98

And yet that part, whose great desert
    you think to reach so far
For your excuse, doth you accuse,
Luke 18:11, 14.   and will your boasting mar.   780
However fair, however square,
    your way and work hath been,
Before mens eyes, yet God espies
    iniquity therein.

99

1 *Sam.* 16:7.   God looks upon th' affection   785
2 *Chron.* 25:2.   and temper of the heart;
Not only on the action,
    and the external part.
Whatever end vain men pretend,   790
    God knows the verity;
And by the end which they intend
    their words and deeds doth try.

100

Heb. 11:6.   Without true Faith, the Scripture saith
    God cannot take delight
In any deed, that doth proceed   795
    from any sinful wight.
1 *Cor.* 13:1, 2, 3.   And without love all actions prove
    but barren empty things.
Dead works they be, and vanitie,
    the which vexation brings.   800

101

Nor from true faith, which quencheth wrath,
    hath your obedience flown:
Nor from true love, which wont to move
    Believers, hath it grown.
Your argument shews your intent,
    in all that you have done:
You thought to scale Heav'ns lofty Wall
    by Ladders of your own.

102

Rom. 10:3.

Your blinded spirit, hoping to merit
    by your own Righteousness,
Needed no Saviour, but your behaviour,
    and blameless carriages;
You trusted to what you could do,
    and in no need you stood:
Your haughty pride laid me aside,
    and trampled on my Blood.

103

All men have gone astray, and done,
    that which Gods Laws condemn:
But my Purchase and offered Grace

Rom. 9:30, 32.
Matt. 11:23, 24; 12:41.

    all men did not contemn.
The *Ninevites*, and *Sodomites*,
    had no such sin as this:
Yet as if all your sins were small,
    you say, All did amiss.

104

Matt. 6:5.

Again you thought and mainly sought
    a name with men t'acquire.
Pride bare the Bell, that made you swell,
    and your own selves admire.
Mean fruit it is, and vile, I wiss,
    that springs from such a root:
Vertue divine and genuine
    wonts not from pride to shoot.

105

	Such deeds as your are worse than poor;
	they are but sins guilt over
Prov. 26:23.	With silver dross, whose glistering gloss
Matt. 23:27.	can them no longer cover.

Such deeds as your are worse than poor;
   they are but sins guilt over
Prov. 26:23.   With silver dross, whose glistering gloss   835
Matt. 23:27.   can them no longer cover.
The best of them would you condemn,
   and ruine you alone,
Although you were from faults so clear,
   that other you had none.   840

106

Prov. 15:8.   Your Gold is brass, your silver dross,
Rom. 3:20.   your righteousness is sin:
And think you by such honesty
   eternal life to win?   845
You make mistake, if for its sake
   you dream of acceptation;
Whereas the same deserveth shame,
   and meriteth Damnation.

107

Those that pretend want   A wond'rous Crowd then 'gan aloud,
of opportunity to repent.   thus for themselves to say,   850
Prov. 27:1.   We did intend, Lord to amend,
James 4:13.   and to reform our way:
Our true intent was to repent,
   and make our peace with thee;
But sudden death stopping our breath,   855
   left us no libertie.

108

Short was our time, for in his prime
   our youthful flow'r was cropt:
We dy'd in youth, before full growth,
   so was our purpose stopt.   860
Let our good will to turn from ill,
   and sin to have forsaken,
Accepted be, O Lord, by thee,
   and in good part be taken.

109

Are Confuted and
Convinced.
Eccles. 12:1.
Rev. 2:21.

To whom the Judge: where you alledge 865
    the shortness of the space,
That from your birth you liv'd on earth,
    to compass saving Grace:
It was Free grace that any space
    was given you at all 870
To turn from evil, defie the Devil,
    and upon God to call.

110

Luke 13:24.
2 *Cor.* 6:2.
Heb. 3:7, 8, 9.

One day, one week, wherein to seek
    God's face with all your hearts,
A favour was that far did pass 875
    the best of your deserts.
You had a season, what was your reason
    such precious hours to waste?
What could you find, what could you mind
    that was of greater haste? 880

111

Eccles. 11:9.
Luke 14:18, 19, 20.

Could you find time for vain pastime,
    for loose licentious mirth?
For fruitless toyes, and fading joyes
    that perish in the birth?
Had you good leasure for carnal Pleasure 885
    in dayes of health and youth?
And yet no space to seek God's face,
    and turn to him in truth?

112

Amos 6:3, 4, 5, 6.

Eph. 5:16.
Luke 19:42.

In younger years, beyond your fears,
    what if you were surprised? 890
You put away the evil day,
    and of long life devised.
You oft were told, and might behold,
    that Death no Age doth spare;
Why then did you your time foreslow, 895
    and slight your Souls welfare?

113

       Had your intent been to repent,
Luke 13:24, 25, &c.   and had you it desir'd,
       There would have been endeavours seen,
Phil. 2:12.   before your time expir'd.   900
       God makes no treasure, nor hath he pleasure,
          in idle purposes:
       Such fair pretences are foul offences,
          and cloaks for wickedness.

114

       Then were brought in, and charg'd with sin,   905
          another Company,
Some plead Examples   Who by Petition obtain'd permission,
of their betters.   to make Apology:
Matt. 18:7.   They argues, We were misled,
          as is well known to thee,   910
       By their Example, that had more ample
          abilities than we:

115

John 7:48.   Such as profest they did detest,
          and hate each wicked way:
       Whose seeming grace whilst we did trace,   915
          our Souls were led astray.
       When men of Parts, Learning and Arts,
          Professing Piety,
       Did thus and thus, it seem'd to us
          we might take liberty.   920

116

Who are told that   The Judge replies, I gave you eyes,
Examples are no Rules.   and light to see your way,
       Which had you lov'd, and well improv'd
Ps. 19:8, 11.   you had not gone astray.   925
Exod. 23:2.   My Word was pure, the Rule was sure,
Ps. 50:17, 18.   why did you it forsake,
       Or thereon trample, and mens example,
          your Directory make?

117

	This you well knew, that God is true	
	and that most men are liars,	920
2 Tim. 3:5.	In word professing holiness,	
	in deed thereof deniers.	
	O simple fools! that having Rules	
	your lives to regulate,	
	Would then refuse, and rather chuse	935
	vile men to imitate.	

118

They urge that they were But Lord, say they, we went astray,
misled by godly mens   and did more wickedlie,
Example: But all their By means of those whom thou hast chose
shifts turn to their   Salvation heirs to be.   940
greater shame. To whom the Judge: What you alledge,
1 *Cor.* 11:1.   doth nothing help the case;
    But makes appear how vile you were,
        and rend'reth you more base.

119

    You understood that what was good,   945
        was to be followed,
    And that you ought that which was naught
        to have relinquished.
Phil. 4:8.   Contrariwayes, it was your guise,
        only to imitate   950
    Good mens defects, and their neglects
        that were regenerate.

120

    But to express their holiness,
        or imitate their grace,
Ps. 32:5.   You little car'd, nor once prepar'd   955
2 *Chron.* 32:26.   your hearts to seek my face.
Matt. 26:75.   They did repent, and truly rent
Prov. 1:24, 25.   their hearts for all known sin:
    You did offend, but not amend,
        to follow them therein.   960

121

Some plead the
Scriptures darkness.
And difference amongst
Interpreters.
2 Pet. 3:16.

We had thy Word, say some, O Lord,
    but wiser men than we
Could never yet interpret it,
    but alway disagree.
How could we fools be led by Rules,   965
    so far beyond our ken,
Which to explain did so much pain,
    and puzzle wisest men?

122

Was all my word abstruse and hard?

They are confuted.
Prov. 14:6.
Isa. 35:8.
Hos. 8:12.

    the Judge then answered: 970
It did contain much truth so plain,
    you might have run and read;
But what was hard you never car'd
    to know nor studied,
And things that were most plain and clear   975
    you never practised.

123

Matt. 11:25.

The Mystery of Pietie
    God unto Babes reveals,
When to the wise he it denies,
    and from the world conceals.

Prov. 2:3, 4, 5.

If to fulfil Gods holy will   980
    had seemed good to you,
You would have sought light as you ought,
    and done the good you knew.

124

Others the fear of
Persecution.
Acts 28:22.

Then came in view another Crew,   985
    and 'gan to make their pleas;
Amongst the rest, some of the best
    had such poor shifts as these:
Thou know'st right well, who all canst tell
    we liv'd amongst thy foes,   990
Who the Renate did sorely hate,
    and goodness much oppose.

125

	We holiness durst not profess,	
John 12:42, 43.	fearing to be forlorn	
	Of all our friends, and for amends	995
	to be the wickeds scorn.	

We holiness durst not profess,
  fearing to be forlorn
Of all our friends, and for amends   995
  to be the wickeds scorn.
We knew their anger would much endanger
  our lives, and our estates:
Therefore for fear we durst appear
  no better than our mates.   1000

126

They are answered.   To whom the Lord returns this word;
  O wonderful deceits!
Luke 12:4, 5.   To cast off aw of Gods strict Law,
Isa. 51:12, 13.   and fear mens wrath and threats.
To fear hell-fire and Gods fierce ire   1005
  less than the rage of men,
As if Gods wrath, could do less scath
  than wrath of bretheren.

127

To use such strife, a temporal life,
  to rescue and secure,   1010
And be so blind as not to mind
  that life that will endure:
This was your case, who carnal peace
  more than true joyes did favour;
Who fed on dust, clave to your lust,   1015
  and spurned at my favour.

128

Luke 9:23, 24, 25;   To please your kin, mens love to win,
16:25.   to flow in worldly wealth,
To save your skin, these things have bin
  more than Eternal health.   1020
You had your choice, wherein rejoyce,
  it was your portion,
For which you chose your Souls t'expose
  unto perdition.

	129	
	Who did not hate friends, life, and state,	1025
Luke 9:26.	with all things else for me,	
Prov. 8:36.	And all forsake, and's Cross up-take,	
John. 3:19, 20.	shall never happy be.	
	Well worthy they to dy for ay,	
	who death then life had rather;	1030
	Death is their due, that so value	
	the friendship of my Father.	
	130	
Others plead for	Others Argue, and not a few,	
Pardon both from Gods	is not God gracious?	
mercy and justice.	His Equity and Clemency	1035
Ps. 78:38.	are they not marvellous?	
	Thus we believ'd; are we deceiv'd?	
	cannot his mercy great,	
	(As hath been told to us of old)	
	asswage his angers heat?	1040
	131	
2 *Kings.* 14:26.	How can it be that God should see	
	his Creatures endless pain,	
	Or hear the groans and rueful moans,	
	and still his wrath retain?	
	Can it agree with Equitie?	1045
	can mercy have the heart	
	To recompence few years offence	
	with Everlasting smart?	
	132	
	Can God delight in such a sight	
	as sinners misery?	1050
	Or what great good can this our blood	
	bring unto the most High?	
Ps. 30:9.	Oh, thou that dost thy Glory most	
Mic. 7:18.	in pard'ning sin display!	
	Lord, might it please thee to release,	1055
	and pardon us this day?	

133

Unto thy Name more glorious fame
    would not such mercy bring?
Would not it raise thine endless praise,
    more than our suffering?
With that they cease, holding their peace,
    but cease not still to weep;
Grief ministers a flood of tears,
    in which their words to steep.

134

They answered.

But all too late, grief's out of date,
    when life is at an end.
The glorious King thus answering,
    all to his voice attend:
God gracious is, quoth he, like his
    no mercy can be found;
His Equity and Clemency
    to sinners do abound.

135

Mercy that now shines
forth in the vessels of
Mercy.

Mic. 7:18.
Rom. 9:23.

As may appear by those that here
    are plac'd at my right hand;
Whose stripes I bore, and clear'd the score,
    that they might quitted stand.
For surely none, but God alone,
    whose Grace transcends mens thought,
For such as those that were his foes
    like wonders would have wrought.

136

Did also long wait
upon such as abused it.

Rom. 2:4.
Hos. 11:4.

And none but he such lenitee
    and patience would have shown
To you so long, who did him wrong,
    and pull'd his judgments down.
How long a space (O stiff neck'd race)
    did patience you afford?
How oft did love you gently move,
    to turn unto the Lord?

THE DAY OF DOOM

137

Luke 13:34.
The day of Grace now past.

With Cords of love God often strove
    your stubborn hearts to tame: 1090
Nevertheless your wickedness,
    did still resist the same.
If now at last Mercy be past
    from you for evermore,
And Justice come in Mercies room,   1095
    yet grudge you not therefore.

138

Luke 19:42, 43.
Jude 4.

If into wrath God turned hath
    his long long suffering,
And now for love you vengeance prove,
    it is an equal thing.   1100
Your waxing worse, hath stopt the course
    of wonted Clemency:
Mercy refus'd, and Grace misus'd,
    call for severity.

139

Rom. 2:5, 6.
Isa. 1:24.
Amos 2:13.
Gen. 18:25.

It's now high time that ev'ry Crime   1105
    be brought to punishment:
Wrath long contain'd, and oft restrain'd,
    at last must have a vent:
Justice severe cannot forbear
    to plague sin any longer,   1110
But must inflict with hand most strict
    mischief upon the wronger.

140

Matt. 25:3, 11, 12.
Prov. 1:28, 29, 30.

In vain do they for Mercy pray,
    the season being past,
Who had no care to get a share   1115
    therein, while time did last.
The man whose ear refus'd to hear
    the voice of Wisdoms cry,
Earn'd this reward, that none regard
    him in his misery.   1120

141

Isa. 5:18, 19.	It doth agree with equity,
Gen. 2:17.	and with Gods holy Law,
Rom. 2:8, 9.	That those should dye eternally
	that death upon them draw.

The Soul that sins damnation wins,　　　　1125
　　for so the Law ordains;
Which Law is just, and therefore must
　　such suffer endless pain.

142

Rom. 6:23.	Eternal smart is the desert,
2 Thess. 1:8, 9.	ev'n of the least offence;　　1130

Then wonder not if I allot
　　to you this Recompence:
But wonder more, that since so sore
　　and lasting plagues are due
To every sin, you liv'd therein,　　　　1135
　　who well the danger knew.

143

Ezek. 33:11.	God hath no joy to crush or 'stroy,
Exod. 34:7; 14:17.	and ruine wretched wights,
Rom. 9:22.	But to display the glorious Ray
	of Justice he delights.　　1140

To manifest he doth detest,
　　and throughly hate all sin,
By plaguing it as is most fit,
　　this shall him glory win.

144

Then at the Bar arraigned are　　　　1145

Some pretend they were	an impudenter sort,
shut out from Heaven	Who to evade the guilt that's laid
by Gods Decree.	upon them, thus retort;
Rom. 9:18, 19.	Who could we cease thus to transgress?
	how could we Hell avoid,　　1150

Whom Gods Decree shut out from thee,
　　and sign'd to be destroy'd?

145

  Whom God ordains to endless pains,
   by Law unalterable,
  Repentance true, Obedience new,
   to save such are unable:
Heb. 22:17. Sorrow for sin, no good can win,
Rom. 11:7, 8.   to such as are rejected;
  Ne can they grieve, nor yet believe,
   that never were elected.

146

  Of Man's fall'n Race, who can true Grace,
   or Holiness obtain?
  Who can convert or change his heart,
   if God withhold the same?
  Had we apply'd our selves, and try'd
   as much as who did most
  God's love to gain, our busie pain
   and labour had been lost.

147

Their pleas taken off. Christ readily makes this Reply,
   I damn you not because
Luke 13:27. You are rejected, or not elected,
2 Pet. 1:9, 10 *compared*   but you have broke my Laws:
with Matt. 19:6. It is but vain your wits to strain,
   the end and means to sever:
  Men fondly seek to part or break
   what God hath link'd together.

148

Acts. 3:19; 16:31. Whom God will save, such he will have,
1 Sam. 2:15.   the means of life to use:
John 3:19. Whom he'll pass by, shall chuse to dy,
John 5:40.   and ways of life refuse.
2 Thess. 2:11, 12. He that fore-sees, and foredecrees,
   in wisdom order'd has,
  That man's free-will electing ill,
   shall bring his will to pass.

	149	
Ezek. 33:11, 12, 13.	High God's Decree, as it is free,	1185
Luke 13:34.	so doth it none compel	
Prov. 8:33, 36.	Against their will to good or ill,	
	it forceth none to Hell.	
	They have their wish whose Souls perish	
	with Torments in Hell-fire,	1190
	Who rather chose their Souls to lose,	
	than leave a loose desire.	

150

Gen. 2:17.	God did ordain sinners to pain	
Matt. 25:41, 42.	and I to Hell send none,	
Ezek. 18:20.	But such as swerv'd, and have deserv'd	1195
	destruction as their own.	
	His pleasure is, that none from bliss	
	and endless happiness	
	Be barr'd, but such as wrong'd him much	
	by wilful wickedness.	1200

151

	You, sinful Crew, no other knew	
	but you might be elect.	
2 Pet. 1:10.	Why did you then your selves condemn?	
Acts. 13:46.	why did you me reject?	
Luke 13:24.	Where was your strife to gain that life	1205
	which lasteth evermore?	
	You never knock'd, yet say God lock'd	
	against you Heav'ns door.	

152

Matt. 7:7, 8.	'Twas no vain task to knock, to ask,	
	whilst life continued.	1210
	Whoever sought heav'n as he ought,	
	and seeking perished?	
Gal. 5:22, 23.	The lowly meek who truly seek	
	for Christ, and for Salvation,	
	There's no Decree whereby such be	1215
	ordain'd to Condemnation.	

153

    You argue than; But abject men,
        whom God resolves to spill,
    Cannot repent, nor their hearts rent;
        ne can they change their will.
    Not for his *Can* is any man
        adjudged into Hell:
    But for his *Will* to do what's ill,
        and nilling to do well.

John 3:19.

154

    I often stood tend'ring my Blood
        to wash away your guilt:
    And eke my Spright to frame you right,
        lest your Souls should be split.
    But you vile Race, rejected Grace,
        when Grace was freely proffer'd:
    No changed heart, no heav'nly part
        would you, when it was offer'd.

John 5:40.

155

    Who wilfully the Remedy,
        and means of life contemned,
    Cause have the same themselves to blame,
        if now they be condemned.
    You have your selves, you and none else,
        your selves have done to dy.
    You chose the way to your decay,
        and perisht wilfully.

John 15:22, 24.
Heb. 2:3.
Isa. 66:3, 4.

156

    These words appall and daunt them all;
        dismai'd, and all amort,
    Like stocks they stand at Christ's left-hand,
        and dare no more retort.
    Then were brought near with trembling fear,
        a number numberless
    Of blind Heathen, and bruitish men,
        that did Gods Laws transgress.

157

Heathen men plead	Whose wicked ways Christ open layes,
want of the written	and makes their sins appear, 1250
Word.	They making pleas their case to ease,
	if not themselves to clear.
	Thy written Word (say they) good Lord,
	we never did enjoy:
	We nor refus'd, nor it abus'd, 1255
	Oh, do not us destroy!

158

Matt. 11:22.	You ne'r abus'd, nor yet refus'd
Luke 12:48.	my written Word, you plead,
	That's true (quoth he) therefore shall ye
	the less be punished. 1260
	You shall not smart for any part
	of other mens offence,
	But for your own transgression
	receive due recompence.

159

	But we were blind, say they, in mind, 1265
1 *Cor.* 1:21.	too dim was Natures Light,
And insufficiency of the	Our only guide, as hath been try'd
Light of Nature.	to bring us to the sight
	Of our estate degenerate,
	and curst by *Adam's* Fall; 1270
	How we were born and lay forlorn
	in bondage and in thrall.

160

	We did not know a Christ till now,
	nor how faln man be saved,
	Else would we not, right well we wot, 1275
	have so our selves behaved.
	We should have mourn'd, we should have turn'd
Matt. 11:21.	from sin at thy Reproof,
	And been more wise through thy advice,
	for our own Souls behoof. 1280

161

They are answered.	But Natures Light shin'd not so bright
	    to teach us the right way:
	We might have lov'd it, and well improv'd it,
	    and yet have gone astray.
	The Judge most High makes this Reply,
	    you ignorance pretend,
	Dimness of sight, and want of light
	    your course Heav'nward to bend.

    1285

162

Gen. 1:27.
Eccles. 7:29.
Hos. 13:9.

How came your mind to be so blind?
    I once you knowledge gave,   1290
Clearness of sight, and judgment right;
    who did the same deprave?
If to your cost you have it lost,
    and quite defac'd the same;
Your own desert hath caus'd the smart,   1295
    you ought not me to blame.

163

Matt. 11:25 *compared
with* 20 & 15.

Your selves into a pit of woe,
    your own transgression led:
If I to none my Grace had shown,
    who had been injured?   1300
If to a few, and not to you,
    I shew'd a way of life,
My Grace to free, you clearly see,
    gives you no ground of strife.

164

'Tis vain to tell, you wot full well,   1305
    if you in time had known
Your Misery and Remedy,
    your actions had it shown.

Rom. 1:20, 21, 22.

You, sinful Crew, have not been true
    unto the Light of Nature,   1310
Nor done the good you understood,
    nor owned your Creator.

165

He that the Light, because 'tis Light,
   hath used to despize,

Rom. 2:12, 15; 1:32. Would not the Light shining more bright,
   be likely for to prize.

Matt. 12:41. If you had lov'd, and well improv'd
   your knowledge and dim sight,
Herein your pain had not been vain,
   your plagues had been more light.

166

Reprobate Infants plead   Then to the Bar, all they drew near
for themselves.   who dy'd in Infancy,
Rev. 20:12, 15   And never had or good or bad
Compared with   effected pers'nally,
Rom . 5:12, 14; 9:11, 13. But from the womb unto the tomb
   were straightway carried,
(Or at the last e're they transgrest)
   who thus began to plead:

167

Ezek. 18:2. If for our own transgression,
   or disobedience,
We here did stand at thy left-hand
   just were the Recompence:
But *Adam's* guilt our souls hath spilt,
   his fault is charg'd on us;
And that alone hath overthrown,
   and utterly undone us.

168

Not we, but he, ate of the Tree,
   whose fruit was interdicted:
Yet on us all of his sad Fall,
   the punishment's inflicted.
How could we sin that had not been,
   or how is his sin our,
Without consent, which to prevent,
   we never had a pow'r?

169

  O great Creator, why was our Nature
   depraved and forlorn?
  Why so defil'd, and made so vild
   whilst we were yet unborn?
  If it be just, and needs we must
   transgressors reck'ned be,
Ps. 51:5. Thy Mercy, Lord, to us afford,
   which sinners hath set free.

170

  Behold we see *Adam* set free,
   and sav'd from his trespass,
  Whose sinful Fall hath split us all,
   and brought us to this pass.
  Canst thou deny us once to try,
   or Grace to us to tender,
  When he finds grace before thy face,
   that was the chief offender?

171

Their Argument taken Than answered the Judge most dread,
off.   God doth such doom forbid,
Ezek. 18:20. That men should dye eternally
Rom. 5:12, 19. for what they never did.
  But what you call old *Adam's* Fall,
   and only his Trespass,
  You call amiss to call it his,
   both his and yours it was.

172

  He was design'd of all Mankind
   to be a publick Head,
  A common Root, whence all should shoot,
   and stood in all their stead.
1 *Cor.* 15:48, 49. He stood and fell, did ill or well,
   not for himself alone,
  But for you all, who now his Fall,
   and trespass would disown.

173

If he had stood, then all his brood
    had been established
In Gods true love, never to move,
    nor once awry to tread: 1380
than all his Race, my Father's Grace,
    should have enjoy'd for ever,
And wicked Sprights by subtile sleights
    could them have harmed never.

174

Would you have griev'd to have receiv'd   1385
    through *Adam* so much good,
As had been your for evermore,
    if he at first had stood?
Would you have said, we ne'r obey'd
    nor did thy Laws regard;   1390
It ill befits with benefits,
    us, Lord, so to reward?

175

Since then to share in his welfare,
    you could have been content,
You may with reason share in his treason,   1395
    and in the punishment.

Rom. 5:12.   Hence you were born in state forlorn,
Ps. 51:5.   with Natures so depraved:
Gen. 5:3.   Death was your due, because that you
    had thus your selves behaved.   1400

176

Matt. 23:30, 31.   You think if we had been as he,
    whom God did so betrust,
We to our cost would ne're have lost
    all for a paltry Lust.
Had you been made in *Adam's* stead,   1405
    you would like things have wrought,
And so into the self-same wo,
    your selves and your have brought.

177

Rom. 9:15, 18.	I may deny you once to try,
The free gift.	or Grace to you to tender, 1410
Rom. 5:15.	Though he finds Grace before my face,
	who was the chief offender:
	Else should my Grace cease to be Grace;
	for it should not be free,
	If to release whom I should please, 1415
	I have no libertee.

178

If upon one what's due to none
    I frankly shall bestow,
And on the rest shall not think best,
    compassions skirts to throw,   1420
Whom injure I? will you envy,
    and grudge at others weal?
Or me accuse, who do refuse
    your selves to help and heal?

179

Matt. 20:15.

Am I alone of what's my own,   1425
    no Master or no Lord?
Or if I am, how can you claim
    what I to some afford?
Will you demand Grace at my hand,
    and challenge what is mine?   1430
Will you teach me whom to set free,
    & thus my Grace confine?

180

Ps. 58:3.	You sinners are, and such a share
Rom. 6:23.	as sinners may expect,
Gal. 3:10.	Such you shall have; for I do save 1435
Rom. 8:29, 30; 11:7.	none but mine own Elect.
Rev. 21:27.	Yet to compare your sin with their,
Luke 12:48.	who liv'd a longer time,
	I do confess yours is much less,
	though every sin's a crime. 1440

181

Matt. 11:22.	A crime it is, therefore in bliss
The wicked all	you may not hope to dwell;
convinced and put to	But unto you I shall allow
silence.	the easiest room in Hell.
Rom. 3:19.	The glorious King thus answering, 1445
Matt. 22:12.	they cease, and plead no longer:
	Their Consciences must needs confess
	his Reasons are the stronger.

182

Behold the formidable	Thus all mens Pleas the Judge with ease
estate of all the	doth answer and confute, 1450
ungodly, as they stand	Until that all, both great and small,
hopeless & helpless	are silenced and mute.
before an impartial	Vain hopes are cropt, all mouths are stopt,
Judge, expecting their	sinners have nought to say,
final Sentence.	But that 'tis just, and equal most 1455
Rev. 6:16, 17.	they should be damn'd for ay.

183

Now what remains, but that to pains
    and everlasting smart,
Christ should condemn the Sons of men,
    which is their just desert; 1460
Oh, rueful plights of sinful wights!
    Oh wretches all forlorn:
'T had happy been that ne're had seen
    the Sun, or not been born.

184

Yea, now it would be good they could 1465
    themselves annihilate,
and cease to be, themselves to free
    from such a fearful state.
Oh happy Dogs, and Swine, and Frogs:
    yea Serpents generation, 1470
Who do not fear this doom to hear,
    and sentence of Damnation!

185

Ps. 139:2, 3, 4.	This is their state so desperate:
Eccles. 12:14.	their sins are fully known;
	Their vanities and villanies 1475
	before the world are shown.
	As they are gross and impious,
	so are their numbers more
	Than motes i'th' Air, or then their hair,
	or sands upon the shore.

186

Divine Justice offended is
    and Satisfaction claimeth:
God's wrathful ire kindled like fire,
    against them fiercely flameth.
Their Judge severe doth quite cashier   1485

Matt. 25:45.   and all their Pleas off take,
That never a man, or dare, or can
    a further Answer make.

187

Matt. 22:12.   Their mouths are shut, each man is put
Rom. 2:5, 6.   to silence and to shame: 1490
Luke 19:42.   Nor have they ought within their thought,
    Christ's Justice for to blame.
The Judge is just, and plague them must,
    nor will he mercy shew
(For Mercies day is past away)   1495
    to any of this Crew.

188

Matt. 28:18.   The Judge is strong, doers of wrong
Ps. 139:7.   cannot his power withstand:
None can by flight run out of sight,
    nor scape out of his hand.   1500
Sad is their state: for Advocate
    to plead their Cause there's none:
None to prevent their punishment,
    or misery bemone.

189

    O dismal day! whither shall they
      for help and succour flee?
    To God above, with hopes to move
      their greatest Enemee:
    His wrath is great, whose burning heat
Isa. 33:14.   no floods of tears can slake:
Ps. 11:6.   His word stands fast, that they be cast
Num. 23:19.   into the burning Lake.

190

    To Christ their Judge, he doth adjudge
      them to the Pit of Sorrow;
Matt. 25:41.   Nor will he hear, or cry, or tear,
      nor respite them one morrow.
Matt. 25:10, 11, 12.   To Heav'n alas, they cannot pass,
      it is against them shut;
    To enter there (O heavy cheer)
      they out of hopes are put.

191

Luke 12:20.   Unto their Treasures, or to their Pleasures,
Ps. 49:7, 17.   all these have them forsaken:
    Had they full Coffers to make large offers,
      their Gold would not be taken
    Unto the place where whilome was
Deut. 32:22.   their Birth and Education?
    Lo! Christ begins for their great sins
      to fire the Earths Foundation;

192

2 Pet. 3:10.   And by and by the flaming Sky
      shall drop like molten Lead
    About their ears, t'increase their fears,
      and aggravate their dread.
    To Angels good that ever stood
      in their integrity,
    Should they betake themselves, and make
      their sute incessantly?

193

Matt. 13:41, 42.

They neither skill, nor do they will
    to work them any ease:
They will not mourn to see them burn,
    nor beg for their release. 1540
To wicked men, their bretheren,
    in sin and wickedness,
Should they make mone? their case is one,

Rev. 20:13, 15.

    they're in the same distress.

194

Ah, cold comfort, and mean support 1545
    from such like Comforters!
Ah, little joy of Company,
    and fellow-sufferers!

Luke 16:28.

Such shall increase their hearts disease,
    and add unto their woe, 1550
Because that they brought to decay
    themselves and many moe.

195

Unto the Saints with sad complaints
    should they themselves apply?

Rev. 21:4.

They're not dejected, nor ought affected 1555
    with all their misery.
Friends stand aloof, and make no proof
    what Prayers or Tears can do:

Ps. 58:10.

Your godly friends are now more friends
    to Christ than unto you. 1560

196

Where tender love mens hearts did move
    unto a sympathy,
And bearing part of others smart
    in their anxiety;

1 *Cor.* 6:2.

Now such compassion is out of fashion, 1565
    and wholly laid aside:
No Friends no near, but Saints to hear
    their Sentence can abide.

197

               One natural Brother beholds another
                    in this astonied fit,   1570
               Yet sorrows not thereat a jot,

Compare   nor pitties him a whit.
Prov. 1:26 *with*   The godly wife conceives no grief,
1 *John* 3:2 &   nor can she shed a tear
2 *Cor.* 5:16.   For the sad state of her dear Mate,   1575
                    when she his doom doth hear.

198

               He that was erst a Husband pierc't
                    with sense of Wives distress,
               Whose tender heart did bear a part
                    of all her grievances,   1580
               Shall mourn no more as heretofore
                    because of her ill plight;
               Although he see her now to be
                    a damn'd forsaken wight.

199

               The tender Mother will own no other   1585
                    of all her numerous brood,
               But such as stand at Christ's right hand
                    acquitted through his Blood.
Luke 16:25.   The pious Father had now much rather
                    his graceless Son should ly   1590
               In Hell with Devils, for all his evils
                    burning eternally,

200

               Then God most high should injury,
Ps. 58:10.   by sparing him sustain;
               And doth rejoyce to hear Christ's voice   1595
                    adjudging him to pain.
               Who having all, both great and small,
                    convinc'd and silenced,
               Did then proceed their Doom to read,
                    and thus it uttered,   1600

	201	

<table>
<tr><td>The Judge
pronounceth the
Sentence of
condemnation.
Matt. 25:41.</td><td>

Ye sinful wights, and cursed sprights,
    that work Iniquity,
Depart together from me for ever
    to endless Misery;
Your portion take in yonder Lake,
    Where Fire and Brimstone flameth:
Suffer the smart, which your desert
    as it's due wages claimeth.

</td><td>1605</td></tr>
</table>

202

<table>
<tr><td></td><td>

Oh piercing words more sharp than swords!
    what, to depart from Thee,

</td><td>1610</td></tr>
<tr><td>*The terrour of it.*</td><td>

Whose face before for evermore
    the best of Pleasures be!
What? to depart (unto our smart)
    from thee *Eternally*:
To be for aye banish'd away,
    with *Devils* company!

</td><td>1615</td></tr>
</table>

203

What? to be sent to *Punishment*,
    and flames of *Burning Fire*,
To be surrounded, and eke confounded
    with Gods *Revengful ire*.   1620
What? to abide, not for a tide
    these Torments, but for *Ever*:
To be released, or to be eased,
    not after years, but *Never*.

204

Oh, *fearful Doom*! now there's no room   1625
    for hope or help at all:
Sentence is past which aye shall last,
    Christ will not it recall.
There might you hear them rent and tear
    the Air with their out-cries: 1630
The hideous noise of their sad voice
    ascendeth to the Skies.

205

Luke 13:28.	They wring their hands, their caitiff-hands,
	and gnash their teeth for terrour;
	They cry, they roar for anguish sore,
	and gnaw their tongues for horrour.
	But get away without delay,
	Christ pitties not your cry:
	Depart to Hell, there may you yell,
Prov. 1:26.	and roar Eternally.

1635

1640

206

It is put in Execution.	That word, *Depart*, maugre their heart,
	drives every wicked one,
	With mighty pow'r, the self-same hour,
	far from the Judge's Throne.
Matt. 25:46.	Away they're chaste by the strong blast
	of his Death-threatning mouth:
	They flee full fast, as if in haste,
	although they be full loath.

1645

207

As chaff that's dry, and dust doth fly
    before the Northern wind:
Right so are they chased away,
    and can no Refuge find.
They hasten to the Pit of Wo,
Matt. 13:41, 42.   guarded by Angels stout;
Who to fulfil Christ's holy will,
    attend this wicked Rout.

1650

1655

208

HELL.	Whom having brought, as they are taught,
Matt. 25:30.	unto the brink of Hell
Mark 9:43.	(That dismal place far from Christ's face,
Isa. 30:33.	where Death and Darkness dwell:
Rev. 21.8.	Where Gods fierce Ire kindleth the fire,
	and vengeance feeds the flame
	With piles of Wood, and Brimstone Flood,
	that none can quench the same,)

1660

209

Wicked Men and Devils cast into it for ever.
Matt. 22:13; 25:46.

With Iron bands they bind their hands,
    and cursed feet together,
And cast them all, both great and small,
    into that Lake for ever.
Where day and night, without respite,
    they wail, and cry, and howl
For tort'ring pain, which they sustain
    in Body and in Soul.

210

Rev. 14:10, 11.

For day and night, in their despight,
    their torments smoak ascendeth.
Their pain and grief have no relief,
    their anguish never endeth.
There must they ly, and never dy,
    though dying every day:
There must they dying every ly,
    and not consume away.

211

Dy fain they would, if dy they could,
    but Death will not be had.
God's direful wrath their bodies hath
    for ev'r Immortal made.
They live to ly in misery,
    and bear eternal wo;
And live they must whilst God is just,
    that he may plague them so.

212

The unsufferable torments of the damned.
Luke 16:24.
Jude 7.

But who can tell the plagues of Hell,
    and torments exquisite?
Who can relate their dismal state,
    and terrours infinite?
Who fare the best, and feel the least,
    yet feel that punishment
Whereby to nought they should be brought,
    if God did not prevent.

213

      The least degree of miserie
         there felt's incomparable,
      The lightest pain they there sustain
Isa. 33:14.   more than intolerable.   1700
Mark 9:43, 44.   But God's great pow'r from hour to hour
         upholds them in the fire,
      That they shall not consume a jot,
         nor by it's force expire.

214

      But ah, the wo they undergo   1705
         (they more than all besides)
      Who had the light, and knew the right,
Luke 12:47.   yet would not it abide.
      The sev'n-fold smart, which to their part,
         and portion doth fall,   1710
      Who Christ his Grace would not imbrace,
         nor hearken to his call.

215

      The *Amorites* and *Sodomites*
Matt. 11:24.   although their plagues be sore,
      Yet find some ease, compar'd to these,   1715
         who feel a great deal more.
      Almighty God, whose Iron Rod,
         to smite them never lins,
      Doth most declare his Justice rare
         in plaguing these mens sins.   1720

216

Luke 16:23, 25.   The pain of loss their Souls doth toss,
Luke 13:28.   and wond'rously distress,
      To think what they have cast away
         by wilful wickedness.
      We might have been redeem'd from sin   1725
         think they, and liv'd above,
      Being possest of heav'nly rest,
         and joying in God's love.

217

Luke 13:34.

But wo, wo, wo our Souls into!
    we would not nappy be;
And therefore bear Gods Vengeance here
    to all Eternitee.
Experience and woful sense
    must be our painful teachers
Who n'ould believe, nor credit give,
    unto our faithful Preachers.

218

Mark 9:44.
Rom. 2:15.

Thus shall they ly, and wail, and cry,
    tormented, and tormenting
Their galled hearts with pois'ned darts
    but now too late repenting.
There let them dwell i'th' Flames of Hell:
    there leave we them to burn,
And back agen unto the men
    whom Christ acquits, return.

219

The Saints rejoyce to see Judgment executed upon the wicked World.
Ps. 58:10.
Rev. 19:1, 2, 3.

The Saints behold with courage bold,
    and thankful wonderment,
To see all those that were their foes
    thus sent to punishment:
Then do they sing unto their King
    a Song of endless Praise:
They praise his Name, and do proclaim
    that just are all his ways.

220

They ascend with Christ into Heaven triumphing.
Matt. 25:46.
1 *John* 3:2.
1 *Cor.* 13:12.

Thus with great joy and melody
    to Heav'n they all ascend,
Him there to praise with sweetest layes,
    and Hymns that never end:
Where with long Rest they shall be blest,
    and nought shall them annoy:
Where they shall see as seen they be,
    and whom they love enjoy.

221

Their Eternal happiness   O glorious Place! where face to face
and incomparable   Jehovah may be seen,
Glory there.   By such as were sinners whilere
                     and no dark vail between.
                Where the Sun shine, and light Divine,   1765
                     of Gods bright Countenance,
                Doth rest upon them every one,
                     with sweetest influence.

222

                O blessed state of the Renate!
                     O wondrous Happiness,   1770
                To which they're brought, beyond what thought
                     can reach, or words express!
Rev. 21:4.   Griefs water-course, and sorrows sourse,
                     are turn'd to joyful streams.
                Their old distress and heaviness   1775
                     are vanished like dreams.

223

                For God above in arms of love
                     doth dearly them embrace,
Ps. 16:11.   And fills their sprights with such delights,
                     and pleasures in his grace;   1780
                As shall not fail, nor yet grow stale
                     through frequency of use:
                Nor do they fear Gods favour there,
                     to forfeit by abuse.

224

Heb. 12:23.   For there the Saints are perfect Saints,   1785
                     and holy ones indeed,
                From all the sin that dwelt within
                     their mortal bodies freed:
                Made Kings and Priests to God through Christs
Rev. 1:6; 22:5.   dear loves transcendency,   1790
                There to remain, and there to reign
                     with him Eternally.

A Short Discourse on Eternity

1

    What Mortal man can with his Span
        mete out Eternity?
Isa. 57:15.   Or fathom it by depth of Wit,
Mark 3:29.   or strength of Memory?
Matt. 25:46.   The lofty Sky is not so high,   5
        Hells depth to this is small:
    The World so wide is but a stride,
        compared therewithall.

2

    It is a main great Ocean,
        withouten bank or bound: 10
    A deep Abyss, wherein there is
        no bottom to be found.
    This World hath stood now since the Flood,
        four thousand years well near,
    And hath before endured more   15
        than sixteen hundred year.

3

    But what's the time from the Worlds prime
        unto this present day,
    If we thereby Eternity
        to measure should assay?   20
    The whole duration since the Creation
        though long, yet is more little,
    If placed by Eternity,
        then is the smallest tittle.

4

Tell every Star both near and far, 25
    in Heav'ns bright Canopee,
That doth appear throughout the year,
    of high or low degree:
Tell every Tree that thou canst see
    in this vast Wilderness, 30
Up in the Woods, down by the Floods,
    in thousand miles progress.

5

The sum is bast, yet not so vast,
    but that thou may'st go on
To multiply the Leaves thereby, 35
    that hang those Trees upon:
And thereunto the Drops, that thou
    imaginest to be
In *April* Show'rs, that bring forth Flow'rs,
    and blossoms plenteously: 40

6

Number the Fowls and living Souls
    that through the Air do Fly,
The winged Hosts in all their Coasts
    beneath the Starry Sky:
Count all the Grass as thou doast pass 45
    through many a pasture-land,
And dewy Drops that on the tops
    of Herbs and Plants do stand.

7

Number the Sand upon the Strand,
    and Atomes of the Air; 50
And do thy best on Man and Beast,
    to reckon every Hair:

2 *Thess.* 1:9.   Take all the Dust, if so thou lust,
Rev. 14:11.   and add to thine Account:
Yet shall the Years of sinners tears, 55
    the Number far surmount.

8

Nought joyn'd to nought can ne're make ought,
nor Cyphers make a Sum:
Nor things Finite, to infinite
by multiplying come:
A Cockle-shell may serve as well
to lade the Ocean dry,
As finite things and Reckonings
to bound Eternity.

9

O happy they that live for aye,
1 Thess. 4:17.   with Christ in Heav'n above!
Rom. 8:38, 39.   Who know withal, that nothing shall
deprive them of his love.
Eternity, Eternity!
Oh, were it not for thee,
The Saints in bliss and happiness
could never happy be.

10

For if they were in any fear,
1 John 4:18.   that this their joy might cease,
John 6:35, 40, 51.   It would annoy (if not destroy)
Rev. 21:4.   and interrupt their peace:
But being sure it shall endure
so long as God shall live;
The thoughts of this unto their bliss,
do full perfection give.

11

Heb. 12:12.   Cheer up, ye Saints, amidst your wants,
and sorrows many a one.
Lift up the head, shake off all dread,
and moderate your mone.
Your sufferings and evil things
2 Cor. 4:17.   will suddenly be past;
Ps. 16:11.   Your sweet Fruitions, and blessed Visions,
for evermore shall last.

12

  Lament and mourn you that must burn
    amidst those flaming Seas: 90
  If once you come to such a doom,
    for ever farewel ease.
  O sad estate and desperate,
    that never can be mended,
  Until Gods Will shall change, or till   95
    Eternity be ended!

Luke 13:28.
Matt. 25:41, 46.
Rev. 14:11.

13

  If any one this Question
    shall unto me propound:
  What, have the years of sinners tears
    no limits, or no bound?   100
  It kills our heart to think of smart,
    and pains that last for ever;
  And hear of fire that shall expire,
    or be extinguish'd never.

Mark 9:43, 44.

14

  I'le Answer make (or let them take   105
    my words as I intend them:
  For this is all the Cordial
    that here I have to lend them)
  When Heav'n shall cease to flow with peace
    and all felicity;   110
  Then Hell may cease to be the place
    of Wo and Misery.

15

  When Heav'n is Hell, when Ill is Well,
    when Vertue turns to Vice,
  When wrong is Right, and Dark is Light,   115
    when Nought is of great price:
  Then may the years of sinners tears
    and sufferings expire,
  And all the hosts of damned ghosts
    escape out of Hell-fire.   120

16

When Christ above shall cease to love,
    when God shall cease to reign,
And be no more, as heretofore,
    the Worlds great Sovereign,
Or not be just, or favour lust,
    or in mens sins delight:
Then wicked men (and not till then)
    to Heav'n may take their flight.

17

When Gods great Power shall be brought lower,
    by forreign Puissance;
Or be decay'd, and weaker made
    through Times continuance:
When drowsiness shall him oppress,
    and lay him fast asleep:
Then sinful men may break their pen,
    and out of Prison creep.

18

When those in Glory shall be right sory
    they may not change their place,
And wish to dwell with them in Hell,
    never to see Christs face:
Then those in pain may freedom gain,
    and be with Glory dight:
Then Hellish Fiends may be Christs Friends,
    and Heirs of Heaven hight.

19

Then, Ah poor men! what, not till then?
    No, not an hour before:
For God is just, and therefore must
    torment them evermore.
ETERNITY! ETERNITY!
    thou mak'st hard hearts to bleed:
The thoughts of thee in misery,
    do make men wail indeed.

20

 When they remind what's still behind,
  and ponder this word NEVER,
Mark 9:43, 44, 45, 46, That they must here be made to bear   155
&c.   Gods Vengeance for EVER:
 The thought of this more bitter is,
  then all they feel beside:
 Yet what they feel, nor heart of steel,
  nor Flesh of Brass can bide.   160

21

 To lye in wo, and undergo
  the direful pains of Hell,
2 Thess. 1:8, 9. And know withall, that there they shall
  for aye, and ever dwell;
 And that they are from rest as far   165
Matt. 25:46.   when fifty thousand year,
Rev. 14:10, 11. Twice told, are spent in punishment,
  as when they first came there.

22

 This, Oh! this makes Hells fiery flakes
  much more intolerable;   170
 This makes frail wights & damned sprights,
  to bear their plagues unable.
 This makes men bite, for fell despite,
  their very tongues in twain:
 This makes them rore for great horror,   175
  and trebleth all their pain.

A Postscript unto the Reader

And now good Reader, I return again
To talk with thee, who has been at the pain
To read throughout, & heed what went before;
And unto thee I'le speak a little more.
Give ear, I pray to thee, unto what I say,   5
That God may hear thy voice another day.
Thou hast a Soul, my friend, and so have I,
To save or lose; a Soul that cannot die,
A soul of greater price than Gold or Gems;
A Soul more worth than Crowns and Diadems;   10
A Soul at first created like its Maker,
And of Gods Image made to be partaker:
Upon the wings of Noblest Faculties,
Taught for to soar above the Starry Skies,
And not to rest, until it understood   15
It self possessed of the chiefest good.
And since the Fall, thy Soul retaineth still
Those Faculties of Reason and of Will,
But Oh, how much deprav'd, and out of frame,
As if they were some others, not the same.   20
Thine Understanding dismally benighted,
And Reason's eye in Sp'ritual things dim-sighted,
Or else stark blind: Thy Will inclin'd to evil,
And nothing else, a Slave unto the Devil;
That loves to live, and liveth to transgress,   25
But shuns the way of God and Holiness.
All thine Affections are disordered;
And thou by head-strong Passions are misled.
What need I tell thee of the crooked way,
And many wicked wand'rings every day?   30
Or that think own transgressions are more
In number, than the sands upon the Shore:
Thou are a lump of wickedness become,
And may'st with horrour think upon they Doom,
Until thy Soul be washed in the flood   35
Of Christ's most dear, soul-cleansing precious blood.
That, that alone can do away thy sin
Which thou wert born, and hast long lived in;
That, only that, can pacifie Gods wrath,

If apprehended by a lively Faith, 40
Now whilst the day and means of Grace to last,
Before the opportunity be past.
But if, O man, thou liv'st a Christless creature,
And Death surprize thee in a state of nature,
(As who can tell but that may be thy case) 45
How wilt thou stand before the Judge's face?
When he shall be reveal'd in flaming fire,
And come to pay ungodly men their hire:
To execute due vengeance upon those
That knew him not, or that have been his foes? 50
What wilt thou answer unto his demands,
When he requires a reason at thy hands
Of all the things that thou has said, or done,
Or left undone, or set thine heart upon?
When he shall thus with thee expostulate, 55
What cause hadst thou thy Maker for to hate,
To take up Arms against thy Soveraign,
And Emnity against him to maintain?
What injury hath God Almighty done thee?
What good hath he with-held that might have won thee? 60
What evil, or injustice, hast thou found
In him, that might unto thine hurt redound?
If neither felt, nor feared injury
Hath moved thee to such hostility;
What made thee then the Fountain to forsake, 65
And unto broken Pits thy self betake?
What reason hadst thou to dishonour God,
Who thee with Mercies never cease to load?
Because the Lord was good, hast thou been evil,
And taken part against him with the Devil? 70
For all his cost to pay him with despite,
And all his love with hatred to requite?
Is this the fruit of Gods great patience,
To wax more bold in disobedience?
To kick against the bowels of his Love, 75
Is this aright his Bounty to improve?
Stand still, ye Heav'ns and be astonished,
That God by man should thus be injured!
Give ear, O earth, and tremble at the sin
Of those that thine Inhabitants have bin. 80

But thou, vile wretch, hast added unto all
Thine other faults, and facts so criminal,
The damning sin of wilful unbelief,
Of all Transgressors hadst thou been the chief;
Yet when time was, thou might'st have been set free 85
From Sin, and Wrath, and punishment by mee.
But thou wouldst not accept of Gospel Grace,
Nor on my terms Eternal Life embrace.
As if that all thy breaches of Gods Law
Were not enough upon thy head to draw 90
Eternal Wrath: Thou hast despis'd a Saviour,
Rejected me, and trampled on my favour.
How oft have I stood knocking at thy door,
And been denied entrance evermore?
How often hath my Spirit been withstood, 95
When as I sent him to have done thee good?
Thou hast no need of nay one to plead
Thy Cause, or for thy Soul to intercede:
Plead for thy self, if thou has ought to say,
And pay thy forfeiture without delay. 100
Behold thou dost ten thousand Talents owe,
Or pay thy Debt, or else to Prison go.
Think, think, O Man, when Christ shall thus unfold
Thy secret guilt, and make thee to behold
The ugly face of all thy sinful errours, 105
And fill thy Soul with his amazing terrours,
And let thee see the flaming Pit of Hell
(Where all that have no part in him shall dwell)
When he shall thus expostulate the case,
How canst thou bear to look him in the face? 110
What wilt thou do without an Advocate?
Or plead, when as thy state is desperate?
Dost think to put him off with fair pretences?
Or wilt thou hide and cover thine offences?
Can any think from him concealed be, 115
Who doth the hidden things of darkness see?
Art thou of force his Power to withstand?
Canst thou by might escape out of his hand?
Dost thou intend to run out of his sight,
And save thy self from punishment by flight? 120
Or wilt thou be eternally accurst,

And bide his Vengeance, let him do his worst?
Oh, who can bear his indignations heat?
Or bide the pains of Hell, which are so great?
If then thou neither canst his Wrath endure,   125
Nor any Ransom after death procure:
If neither Cryes nor Tears can move his heart
To pardon thee, or mittigate thy smart,
But unto Hell thou must perforce be sent
With dismal horrour and astonishment: 130
Consider, O my Friends, what cause thou hast
With fear and trembling (while as yet thou may'st)
To lay to heart thy sin and misery,
And to make out after the Remedy.
Consider well the greatness of my danger,   135
O Child of wrath, and object of Gods anger,
Thou hangest over the Infernal Pit
By one small threed, and car'st thou not a whit?
There's but a step between thy Soul and Death,
Nothing remains but stopping of thy breath,   140
(Which may be done to morrow, or before)
And then thou art undone for evermore.
Let this awaken thy Security,
And make thee look about thee speedily,
How canst thou rest an hour or sleep a night,   145
Or in thy Creature-comforts take delight;
Or with vain Toyes thy self forgetfull make
How near thou art unto the burning Lake?
How canst thou live without tormenting fears?
How canst thou hold from weeping floods of tears,   150
Yea, tears of blood, I might almost have sed,
If such like tears could from thine eyes be shed?
To gain the world what will it profit thee,
And loose thy Soul and self eternallie?
Eternity on one small point dependeth: 155
The man is lost that this short life mispendeth,
For as the Tree doth fall, right so it lies;
And man continues in what state he dies.
Who happy die, shall happy rise again;
Who cursed die, shall cursed still remain;   160
If under Sin, and Wrath, Death leaves thee bound,
At Judgment under Wrath thou shalt be found:

And then wo, wo that ever thou wert born,
O wretched man, of Heav'n and Earth forlorn!
Consider this, all ye that God forget, 165
Who all his threatenings at nought do set,
Lest into pieces he begin to tear
Your Souls, and there be no deliverer.
O you that now sing care and fear away,
Think often of the formidable Day, 170
Wherein the Heavens with a mighty noise,
And with a hideous, heart-confounding voice,
Shall pass away together, being roll'd,
As men are wont their garments for to fold;
When th' Elements with fervent heat shall melt, 175
And living Creatures in the same shall swelt,
And altogether in those Flames expire,
Which set the Earths Foundations on fire.
Oh, what amazement will your hearts be in,
And how will you to curse your selves begin 180
For all your damned sloth, and negligence,
And unbelief, and gross Impenitence,
When you shall hear that dreadful Sentence past,
That all the wicked into Hell be cast?
What horrour will your Consciences surprise, 185
When you shall hear the fruitless doleful cries
Of such as are compelled to depart
Unto the place of everlasting smart?
What, when you see the sparks fly out of Hell,
And view the Dungeon where you are to dwell, 190
Wherein you must eternally remain
In anguish, and intolerable pain?
What, when your hands & feet are bound together,
And you are cast into that Lake for ever?
Then shall you feel the truth of what you hear, 195
That hellish pains are more than you can bear,
And that those Torments are an hundred fold
More terrible than ever you were told.
Nor speak I this, good Reader, to torment thee
Before the time, but rather to prevent thee 200
From running head-long to thine own decay,
In such a perillous and deadly way.
We, who have known and felt Jehovah's terrours,

Perswade men to repent them of their errours,
And turn to God in time, e're his Decree 205
Bring forth, and then there be no Remedee!
If in the night, when thou art fast asleep,
Some friend of thine, that better watch doth keep,
Should see thy house all on a burning flame,
And thee almost inclosed with the same: 210
If such a friend should break thy door & wake thee,
Or else by force out of the peril take thee:
What? wouldst thou take his kindness in ill part?
Or frown upon him for his good desert?
Such, O my friend, such is thy present state, 215
And danger, being unregenerate.
Awake, awake, and then thou shalt perceive
Thy peril greater then thou wilt believe.
Lift up thine eyes, and see Gods wrathful ire,
preparing unextinguishable fire 220
For all that live and die impenitent.
Awake, awake, O Sinner, and repent,
And quarrel not, because I thus alarm
Thy Soul, to save it from eternal harm.
Perhaps thou harbourest such thoughts as these: 225
I hope I may enjoy my carnal ease
A little longer, and my self refresh
With those delights that gratifie the flesh,
And yet repent before it be too late,
And get into a comfortable state: 230
I hope I have yet many years to spend,
And time enough those matters to attend.
Presumptuous heart! Is God engag'd to give
A longer time to such as love to live
Like Rebels still, who think to stain his Glory 235
By wickedness, and after to be sory?
Unto thy lust shall he be made a drudge,
Who thee, and all ungodly men, shall judge?
Canst thou account sin sweet, and yet confess,
That first, or last, it ends in bitterness? 240
Is sin a thing that must procure thee sorrow?
And wouldst thou dally with't another morrow?
O foolish man, who lovest to enjoy
That which will thee distress, or else destroy!

What gained Sampson by his Delilah? 245
What gained David by his Bathsheba?
The one became a Slave, lost both his eyes,
And made them sport that were his Enemies:
The other penneth, as a certain token
Of Gods displeasure, that his bones were broken, 250
Besides the woes he after met withal,
To chasten him for that his grievous Fall:
His own Son Ammon using crafty wiles,
His Daughter Thamar wickedly defiles;
His second Son more beautiful than good, 255
His hands embreweth in his Brothers Blood:
And by and by aspiring to the Crown,
He strives to pull his gentle Father down:
With hellish rage, him fiercely persecuting,
And bruitishly his concubines polluting. 260
Read whoso list, and ponder what he reads,
And he shall find small joy in evil deeds.
Moreover this consider, that the longer
Thou liv'st in sin, thy sin will grow the stronger.
And then it will an harder matter prove, 265
To leave those wicked haunts that thou dost love.
The Black-moor may as eas'ly change his skin,
As old transgressors leave their wonted sin.
And who can tell what may become of thee,
Or where thy Soul in one days time may be? 270
We see that Death ner old nor young men spares,
But one and other takes at unawares.
For in a moment, whil'st men Peace do cry,
Destruction seizeth on them suddenly.
Thou who this morning art a lively wight, 275
May'st be a Crops and damned Ghost ere night.
Oh, dream not then, that it will serve the turn,
Upon thy death bed for thy sins to mourn.
But think how many have been snatcht away,
And had no time for mercy once to pray. 280
It's just with God Repentance to deny
To such as put it off until they dy.
And late Repentance seldom proveth true,
Which if it fail, thou know'st what must ensue.
For after this short life is at an end, 285

What is amiss thou never canst amend.
Believe, O man, that to procrastinate,
And put it off until it be too late,
As 'tis thy sin, so is it Satans wile,
Whereby he doth great multitudes beguile. 290
How many thousands hath this strong delusion
Already brought to ruine and confusion,
Whose Souls are now reserv'd in Iron Chains,
Under thick darkness to eternal pains?
They thought of many years, as thou dost now, 295
But were deceived quite, and so may'st thou.
Oh, then my friend, while not away thy time,
Nor by rebellion aggravate thy Crime.
Oh put not off Repentance till to morrow,
Adventure not without Gods leave to borrow 300
Another day to spend upon thy lust,
Lest God (that is most holy, wise, and just)
Denounce in wrath, and to thy terrour say:
This night shall Devils fetch thy Soul away.
Now seek the face of God with all thy heart; 305
Acknowledge unto him how vile thou art.
Tell him thy sins deserve eternal wrath,
And that it is a wonder that he hath
Permitted thee so long to draw thy breath,
Who might have cut thee off by sudden death, 310
And sent thy Soul into the lowest Pit,
From whence no price should ever ransom it,
And that he may most justly do it still
(Because thou hast deserv'd it) if he will.
Yet also tell him that, if he shall please, 315
He can forgive thy Sins, and thee release.
And that in Christ his Son he may be just,
And justifie all those that on him trust:
That though thy sins are of a crimson dy,
Yet Christ his Blood can cleanse thee thorowly. 320
Tell him, that he may make his glorious Name
More wonderful by covering thy shame;
That Mercy may be greatly magnify'd,
And Justice also fully satisfy'd,
If he shall please to own thee in his Son, 325
Who hath paid dear for Men's Redemption.

Tell him thou hast an unbelieving heart,
Which hindereth thee from coming for a part
In Christ: and that although his terrours aw thee,
Thou canst not come till he be pleas'd to draw thee. 330
Tell him thou know'st thine heart to be so bad,
And thy condition so exceeding sad,
That though Salvation may be had for nought,
Thou canst not come and take, till thou be brought.
Oh beg of him to bow thy stubborn Will 335
To come to Christ, that he thy lusts may kill.
Look up to Christ for his attractive pow'r,
Which he exerteth in a needful hour;
Who saith, whenas I lifted up shall be,
Then will I draw all sorts of men to me. 340
O wait upon him with true diligence,
And trembling fear in every Ordinance.
Unto his call earnest attention give,
Whose voice makes deaf men hear, and dead men live.
Thus weep, and mourn, thus hearken, pray and wait, 345
Till he behold, and pitty thine estate,
Who is more ready to bestow his Grace,
Then thou the same art willing to imbrace;
Yea, he hath Might enough to bring thee home,
Though thou hast neither strength nor will to come. 350
If he delay to answer thy request,
Know that oft-times he doth it for the best:
Not with intent to drive us from his door,
But for to make us importune him more;
Or else to bring us duly to confess, 355
And be convinc'd of our unworthiness.
Oh, be not weary then, but persevere
To beg his Grace till he thy suit shall hear:
And leave him not, nor from his foot-stool go,
Till over thee Compassions skirt he throw. 360
Eternal Life will recompence thy pains,
If found at last, with everlasting gains.
For if the Lord be pleas'd to hear thy cryes,
And to forgive thy great iniquities,
Thou wilt have cause for ever to admire, 365
And laud his Grace, that granted thy desire.
Then shalt thou find thy labour is not lost:

But that the good obtain'd surmounts the cost.
Nor shall thou grieve for loss of sinful pleasures,
Exchang'd for heavenly joyes and lasting treasures. 370
The yoke of Christ, which once thou didst esteem
A tedious yoke, shall then most easie seem.
For why? The love of Christ shall thee constrain
To take delight in that which was thy pain.
The wayes of Wisdom shall be pleasant wayes, 375
And thou shalt chuse therein to spend thy dayes;
If once thy Soul be brought to such a pass:
O'bless the Lord, and magnifie his Grace.
Thou, that of late hadst reason to be sad,
May'st now rejoyce, and be exceeding glad, 380
For thy condition is as happy now,
As erst it was disconsolate and low.
Thou art become as rich as whilome poor,
As blessed now, as cursed heretofore.
For being cleansed with Christs precious Blood, 385
Thou hast an int'rest in the chiefest good:
Gods anger is towards thy Soul appeased,
And in his Christ he is with thee well pleased.
Yea, he doth look upon thee with a mild
And gracious aspect as upon his child. 390
He is become thy Father and thy Friend,
And will defend thee from the cursed Fiend.
Thou need'st not fear the roaring Lyon's rage,
Since God Almighty doth himself engage
To bear thy Soul in Everlasting Armes, 395
Above the reach of all destructive harms.
What ever here thy sufferings may be,
Yet from them all the Lord shall rescue thee.
He will preserve thee by his wond'rous might
Unto that rich Inheritance in light. 400
Oh, sing for joy, all ye regenerate,
Whom Christ hath brought into this blessed state!
O love the Lord, all ye his Saints, who hath
Redeemed you from everlasting wrath:
Who hath by dying made your Souls to live, 405
And what he dearly bought doth freely give:
Give up your selves to walk in all his wayes,
And study how to live unto his praise.

The time is short you have to serve him here:
The day of your deliv'rance draweth near. 410
Lift up your heads, ye upright ones in heart,
Who in Christ's purchase have obtain'd a part.
Behold, he rides upon a shining Cloud,
With Angels voice, and Trumpet sounding loud;
He comes to save his folk from all their foes, 415
And plague the men that Holiness oppose.
So come, Lord Jesus, quickly come we pray:
Yea come, and hasten our Redemption day.

A Song of Emptiness,

To fill up the Empty Pages following.

Vanity of Vanities

Vain, frail, short liv'd, and miserable Man,
Learn what thou art when thine estate is best:
A restless Wave o'th' troubled Ocean,
A Dream, a lifeless Picture finely drest:

A Wind, a Flower, a Vapour, and a Bubble, 5
A Wheel that stands not still, a trembling Reed,
A rolling Stone, dry Dust, light Chaff, and Stubble,
A Shadow of Something, but nought indeed.

Learn what deceitful toyes, and empty things,
This World, and all its best Enjoyments bee: 10
Out of the Earth no true Contentment springs,
But all things here are vexing Vanitee.

For what is *Beauty*, but a fading Flower?
Or what is *Pleasure*, but the Devils bait,
Whereby he catcheth whom he would devour, 15
And multitudes of Souls doth ruinate?

And what are *Friends* but mortal men, as we?
Whom Death from us may quickly separate;
Or else their hearts may quite estranged be,
And all their love be turned into hate. 20

And what are *Riches* to be doted on?
Uncertain, fickle, and ensnaring things;
They draw Mens Souls into Perdition,
And when most needed, take them to their wings.

Ah foolish Man! that sets his heart upon 25
Such empty Shadows, such wild Fowl as these,
That being gotten will be quickly gone,
And whilst they stay increase but his disease

As in a Dropsie, drinking draughts begets,
The more he drinks, the more he still requires: 30
So on this World whoso affection sets,
His Wealths encrease encreaseth his desires.

O happy Man, whose portion is above,
Where Floods, where Flames, where Foes cannot bereave him;
Most wretched man, that fixed hath his love 35
Upon this World, that surely will deceive him!

For, what is *Honour*? What is *Sov'raignty*,
Whereto mens hearts so restlesly aspire?
Whom have they Crowned with Felicity?
When did they ever satisfie desire? 40

The Ear of Man with hearing is not fill'd:
To see new sights still coveteth the Eye:
The craving Stomack though it may be still'd,
Yet craves again without a new supply.

All Earthly things, man's Cravings answer not, 45
Whose little heart would all the World contain,
(If all the World should fall to one man's Lot)
And notwithstanding empty still remain.

The *Eastern Conquerour* was said to weep,
When he the *Indian* Ocean did view, 50
To see his Conquest bounded by the Deep,
And no more Worlds remaining to subdue.

Who would that man in his Enjoyments bless,
Or envy him, or covet his estate,
Whose gettings do augment his greediness,   55
And make his wishes more intemperate?

Such is the wonted and the common guise
Of those on Earth that bear the greatest Sway:
If with a few the case be otherwise
They seek a Kingdom that abides for ay.   60

Moreover they, of all the Sons of men,
that Rule, and are in highest places set,
Are most inclin'd to scorn their Bretheren
And God himself (without great grace) forget.

For as the Sun doth blind the gazer's eyes,   65
That for a time they nought discern aright:
So Honour doth befool and blind the Wise,
And their own Lustre 'reaves them of their sight.

Great are their Dangers, manifold their Cares,
Thro which, whilst others Sleep, they scarcely Nap;   70
And yet are oft surprized unawares,
And fall unweeting into Envies Trap.

The mean Mechanick finds his kindly rest,
All void of fear Sleepeth the County-Clown,
When greatest Princes often are distrest,   75
And cannot Sleep upon their Beds of Down.

Could *Strength* or *Valour* men Immortalize,
Could *Wealth* or *Honour* keep them from decay,
There were some cause the same to Idolize,
And give the lye to that which I do say.   80

But neither can such things themselves endure
Without the hazard of a Change one hour,
Nor such as trust in them can they secure
From dismal dayes, or Deaths prevailing pow'r.

If *Beauty* could the beautiful defend   85
From Death's dominion, than fair *Absalom*
Had not been brought to such a shameful end:
But fair and foul into the Grave must come.

If *Wealth* or *Scepters* could Immortal make,
then wealthy *Croesus*, wherefore art thou dead? 90
If *Warlike force*, which makes the World to quake,
Then why is *Julius Caesar* perished?

Where are the *Scipio's* Thunder-bolts of War?
Renowned *Pompey, Caesars* Enemie?
Stout *Hannibal, Romes* Terror known so far? 95
Great *Alexander*, what's become of thee?

If *Gifts* and *Bribes* Death's favour might but win,
If *Power*, if force, or *Threatnings* might it fray,
All these, and more, had still surviving been:
But all are gone, for Death will have no Nay. 100

Such is this World with all her Pomp and Glory,
Such are the men whom worldly eyes admire:
Cut down by Time, and now become a Story,
That we might after better things aspire.

Go boast thy self of what thy heart enjoyes, 105
Vain Man! triumph in all thy worldly Bliss:
Thy best enjoyments are but Trash and Toyes:
Delight thy self in that which worthless is.

*Omnia praetereunt praeter amare Deum.**

---

*"All things pass except the love of God."

GOD'S CONTROVERSY WITH NEW-ENGLAND

Written in the time of the great drought

Anno 1662

By a lover of New-England's Prosperity

Isaiah 5.4
What could have been done more to my vineyard,
that I have not done in it? wherefore, when I
looked that it should bring forth grapes,
brought it forth wilde grapes?

The Author's request unto the Reader.

Good christian Reader judge me not
    As too Censorious,
For pointing at those faults of thine
    Which are notorious.
For if those faults be none of thine   5
    I do not thee accuse:
But if they be, to hear thy faults
    Why shouldest thou refuse.

I blame not thee to spare my self:
    But first at home begin,   10
And judge my self, before that I
    Reproove anothers sin.
Nor is it I that thee reproove
    Let God himself be heard
Whose awfull providence's voice   15
    No man may disregard.

Quod Deus omnipotens regali voce minatur,
Quod tibi proclamant uno simul ore prophetae,
Quodq' ego cum lachrymis testor de numinis irâ,
Tu leve comentu ne ducas, Lector Amice.*   20

---

*"What God almighty warns you with a ruler's voice,
What the prophets proclaim unto you, crying in unison,
And what I with many tears testify concerning God's wrath,
Do not, Dear Reader, consider lightly."

New-England planted, prospered, declining, threatned, punished.

 Beyond the great Atlantick flood
  There is a region vast,
 A country where no English foot
  In former ages past:
 A waste and howling wilderness,   25
  Where none inhabited
 But hellish fiends, and brutish men
  That Devils worshiped.

 This region was in darkness plac't
  Far off from heavens light,   30
 Amidst the shaddows of grim death
  And of Eternal night.
 For there the Sun of righteousness
  Had never made to shine
 The light of his sweet countenance,   35
  And grace which is divine:

 Until the time drew nigh wherein
  The glorious Lord of hostes
 Was pleasd to lead his armies forth
  Into those forrein coastes.   40
 At whose approach the darkness sad
  Soon vanished away,
 And all the shaddows of the night
  Were turnd to lightsome day.

 The dark and dismal western woods   45
  (The Devils den whilere)
 Beheld such glorious Gospel-shine,
  As none beheld more cleare.
 Where sathan had his scepted sway'd
  For many generations,   50
 The King of Kings set up his throne
  To rule amongst the nations.

The stubborn he in pieces brake,
    Like vessels made of clay:
And those that sought his peoples hurt   55
    He turned to decay.
Those curst Amalekites, that first
    Lift up their hand on high
To fight against Gods Israel,
    Were ruin'd fearfully.   60

Thy terrours on the Heathen folk,
    O Great Jehovah, fell:
The fame of thy great acts, o Lord,
    Did all the nations quell.
Some hid themselves for fear of thee   65
    In forrests wide & great:
Some to thy people croutching came,
    For favour to entreat.

Some were desirous to be taught
    The knowledge of thy wayes,   70
And being taught, did soon accord
    Therein to spend their dayes.
Thus were the fierce and barbarous
    Brought to civility,
And those that liv'd like beasts (or worse)   75
    To live religiously.

O happiest of dayes wherein
    The blind received sight,
And those that had no eyes before
    Were made to see the light!   80
The wilderness hereat rejoyc't,
    The woods for joy did sing,
The vallys & the little hills
    Thy praises ecchoing.

Here was the hiding place, which thou,   85
    Jehovah, didst provide
For thy redeemed ones, and where
    Thou didst thy jewels hide
In per'lous times, and saddest dayes
    Of sack-cloth and of blood,   90
When th' overflowing scourge did pass
    Through Europe, like a flood.

While almost all the world beside
    Lay weltring in their gore:
We, only we, enjoyd such peace   95
    As none enjoyd before.
No forrein foeman did us fray,
    Nor threat'ned us with warrs:
We had no enemyes at home,
    Nor no domestick jarrs.   100

The Lord had made (such was his grace)
    For us a Covenant
Both with the men, and with the beasts,
    That in this desert haunt:
So that through places wilde and waste   105
    A single man, disarm'd,
Might journey many hundred miles,
    And not at all be harm'd.

Amidst the solitary woods
    Poor travellers might sleep   110
As free from danger as at home,
    Though no man watch did keep.
Thus were we priviledg'd with peace,
    Beyond what others were.
Truth, Mercy, Peace, with Righteousness,   115
    Took up their dwelling here.

Our Governour was of our selves,
    And all his Bretheren,
For wisdom and true piety,
    Select, & chosen men.   120
Who, Ruling in ye fear of God,
    The righteous cause maintained,
And all injurious violence,
    And wickedness, restrained.

Our temp'rall blessings did abound: 125
    But spirituall good things
Much more abounded, to the praise
    Of that great King of Kings.
Gods throne was here set up; here was
    His tabernacle pight: 130
This was the place, and these the folk
    In whom he took delight.

Our morning starrs shone all day long:
    Their beams gave forth such light,
As did the noon-day sun abash,   135
    And's glory dazle quite.
Our day continued many yeers,
    And had no night at all:
Yea many thought the light would last,
    And be perpetuall.   140

Such, O New-England, was thy first,
    Such was thy best estate:
But, Loe! a strange and suddain change
    My courage did amate.
The brightest of our morning starrs   145
    Did wholly disappeare:
And those that tarried behind
    With sack-cloth covered were.

Moreover, I beheld & saw
Our welkin overkest, 150
And dismal clouds for sun-shine late
O'respread from East to West.
The air became tempestuous;
The wilderness gan quake:
And from above with awfull voice 155
Th' Almighty thundring spake.

Are these the men that erst at my command
Forsook their ancient seats and native soile,
To follow me into a desart land,
Contemning all the travell and the toile, 160
Whose love was such to purest ordinances
As made them set at nought their fair inheritances?

Are these the men that prized libertee
To walk with God according to their light,
To be as good as he would have them bee, 165
To serve and worship him with all their might,
Before the pleasures which a fruitfull field,
And Country flowing-full of all good things, could yield?

Are these the folk whom from the brittish Iles,
Through the stern billows of the watry main, 170
I safely led so many thousand miles,
As if their journey had been through a plain?
Whom having from all enemies protected,
And through so many deaths and dangers well directed,

I brought and planted on the Western-shore, 175
Where nought but bruits and salvage wights did swarm
(Untaught, untrain'd, untam'd by Vertue's lore)
That sought their blood, yet could not do them harm?
My fury's flaile them thresht, my fatall broom
Did sweep them hence, to make my people elbow-room. 180

Are these the men whose gates with peace I crown'd,
To whom for bulwarks I Salvation gave,
Whilst all things else with rattling tumults sound,
And mortall frayes send thousands to the grave:
Whilest their own brethren bloody hands embrewed 185
In brothers blood, and fields with carcases bestrewed?

Is this the people blest with bounteous store,
By land and sea full richly clad and fed,
Whom plenty's self stands waiting still before,
And powreth out their cups well tempered? 190
For whose dear sake an howling wildernes
I lately turned into a fruitfull paradeis?

Are these the people in whose hemisphere
Such bright-beam'd, glist'ring, sun-like starrs I placed,
As by their influence did all things cheere, 195
As by their light blind ignorance defaced,
As errours into lurking holes did fray,
As turn'd the late dark night into a lightsome day?

Are these the folk to whom I milked out
And sweetnes stream'd from Consolations brest; 200
Whose soules I fed and strengthened throughout
With finest spirituall food most finely drest?
On whom I rained living bread from Heaven,
Withouten Errour's bane, or Superstition's leaven?

With whom I made a Covenant of peace, 205
And unto whom I did most firmly plight
My faithfulness, If whilst I live I cease
To be their Guide, their God, their full delight;
Since them with cords of love to me I drew,
Enwrapping in my grace such as should them ensew. 210

Are these the men, that now mine eyes behold,
Concerning whom I thought, and whilome spake,
First Heaven shall pass away together scrold,
Ere they my lawes and righteous wayes forsake,
Or that they slack to runn their heavenly race? 215
Are these the same? or are some others come in place?

If these be they, how is it that I find
In stead of holyness Carnality,
In stead of heavenly frames an Earthly mind,
For burning zeal luke-warm Indifferency, 220
For flaming Love, key-cold Dead-heartedness,
For temperance (in meat, and drink, and cloaths) excess?

Whence cometh it, that Pride, and Luxurie
Debate, Deceit, Contention and Strife,
False-dealing, Covetousness, Hypocrisie 225
(With such like Crimes) amongst them are so rife,
That one of them doth over-reach another?
And that an honest man can hardly trust his Brother?

How is it, that Security, and Sloth,
Amongst the best are Common to be found? 230
That grosser sinns, in stead of Graces growth,
Amongst the many more and more abound?
I hate dissembling shews of Holiness.
O practise as you talk, or never more profess.

Judge not, vain world, that all are hypocrites 235
That do profess more holiness then thou:
All foster not dissembling, guilefull sprites,
Nor love their lusts, though very many do.
Some sin through want of care and constant watch,
Some with the sick converse, till they the sickness catch. 240

Some, that maintain a reall root of grace,
Are overgrown with many noysome weeds,
Whose heart, that those no longer may take place,
The benefit of due correction needs.
And such as these however gone astray 245
I shall by stripes reduce into a better way.

Moreover some there be that still retain
Their ancient vigour and sincerity;
Whom both their own, and others sins, constrain
To sigh, and mourn, and weep, and wail, and cry: 250
And for their sakes I have forborn to powre
My wrath upon Revolters to this present houre.

To praying Saints I always have respect,
And tender love, and pittifull regard:
Nor will I now in any wise neglect 255
Their love and faithfull service to reward;
Although I deal with others for their folly,
And turn their mirth to tears that have been too too jolly.

For thinke not, O Backsliders, in your heart,
That I shall still your evill manners beare: 260
Your sinns me press as sheaves do load a cart;
And therefore I will plague you for this geare.
    Except you seriously, and soon, repent,
Ile not delay your pain and heavy punishment.

    And who be those themselves that yonder shew? 265
The seed of such as name by dreadfull Name!
On whom whilere compassions skirt I threw
Whilest in their blood they were, to hide their shame!
    Whom my preventing love did neer me take!
Whom for mine own I mark't, lest they should me forsake! 270

    I look't that such as these to vertue's Lore
(Though none but they) would have Enclin'd their ear:
That they at least mine image should have bore,
And sanctify'd my name with awfull fear.
    Let pagan's Bratts pursue their lusts, whose meed 275
Is Death: For christians children are an holy seed.

    But hear O heavens! Let Earth amazed stand;
Ye Mountains melt, and Hills come flowing down:
Let horrour seize upon both Sea and Land;
Let Natures self be cast into a stown. 280
    I children nourisht, nurtur'd and upheld:
But they against a tender father have rebell'd.

    What could have been by me performed more?
Or wherein fell I short of your desire?
Had you but askt, I would have op't my store, 285
And given what lawfull wishes could require.
    For all this bounteous cost I lookt to see
Heaven-reaching-hearts, and thoughts, Meekness, Humility.

    But lo, a sensuall Heart all void of grace,
An Iron neck, a proud presumptuous Hand; 290
A self-conceited, still, stout, stubborn Race,
That fears no threats, submitts to no command:
    Self-will'd, perverse, such as can beare no yoke;
A generation even ripe for Vengeance stroke.

Such were the Carnall Brood of Israelites 295
That Josua and the Elders did ensue,
Who growing like the cursed Cananites
Upon themselves my heavy judgements drew.
Such also was that fleshly Generation,
Whom I o'rewhelm'd by waters deadly inundation. 300

They darker light, and lesser meanes misused;
They had not such Examples them to warn:
You clearer Rules, and precepts, have abused;
And dreadfull monuments of others harm.
My gospels glorious light you do not prize: 305
My Gospels endless, boundless grace you clean despize.

My painfull messengers you disrespect,
Who toile and sweat and sweale themselves away,
Yet nought at all with you can take effect,
Who hurrie headlong to your own decay. 310
In vain the Founder melts, and taketh pains:
Bellows and Lead's consum'd, but still your dross remains.

What should I do with such a stiff-neckt race?
How shall I ease me of such Foes as they?
What shall befall despizers of my Grace? 315
I'le surely beare their Candle-stick away,
And Lamps put out. Their glorious noon-day light
I'le quickly turn into a dark Egyptian night.

Oft have I charg'd you by my Ministers
To gird your selves with sack cloth, and repent. 320
Oft have I warnd you by my Messengers;
That so you might my wrathfull ire prevent:
But who among you hath this warning taken?
Who hath his crooked wayes, and wicked works forsaken?

Yea many grow to more and more excess; 325
More light and loose, more Carnall and prophane.
The sins of Sodom, Pride, and Wantonness,
Among the multitude spring up amain.
Are these the fruits of pious Education,
To run with greater speed and Courage to Damnation? 330

If here and there some two, or three, shall steere
A wiser Course, then their Companions do,
You make a mock of such; and scoff, and jeere
Becaus they will not be so bad as you.
Such is the Generation that succeeds 335
The men, whose eyes have seen my great and awfull deeds.

Now therefore hearken and encline your ear,
In judgement I will henceforth with you plead;
And if by that you will not learn to fear,
But still go on a sensuall life to lead: 340
I'le strike at once an All-Consuming stroke;
Nor cries nor tears shall then my fierce intent revoke.

 Thus ceast his Dreadful-threatning voice
  The High & lofty-One.
 The Heavens stood still Appal'd thereat; 345
  The Earth beneath did groane:
 Soon after I beheld and saw
  A mortall dart come flying:
 I lookt again, & quickly saw
  Some fainting, others dying. 350

 The Heavens more began to lowre,
  The welkin Blacker grew:
 And all things seemed to forebode
  Sad changes to ensew.
 From that day forward hath the Lord 355
  Apparently contended
 With us in Anger, and in Wrath;
  But we have not amended.

 Our healthfull dayes are at an end,
  And sicknesses come on 360
 From yeer to yeer, becaus our hearts
  Away from God are gone.
 New-England, where for many yeers
  You scarcely heard a cough,
 And where Physicians had no work, 365
  Now finds them work enough.

Now colds and coughs, Rhewms, and sore-throats,
    Do more and more abound:
Now Agues sore & Feavers strong
    In every place are found.   370
How many houses have we seen
    Last Autumn, and this spring,
Wherein the healthful were too few
    To help the languishing.

One wave another followeth,   375
    And one disease begins
Before another cease, becaus
    We turn not from our sins.
We stopp our ear against reproof,
    And hearken not to God: 380
God stops his ear against our prayer,
    And takes not off his rod.

Our fruitful seasons have been turnd
    Of late to barrenness,
Sometimes through great & parching drought,   385
    Sometimes through rain's excess.
Yea not the pastures & corn fields
    For want of rain do languish:
The cattell mourn, and hearts of men
    Are fill'd with fear and anguish.   390

The clouds are often gathered,
    As if we should have rain:
But for our great unworthiness
    Are scattered again.
We pray & fast, & make fair shewes,   395
    As if we meant to turn:
But whilest we turn not, God goes on
    Our fields & fruits to burn.

And burnt are all things in such sort,
    That nothing now appeares, 400
But what may wound our hearts with grief,
    And draw foorth floods of teares.
All things a famine do presage
    In that extremity,
As if both men, and also beasts, 405
    Should soon be done to dy.

This O New-England hast thou got
    By riot, and excess:
This hast thou brought upon thy self
    By pride and wantonness. 410
Thus must thy worldlyness be whipt.
    They, that too much do crave,
Provoke the Lord to take away
    Such blessings as they have.

We have been also threatened 415
    With worser things then these:
And God can bring them on us still,
    To morrow if he please.
For if his mercy be abus'd,
    Which holpe us at our need 420
And mov'd his heart to pitty us,
    We shall be plagu'd indeed.

Beware, O sinful-Land, beware;
    And do not think it strange
That sorer judgements are at hand, 425
    Unless thou quickly change.
Or God, or thou, must quickly change;
    Or else thou art undon:
Wrath cannot cease, if sin remain,
    Where judgement is begun. 430

Ah dear New England! dearest land to me:
Which unto God hast hitherto been dear,
And mayst be still more dear than formerlie,
If to his voice thou wilt incline thine ear.

Consider wel & wisely what the rod, 435
Wherewith thou art from yeer to yeer chastized,
Instructeth thee: Repent, and turn to God,
Who wil not have his nurture be despized.

Thou still hast in thee many praying saints,
Of great account, and precious with the Lord, 440
Who dayly powre out unto him their plaints,
And strive to please him both in deed and word.

Cheer on, sweet souls, my heart is with you all,
And shall be with you, maugre Sathan's might:
And whereso'ere this body be a Thrall, 445
Still in New-England shall be my delight.

MEAT OUT OF THE EATER

or

Meditations Concerning

The Necessity, End, and Usefulness of Afflictions

Unto God's Children.

All Tending to Prepare Them for,

and Comfort Them under the

Cross.

Tolle Crucem.

All Christians must be Cross-bearers.

If any man will my Disciple be,

Let him take up his Cross and follow me.

> *None can with me and mine partake*

> *Who doth not all for me forsake.*

Meditation I

*All Christians must be Sufferers,
That Would be Christ His Followers.*

1

    All that resolve to be
    Christs faithful Followers,
Acts 14:22.   Must be contented in *this* world
    To be great Sufferers.
Matt. 10:37, 38;   They must renounce themselves   5
16:24, 25.   And their own Wills deny,
    Take up their Cross and follow Christ
    Through Sufferings chearfully.

2

    Not only lighter Griefs
Matt. 10:39.   This Cross of ours implies: 10
    But when the Lord us calls thereto;
Heb. 12:4.   Greatest Extremities.
    This must be taken up,
    (Willingly undergone)
    For *Christ's* dear sake who suffred more   15
    For our Redemption.

3

    The Christian that expects
    An Earthly Paradise
When Christ bids him take up the cross
    And bear it, is unwise.   20
    We must not on the knee
    Be alway dandled,
Nor must we think to ride to Heaven
    Upon a Feather-bed.

4

 Our way to heavenly Rest, 25
Is all against the Stream;
We must not fail with Wind and Tide
 As too too many dream;
But row against them both,
 And many Storms endure; 30
Till we arrive at that sweet port,
 Where Saints shall rest secure.

5

 Our way is up the Hill,
Which mounteth to the Skies:
But that's the way to Death and Hell 35
 Which low and down-hill lies.
'Tis easy to descend,
 And down the Hill to roll;
But this is labour to ascend,
 And painful to the Soul. 40

6

 But who would not take pain
Against the Hill to climbe,
That so they may true Rest attain
 And Happiness in time?
Rather than down the Hill 45
 With present ease to Run
(As most men do) until they be
 Eternally undone.

7

Matt. 7:13, 14. Strait is the way and path
Which leadeth unto Life: 50
Luke 13:24. Heav'n is not gaind by Ease and Sloth,
 But by an earnest Strife.
But broad are all the Waies
 That to Destruction lead,
And many many are the feet 55
 That daily therein tread.

8

>Let others take their Choice,
>And Run what way they please:
>Let them enjoy their Lusts, and take
>Their Fill of Carnal ease: 60
>Choose thou the narrow path,
>My soul, and walk therein;
>Thou know'st this is the ready Way,
>Eternal Life to win.

Meditation II

God doth in Mercy scourge His own.
In Wrath he others lets alone.

1

>If in this narrow path
>And way that is so strait
>You meet with Difficulties great;   1 *Pet.* 4:12.
>Be not disconsolate.
>The Straitness of the way   5
>Betokeneth Opposition,
>Afflictions, Dangers, Crosses, Snares
>In this our frail Condition.

2

>These are the Common Lot
>Of all God's Children Dear,   10
>Through many Sorrows they must pass
>The Lord that truly fear.
>There's no Calamity
>Doth unto thee befall,
>But such as common is to men,   15   1 *Cor.* 10:13.
>Yea, to the best of all.

3

Though various are the Wayes
And Sufferings whereby
God doth His Children excercise,
Correct and also try: 20
Yet all must bear the Cross;
2 *Tim.* 2:12. Before they wear the Crown;
All must partake of Chastening,
Whom God vouchsafes to own.

4

It is in mercy then 25
That God Chastiseth His
And lets them not Correction want
Whenas they do amiss.
They are in Trouble now
Ps. 94:12, 13. That he may give them Rest, 30
When as the pit shall digged be
For Such as them Opprest.

5

All that Christ's members are,
Must be made like their Head:
He is a *Bastard* not a Child 35
Heb. 12:8. That's never chastened.
God letteth some alone,
Hos. 4:14. Leaves them to take their Course,
And by his Rod reclaims them not;
They sin without Remorse. 40

6

They will not cross themselves,
Nor their own wills deny:
God will not cross them nor correct,
To do them good thereby.
Eccles. 8:11. They wax more impudent, 45
And bolder to do evil,
Matt. 25:41. Thro' God's forbearance, till at length
He hurl them to the Devil.

7

	This is a fearful case	
Ps. 18:11, 12.	To be thus left to God:	50
	Great mercy 'tis to be subdu'd	
Ps. 94:12.	By scourging with the Rod:	
	My soul be thankful then	
Job 7:17, 18.	That God thee thus corrects,	
Isa. 1.	Who might have let thee head long run	55
	With those whom He rejects.	

Meditation III

The third doth further hint at th' Ends
For which the Lord Affliction sends.

1

God doth chasten his own
In Love, their souls to save:
And lets them not run wild with them
That no Correction have.

Prov. 23:14. Now as the Rod restrains 5
From posting down to Hell;
So by the same God doth Excite
And teach us to do well.

2

Affliction is Christ's School,
Ps. 94:12. Wherein He teacheth His 10
To know and do their duty, and
To mend what is amiss.
For though Afflictions may
Unto the Flesh be painfull;
David and other Saints of God 15
Have found them very gainful.

3

Ps. 119:67. Before I was chastis'd,
  Saith he, I went astray:
  But since I've learnt with better Care
  To keep Thy Precepts way. 20
Ps. 119:71. 'Tis good for mee that I
  Have been afflicted sore
  That I might learn to know thy Lawes
  And swerve therefrom no more.

4

Isa. 48:10. These are God's Fining Pot, 25
  Wherein He melts His Gold,
  Consumes the Dross and maketh it
  More lovely to behold.
Matt. 3:2, 3. These are His Fullers Sope
  To wash our spots away. 30
Dan. 11:35. That being thus refin'd and Wash'd
  Him glorifie we may.

5

  As sharpest Winter Frosts
  Do clarifie the Aire
  And cleanse our blood, soften the earth 35
  And it for feed prepare,
  Making it fruitfuller:
  So do Afflictions sore
  Correct the Rankness of our hearts,
  Cleanse and Subdue them more. 40

6

  Much Honey turns to Gall
  And Cholerick Excess;
  And too-too-much Prosperity
Deut. 32:15. Breeds Pride and Wantonness:
Isa. 27:9. Afflictions purge them out, 45
Heb. 12:10, 11. Like bitter Aloe,
  Which though unpleasant to the Taste,
  Far wholesomer may be.

7

    Full Diet, dainty Fare,
      With Idleness and Ease   50
Ezek. 16:49, 50.   Heap up bad Humours and Contract,
      Many a foul Disease,
    To Soul and Body too,
      Dang'rous and Troublesome,
    Which must be purged out in time   55
      With some *Catholicum*.

8

    Strong wine makes weak heads *giddy*,
      Procuring Drunkenness;
Jer. 9:7, 8.   Long peace and plenty likewise breed
      Intemperance and Excess.   60
    We soon are surfeited
      With strong delicious matter:
    And therefore God who *knowes our frame*
      Mingleth our Wine with Water.

9

    Afflictions are like Ballast   65
      I'th' Bottom of a Ship;
    For tho perhaps without the same
      We might more lightly Skip:
    Yet every little puff
      Would quickly set us over,   70
    And sink us in the Ocean Sea
      No more for to Recover.

10

    Our hearts are over-run
Jer. 4:3, 4.   Much like a Fallow-field.
    Which must be broke and plowed up   75
      Before it Fruit can yeild:
    Afflictions are God's Plough
Ps. 129:2, 3.   Where-with He breaketh us,
    Tears up our *lusts* those noisome *weeds*
Jer. 31:18, 19.   And fitteth us for Use.   80

11
Grace in prosperity
Lies hid unoccupy'd:
But is by Chastening set to work,
And by the Cross descri'd.
The Cross to Vertue trains; 85
It Tries, it makes to grow;
It sanctifies, purgeth and heals;
It humbleth and layes low.

Meditation IV

*The Fourth by various Arguments
Strives to beat down all Discontents,
And overcome Discouragements.*

1

Since then our gracious God
And Father that's above
For such great Ends useth His Rod,
Heb. 12:6.   In faithfulness and Love:
Why shouldst thou once Repine, 5
Or murmur at the Cross,
Impatient man? without such blows
Thy soul would suffer Loss.

2

1 *Pet.* 1:6.   Except that need there be,
And thy soul's health require, 10
He useth not severity,
Nor stirreth up His Ire.
Job 34:23.   He lays on thee no more
Than what may reach the End,
And do thy Soul the Good for which 15
He doth Affliction send.

3

Lam. 3:33.

He that unwillingly
Afflicts the Sons of men,
Cannot take pleasure in the Grief
Of His own Childeren.
He layes on His no Crosses,
But that they may attain
Some higher Good: He sends no Losses
But for their greater Gain.

4

Burning and Cutting 'bide,
Hunger and Thirst endure
Thou willt, thy body from grim *Death*
Or Sickness to recure:
Thy Soul is much more worth,
And its Salvation Dear;
Why then what may *Soul-health* procure
Shouldst thou refuse to bear?

5

Christ never flattered thee
Nor promis'd carnal ease,
Nor worldly Honour, Pleasure, Gain,
Security or Peace.
He told the worst at first,
(It was thine A, B, C.)

Matt. 16:24.

That every one must bear the Cross
That would His follower be.

6

1 *Pet.* 4:12.

Why shouldst thou think it strange
To meet with fiery Tryal,
Or to be put upon the Task
Of serious Self-Denial?
Thou owest more to Christ,
Who shed His dearest Blood,
And bare Gods Wrath for to procure
Thine everlasting Good.

7

	The Son of God Himself,	
	By whom the World was made,	50
Heb. 5:8, 9; 12:2, 3.	Took up the Cross, endured Death	
	And so our Ransome paid.	
	He had no need to dye;	
	But we had been undone,	
	Unless that He our punishment	55
	And pain had undergone.	

8

Luke 24:26.	He past through Sufferings	
	Into His glorious state:	
Matt. 10:24, 25.	It's fit that Members be content	
	Their Head to imitate.	60
Rom. 8:26.	Himself hath born the Curse,	
Gal. 3:13.	And ta'ne away the sting:	
1 Cor. 15:55, 56.	So that the Cross is now become	
	A sanctified Thing.	

9

	Therefore take up the Cross	65
	The Rod in Meekness kiss:	
	Be silent and him reverence, who	
Ezra 9:13.	Thy God and Father is.	
Heb. 12:10.	Who less afflicteth thee	
	Than thou deserved hast;	70
	Yea, and afflicteth thee, that so	
	A gainer be thou maist.	

10

Jer. 30:11.	Measure and Moderation	
	In Chastning He respecteth.	
	And none of His beyond their strength	75
1 Cor. 10:13.	By pain or grief dejecteth.	
	Although He burn the Dross	
	He will not waste His Gold	
Luke 21:18.	If with the one hand he cast down	
	His other doth uphold.	80

11

Matt. 12:20.
      The smothering smoaking Flax
      Hee'll not extinguish quite
      To break a bruised shaken Reed
      Is none of His Delight.

Isa. 57:16.
      Hee'll not contend for ay,   85
      Nor evermore Upbraid,
      Lest that the Spirit before Him fail
      And souls that He hath made.

12

      Thou cravest oft a pledge

Heb. 12:7.
      Of Christ's free love to thee.   90
      A pledge thou hast, if Chastening
      Thou bearest fruitfully.
      God deals with us like sons
      If Scourging we endure,
      For unto patient Suffering   95
      He will his sons inure.

13

      What if thy strength thee fail?
      If Sicknesses increase?

Ps. 27:10.
      If Creature-comforts thee forsake?
      If dearest Friends decease?   100

Ps. 46:1, 2, 3.
      If wants do multiply,
      And woes come on amain?
      If Men and Devils should conspire
      To aggravate thy pain?

14

      Droop not faint-hearted man,   105
      Thou art not yet undone:

Ps. 73:26.
      So long as God himself survives,
      And is thy Portion.

Judg. 14:14.
      Out of the Eater He
      Will surely bring forth Meat: 110
      And Spiritual good more sweet than hony
      Our of Affliction great.

Meditation V

The fifth perswades to Patience,
From that Rich future Recompense;
Minding us of our Heavenly Rest,
Which should revive us when distrest.

1

  Meekly to bear Christ's yoke
  It is an Honour high:
Thou Christ wilt surely them reward
  Who bear it patiently.
2 *Cor.* 4:17.   For this short Grief of ours,   5
  And our Affliction light
Shall work of glorious Happiness,
  A far more lasting weight.

2

Ps. 97:11.   For just men light is sown
  (Reward laid up in store)   10
Ps. 126:5.   Who sow in tears shall reap in joy,
  And after mourn no more.
They'll one day wear a Crown,
  Who now the Cross sustain:
1 *Cor.* 15:58.   In Christ our Lord no suffering,   15
  Nor labour shall be vain.

3

1 *Tim.* 2:12.   Reign with him long shall they,
  With him that suffer do:
Who follow him in's Death, partake
  Shall of his Glory too.   20
Isa. 64:6.   Not that our services,
  Deserve such Recompence:
2 *Thess.* 1:10.   But he resolveth to set forth
  His own Munificence.

4

  Who can expect a Crop
   Or Harvest to obtain,
  That breaks no ground, that sows no seed,
   That undergoes no pain?
   To triumph who can hope
   That doth the Battel shun?
  Eternal Glory whoso findes,
   Must first through rough ways run.

5

Ps. 39:12. Thou art a Pilgrim here;
   This world is not thy home:
  Then be content with Pilgrims fare,
   Till thou to Heaven come.
   What if thou tossed art
   With boisterous winds and seas?
Heb. 4:9. Behold the Haven where thou shalt
   Enjoy long rest and ease.

6

   What if thy conflict with
   The roaring Lion be?
  If thou be call'd to fight against
   World, Flesh, and Devil, all three.
1 *John* 4:4. Stronger is Christ in thee
   Then strongest Enemy,
Rom. 16:20. Who Satan under thy Souls feet
   Shall tread down speedily.

7

  Souldier be strong, who fightest
Heb. 2:10. Under a Captain Stout:
  Dishonour not thy conquering Head
   By basely giving out.
   Endure a while, Bear up,
   And hope for better things:
  War ends in peace; and Morning light
   Mounts up on Midnights wing.

8

       Through Changes manifold,
       And Dangers perilous,
Isa. 43:2.   Through fiery flames, and water-floods,
       Through ways calamitous.   60
Heb. 11:14, 16. We travel towards Heaven
       A quiet Habitation:
Matt. 23:34.   Christ shews a Kingdom there prepar'd
       Ev'n from the worlds foundation.

9

       O Heaven, most holy place,   65
2 *Cor.* 9:4, 8. Which art our country dear!
       What cause have I to long for thee,
       And Beg with many a tear.
       Earth is to me a Prison;
       This Body is useless weight: 70
       And all things else vile, vain, and nought,
       To one in such ill plight.

10

       O Christ make haste; from bands,
       Of Sin and Death me free,
       And to those Heavenly Mansions,   75
       Be pleas'd to carry me.
       Where glorified Saints
1 *Thess.* 4:17. For ever are possest,
       Of God in Christ their chiefest Good,
       And from all troubles Rest.   80

Meditation VI

Christ's Sufferings are our Copy-Book,
Whereon we often ought to look.

1

Heb. 12:2, 3.   Let every suffering Saint
    Consider Jesus Christ,
What Sufferings great he under-went,
    Who is our Blest High-Priest.
What Misery can'st thou name,   5
    He hath not undergone,
Isa. 53:9.   Who was most innocent and just,
    And nought amiss had done.

2

When we are like to faint,
    And when our spirits fail,   10
When discontents, discouragements,
    And terrours us assail:
When thou art apt to say,
    No grief was e're like mine,
Then think of Christ, and sure thou'lt say,   15
    His far exceeded thine.

3

    Art thou a prisoner?
Matt. 27:2;   Our Lord himself was Bound,
26:65, 67, 68.   Art thou disgrac'd? why, he was scorn'd,
    And trampled to the ground.   20
Blindfolded, spit upon,
    Most wrongfully accused,
Matt. 27: 28, 30.   Reviled, mocked, buffetted,
    And wickedly abused.

4

2 Cor. 8:9.	Art thou in poverty? 25
Matt. 8:20.	Why, Christ himself was poore,
	And had not where to lay his head;
	It's like he gives thee more.
	Art thou in heaviness?
Isa. 5:3.	He was a man of Grief; 30
Matt. 26:38.	Whose Soul was sorrowful to Death,
	To purchase our relief.

5

	Or do temptations vex thee?
Heb. 2:4; 4:15.	He tempted was likewise:
	He pitieth when such things perplex thee, 35
	And helps thee when thou cries.
	Do Sin and wrath distress thee?
Matt. 27:46.	None so distrest as he,
	Who underwent God's direful wrath
	From wrath our Souls to free. 40

6

	If thus our Generall,
John 12:26.	No danger hath declin'd:
	Well may his Souldiers be content,
	Some hardship for to find.
	If he hath suffered, 45
	In whom no guilt was found,
	Well may we suffer for our faults,
	Whose sins so much abound.

7

	If God's dear Son hath dy'd,
	And born his Fathers Ire: 50
	Well may the sinful sons of men
Isa. 53:4, 6.	Pass through a gentle fire.
	Since only for our sake,
	All this he under-went:
	What cause have we with our light Cross, 55
	To be right well content.

8

John 18:11.	He drank up all the Dregs,
Gal. 3:13.	And bitterest of the Cup,

    The Cup, he gives us, is allay'd,
      And but a little sup.   60
    Oh then my sinful soul!
      If Christ to suffering call,
    Take up thy Cross, and willingly,
      Follow thy Generall.

Meditation VII

The worldly man's Prosperity,
Is onely gilded Misery.

1

    Although God's dealings are
      Exceeding various,
    Respecting outward things, which be
      Adverse or prosperous:

Eccles. 9:1, 2.   That none can certainly,   5
      Discern God's love, or hate,
    By being in Affliction,
      Or in a Prosperous state.

2

    (For now and then a Saint,
      Enjoyes Prosperity: 10
    And sometimes wicked men are plagu'd,
      And are in misery.)

Acts 14:22.	Yet commonly we see
Job 21:7, 8, 9, 10, 13.	Affliction is the Lot,

    Of precious Saints, whilst others thrive,   15
      I'th' world, who serve him not.

3

	They are afflicted less,	
	Then God's own Children dear;	
Ps. 17:14.	And it's no wonder, if we mind,	
	They have their Portion here.	20
	Yet silly sinful Flesh	
Ps. 73:3, 4, 5.	At this is apt to grumble:	
	And at the scandal of the Cross	
	There are too many stumble.	

4

	They flourish like a tree,	25
	They have the word at will:	
Job 21:24.	Their Breasts are flowing-full of Milk,	
	Marrow their bones doth fill.	
	They have no sorrows great	
	Their vigour to decay:	30
	Nor is their moisture radical	
	Consum'd and sweal'd away.	

5

While better men are sick,
Their bodies are in health,
Whil'st others are distrest with wants,   35
They flow in worldly wealth.
They have their time of peace,
While others are in trouble.
If other men have plenty too,
They have it more then double.   40

6

Amos 6:4, 5, 6.	They live and lie at ease,	
	While others are in pain:	
	And meet not with Calamity	
	Their mirth for to restrain.	
	While godly men are weeping,	45
	And laying sin to heart:	
	They're feasting, singing, or else sleeping,	
	Because they feel no smart.	

7

	Their eyes stand out with fat;	
Ps. 73:7.	They've more then heart can wish:	50

        Honey and milk, butter and oil,
            Do drop into their dish.
        The World them dandleth,
            Like Darlings on her lap,
        And streams delights into their mouth   55
            From this and th'other Pap.

8

        They prosper in their way,
Ps. 37:7.   And bring their ends to pass,
Ps. 49:18.   Judging themselves as happy men,
            As ever any was.   60
        Because they have success,
        They bless themselves therein:
        They think God loves, and favours them,
            Though they still love their sin.

9

Ps. 55:19.   Because they have no changes,   65
            Therefore they fear not God:
        They do not dread to anger him,
            Because they feel no Rod.
Eccles. 8:11.   God doth not execute
            His Sentence speedily   70
        'Gainst wicked works: therefore they're bold
            To do more wickedly.

10

        God gives them outward things,
            And they the same bestow,
James 4:3.   Upon their Lusts: they serve the world,   75
Luke 16:13.   And unto Mammon bow.
        In him they put their trust;
            Him they most highly prize:
        Unto this Idol every day
            They offer Sacrifice.   80

11

    For having made the World
The God whom they adore,
They rake and scrape, they pill and pull,
    And covet more and more.
    The World doth fill their Head   85
    And occupy their Heart:
But God, to whom both these belong,
    They leave for him no part.

12

1 *Tim.* 6:17.   Their Riches make them proud,
    And puff them up in mind.   90
Their plenty doth besot them too,
    And make them worse then blind.
Rev. 3:17.   They see no need of Christ,
Matt. 19:22, 23, 24.   But by his Grace set lite,
Despise a Saviour, shut their eyes,   95
    Against the Gospel's Light.

13

Deut. 32:15.   They being fat and full,
    Are wanton, *Jesurun*-like,
They kick and spurn, against God's love:
    And at his Bowels strike.   100
Isa. 1:2.   Whilst he them nourisheth,
    Against him they rebell:
John 18:44.   And under Satan's Banner fight,
    Like wicked Imps of hell.

14

Prov. 3:22.   Thus their prosperity,   105
    Through God Almighty's curse,
Doth make them wax more insolent,
Ps. 69:22.   And grow still worse and worse.
Their table is their snare,
    Their Delicates a bait,   110
Which leads them to turn Belly gods,
    And grow intemperate.

15

Prov. 23:31, 33.
    Their over-flowing Cups,
      Entice to Drunkeness:
    And then expose to filthy Lusts
      Their pampered Carcasses.
    The greater strength they have,
      The stronger to do evil;
    The healthfuller their Bodies be:
      More fit to serve the Devil.

16

2 Chron. 36:15, 16.
    God warns them by his word,
      They're deaf and do not hear:
    He cuts down others with his sword,
      They neither feel nor fear.
Ezek. 23:9, 10, 11.
    If God vouchsafe to scourge them,
      Yet they like mad-men feel not:
Isa. 42:25.
    Or if they feel, their hearts are hard;
      Repent, and turn they will not.

17

Jer. 5:3.
Exod. 8:27, 28
compared with
Exod. 8:34.
2 Pet. 2:22.
    Whil'st that the smart is on,
      Perhaps they promise fair:
    But *Pharaoh*-like, when respite comes,
      They shew you what they are.
    To wallewing in the mire
      Like filthy unclean Hogs,
    And to their vomit back again
      They run like greedy Dogs.

18

    Since then they chuse their Bane,
      And will no warning take:
    They have their Choice, and may thereof
Isa. 1:5.
      Their best advantage make.
Hos. 4:14.
    God will no more take pains
      To scourge them for their sin:
    But lets them glut themselves therewith,
      And end as they begin.

19

Ps. 81:11, 12.	He winketh at their faults,	145
	And lets them take their course;	
Matt. 23:32.	Yea gives them up unto their lusts,	
	To sin without remorse:	
Matt. 25:41.	Till having fill'd their measures,	
	The Lord to Judgment call;	150
	Where opening all his fiery Treasures,	
	Hee'l pay them once for all.	

Meditation VIII

Saints happier be when most distrest,
Then wicked men are at the best.

1

We have the wicked view'd,
And seen his best estate:
And who would chuse with him to share,
Except a Reprobate?
Prov. 1:32.　　For sure the Simple's ease　　　　5
Shall turn to his decay:
And the Prosperity of Fools
Shall utterly them slay.

2

Ps. 92:7.　　When wicked men like Grass
Do springing up arise,　　　　　　　　10
When they are in a flourishing case
That work iniquities:
'Tis for their cutting down
To perpetuity;
It's but to ripen them for woe,　　　　15
And endless Misery.

3

Luke 16:23, 24, 25.
>The less Affliction here
>They feel, the more's to come:
>The greater Blessings they abuse,
>The heavier is their Doom.   20
>Now let us take a Saint
>Whom men account accurst,
>Because they judge him plagu'd of God,
>And view him at his worst.

4

>Suppose his case as bad,   25
>As bad it well can be:
>And his Calamity more sad
>Then commonly we see.
>Dispose him where you will,
>Do with him what you can: 30
>Yet God is present with him still;
>He is a happy man.

5

>Let Sickness come upon him
James 5:11.
>Or great Tormenting Pain:
>Bod will not lose him, but a Saint,   35
Acts 23:11.
>A Saint shall still remain.
>In prison him immure,
>All comforts from him take:
>You cannot rob him of his God,
>Nor him unhappy make.   40

6

Isa. 43:2.
>Plunge him into the mire,
>Or water; God is near:
Ps. 42:7, 8.
>Cast him into the burning Fire:
>God will be with him there.
>If many roaring waves   45
>Of great Affliction roll
>Over his head: God so supports,
>They cannot sink his Soul.

7

(*Jacob* in servitude.
Joseph in Prison Chains, 50
Moses in his long Banishment
Heaven's Favourite still remains.
Three Children in the Fire
Daniel i'th' Lions Den
Have God to guard them: so had *Paul* 55
When Shipwrack'd. Happy Men!)

8

Deut. 33:27. The Everlasting Arms
Are underneath his head
To bear him up; and hence it comes
He is not swallowed, 60
Ps. 44:17, 18, 22. Nor suffered wickedly
From God to turn aside:
As by his carriage will appear
When troubles him betide.

Meditation IX

*The Carriage of a Child of God
Under his Fathers smarting Rod.*

1

He sees a hand of God
In his Afflictions all,
Job 1:21; 2:10. And owns it for to be his Rod,
Whatever Cross befall.
For whosoever be 5
Th' immediate Instrument,
2 *Sam.* 16:11. He knows right well that God himself
Was the Efficient.

2

	And that Afflictions
	Rise not out of the Dust: 10
Job 5:6.	Nor are they order'd by the will
	Of Man, or Devils lust.
	If that the Grief be small
	Or the Chastisment light:
1 Kings 22:48, 49.	Yet since God sends it not in vain, 15
	Light strokes he dare not slight.

3

Heb. 12:6.	If greater be the Blow,
	It doth not him dismay:
	Because he knows a Fathers hand
Joel 2:12.	Such stripes may on him lay. 20
Amos 4:12.	But he prepares himself
	Betimes to meet the Lord
	By true Repentance, as he hath
	Commanded in his Word.

4

Lam. 3:40.	To search and try his wayes, 25
Job 10:2.	To find out what's amiss,
Job 34:31, 32.	To leave his sins, to loath himself
Job 39:9, 10, 11, 15.	His first great Business is.
	And having once found out
	What sin hath God offended; 30
Job 42:6.	He seriously bewails it, and
	Endeavours to amend it.

5

Heb. 6:8.	Unto the cleansing Blood
Ps. 51.	Of Jesus Christ he flies;
	And to his wounded Conscience 35
Job 2.	That Soveraign Balm applies:
Heb. 9:14.	Which can both cleanse and heal;
	Both pacifie God's wrath,
Rev. 1:5.	And cure a guilty sin-sick Soul,
	When 'tis improv'd by Faith. 40

6

And though he be unworthy
To look God in the face;
Heb. 4:15, 16. Yet through the Merits of his Son
He begs and hopes for Grace:
Job 19:25, 26, 27. Being right well assur'd, 45
Lam. 3:31, 32. That though the Lord chastise him,
Yet will he not cast off his Soul,
Nor utterly despise him.

7

But if by all his search
He cannot find the cause 50
For which the Lord afflicteth him
Or from his Soul withdraws:
Yet he believeth, that
For just and holy ends,
To humble, purge, and better him 55
The Lord Affliction sends.

8

Job 10:2, 7. And though he cannot say,
I have at random run,
Or wickedly by some known sin
Job 7:2. Away from God have gon: 60
Job 9:3. Yet so much sin he sees
Both in his heart and wayes,
As God may judge it meet therefore
To scourge him all his dayes.

9

1 *Pet.* 5. Himself he humbleth under 65
The mighty hand of God:
1 *Sam.* 3:18. And for the sake of that sweet hand
Doth kiss the sharpest Rod.
Job 2:40. He taketh up his Cross,
Denieth his own will, 70
Advanceth God's above his own,
And yieldeth to him still.

10

Lam. 3:23, 30.	Unto the yoke of Christ
	He doth his neck submit:
	He turns his cheek to him that smites, 75
	And meekly taketh it.
Lam. 3:22, 23, 25.	Yea when his grief is most,
	And sorest is his pain:
	He still endeavoureth good thoughts
	Of God for to retain. 80

11

His earnest care and prayer
When greatest is his smart,
Is that he never may blaspheme
God with his mouth or heart.
He beggeth Patience   85
In his extremities
To bear Gods hand, that so his heart
May not against him rise.

12

Ps. 73:13, 14, 15, 22.	If murmuring thoughts do rise
	(Or hearts begin to swell) 90
	He strives to beat them down again;
	He hates such thoughts like Hell.
	God he resolves to love,
	Deal with him as he will:
	And in his mercy to confide 95
Job 13:15.	Although he should him kill.

13

	To God that smiteth him
	He strives to get more near.
	He will not cease to pray, although
	God seem to stop his ear. 100
Ps. 88:1, 2, 9, 13.	Though God hath long delay'd
Ps. 42:7, 8, 9.	To answer his request,
	Yet will he seek, and never cease,
	Whilst life is in his brest.

14

Ps. 40:1, 2, 4.	He waiteth patiently 105
	Untill deliverance come,
Isa. 28:16.	And will not use dishonest means
	To shun what's troublesome.
	He hates all sinful sleights
	To get his Cross from under: 110
Ps. 116:16.	And will not break his Bonds, but stay
	Till God them cut asunder.

15

Gen. 8:13, 14, 16.   *Noah* would not leave his Ark,
                          Nor out of Prison break
                          Although he saw the Ground was dry,   115
                          Till God did to him speak.
1 Sam. 26:9, 11.   *David* refus'd to kill,
                          King *Saul* his mortal Foe,
                          That persecuted him to Death,
                          And wrought him so much woe.   120

16

He rather chose to wait,
Till God should plead his Cause,
And of his Enemy him avenge,
Then for to break God's Laws.
Thus every Saint will rather, 125
Job 36:22.   Chuse Suffering, then to Sin;
He will not God offend, Self-ease
Or Safety for to win.

17

Matt. 26:70, 75.   But if through Humane frailty,
                          And over-bearing power,   130
                          Of Strong Temptation, he do swerve,
                          And fall i'th' evil hour;
Luke 22:32.   (As sometimes *Peter* did,)
                          It grieveth him full sure,
                          He weeps and mourns, repents, returns,   135
                          Grows stronger then before.

18

Ps. 119:67, 71.
Eccles. 7:3.

The longer God afflicts him,
　The better he is for it,
Love's Holiness the more, loath's sin
　And learneth to abhor it.
The more he is bereft,
　And stript of outward things:
The less he dotes on these wild Fowl,
　That take them to their wings.

19

When creature comforts fail,
　When sorrows him surround,
He takes the faster hold of God,
　In whom true Comfort's found.
When Conduit-pipes are stopt,
　When Streams are vanished,
The more he to the Fountain hastes,
　And lives at the well-head.

20

1 *Sam.* 30:6.

Gen. 32:26. 28.

Thus *David* comforted
　And cheer'd himself in God,
When all was gone, although he felt
　The anguish of the Rod.
Thus *Jacob* took fast hold,
　And wrestled with the Lord,
When as he was distrest for fear
　Of cruel *Esau's* sword.

21

Prince-like he wrestled
　And would not let him go,
Until he had a Blessing got
　To shield him from his Foe.
Thus every suffering Saint
　By wrestling shall prevail,
And having overcome at last
　Be styled *Israel*.

Meditation X

Although Affliction tanne the Skin,
Such Saints are Beautiful within.

1

Cant. 2:14. How amiable is
The face of suffering Saints,
Where God thus quieteth their hearts
And stilleth their complaints!
Where 'tis their daily care,   5
And earnest hearts desire,
To love, and bless, and honour God
In middest of the fire.

2

Ps. 139:21, 22, 23, 24. Where nothing grieves them more
Then what their God doth grieve: 10
Where nothing pleaseth them like that
Which make them sin to leave.
Where though they have a will
And wishes of their own:
Matt. 16:24. Yet at the foot of Jesus Christ   15
They meekly lay them down.

3

These are the happy men,
James 6:11 Judge of them what thou please
compared with Vain world, amongst thy Darlings all
Job 42:6, 7, 8. Thou hast not one like these.   20
As God is dear to them,
So they to him are dear,
And he to all the world ere long
Will make it to appear.

                        4
Ps. 45:13.   The Daughter of the King,   25
                        All glorious is within,
                        How Black soever and Sun-Burnt,
                        May seem her outward Skin.
Cant. 1:5, 6.   Because I Blackish am,
                        Upon me--look not ye,   30
                        Because that with his Beams the Sun
                        Hath looked down on me.

                        5

                        A patient suffering Saint
                        Is a right comely one:
                        Though black as *Kedar's* Tents, and as 35
                        Curtains of *Solomon*.
                        Thus beautifie my soul
                        Dear Saviour; thus adorn it.
                        As for the Trappings of the world,
                        And Bravery, I can scorn it.   40

                        6

                        Some deck the outside fair;
Matt. 23:25, 26, 27, 28. But are like Graves within:
                        Some sweep and wash their houses clean;
                        Whose hearts most nasty been.
                        Some bodies fat and fair   45
                        Have Souls both foul and lean:
                        But howsoe're my Body fare,
                        Lord make my soul more clean.

A conclusion Hortatory

To those that are, or hereafter may be in Affliction.

1

    And now my Christian Friend,
      That shalt these Lines peruse;
    Oh that they might thine heart perswade
      The Cross of Christ to chuse!
    And to esteem it more 5
      Then greatest Worldly Treasures!
2 *Cor.* 4:17.   Light grief would bring thee glorious joys,
      Short pain Eternal Pleasures.

2

    I have endeavoured
      The Cross for to adorn, 10
    By setting forth its comeliness,
      Although the world it scorn.
    I have discours'd in brief
      What profit comes thereby,
    That thou might'st be encouraged 15
      To bear it patiently.

3

    I have before thine eyes,
      An humble gracious Saint,
    Bearing the Cross upon his Back,
      Endeavoured to paint. 20
    Now strive to immitate,
      After this Copy write:
    This is the onely end for which,
      I did the same endite.

4

 I would not for this world,
  Were it a world of Gold,
(Yea for a thousand times as much
  And more then can be told,)
 I would not Rules prescribe,
  And unto thee commend,
And yet me self be negligent,
  Those Rules for to attend.

5

 It is my daily Prayer,
  Lord let me never teach,
That unto others which my self
  Have little care to reach.
 I have not told thee Tales,
  Of things unseen, unfelt,
But speak them from Experience:
  Believe it how thou wilt.

6

 Yet I shall tell the Truth,
  And nothing from thee keep;
Before I wrote this sentence out
  I sat down twice to weep
 Tears of remorse and sorrow
  Because I am so poore
In these rich graces, and because
  I have attain'd no more.

7

 That having been so long
  A Scholar in this School,
I have so little progress made,
  And been so great a fool.
 But I shall say no more,
  But pass from this discourse.
My weeping tears do blind mine eyes,
  And me thereto enforce.

8

Heb. 12:5.
My son despise not thou
The Lords chastising hand,
Nor faint when thou corrected art:
But turn at his command.   60
Oh be not obstinate
(No better then before)
Lev. 26:18.
Lest God provoked be to smite,
And lay on seven times more.

9

For thus he threateneth,   65
If that ye will not be,
Lev. 26:23, 24.
By all my strokes reformed yet
But still walk cross to me.
Then will I also walk
Contrary unto you,   70
In wrath and fury, and seven times
More plagues will on you throw.

10

Dear Brother, Christian Friend,
Be wise for thine own ease,
And do not wilfully thy God   75
And Father mild displease.
Lam. 3:33, 34.
He loveth not to grieve,
Nor Crush the sons of men:
Why should'st thou love to anger him,
Or for to grieve him then?   80

11

It may be thou hast been
Some head-strong Bullock like,
Kicking and spurning at the Rod,
And running on the Pike.
Now then bemoan thy self,   85
And cry, Lord turn thou me,
That have a stubborn sinner been,
And I shall turned be.

12

	If *Ephraim* thus repent	
Jer. 31:18, 19, 20.	And pray; God quickly hears,	90
	Embraceth him as his dear Child,	
	And wipes away his tears.	
	God listeneth for to hear,	
	The voice of True returners,	
	And is most ready to speak peace,	95
	To broken-hearted mourners.	

13

Oh let *New-England* turn,
When gentler Warning's given:
Lest by our sins the Lord to use
    Severity be driven.   100
It will be to our cost
To put him thereupon:
Oh therefore let's repent in time,
    Before we be undone.

14

	Incorrigibleness,	105
	God's Anger will increase:	
	True penitence, and Faith in Christ:	
	This anger will appease.	
	And nothing else can do't,	
	Lord give us hearts to say,	110
Hos. 14:2.	Turn us to thee, and all our sins,	
	Purge out and wash away.	

15

Hos. 6:1, 2.	Come let's return to God,	
	He hath us torn, He'll heal:	
	He hath us smitten with his Rod,	115
	And bind us up he will.	
	After two dayes are past,	
	He will us so revive,	
	And on the third day raise us up,	
	That we in's sight shall live.	120

Ps. 80.   *Turn us again Lord God of Hosts,*
And make thy Countenance,
To shine upon us, and so we
Shall have deliverance.

                                              Amen.

RIDDLES UNRIDDLED,
or
Christian Paradoxes

Broke open, smelling like sweet
Spice New taken out of Boxes.

Each Paradox, is like a Box,
    That Cordials rare incloseth:
This Key unlocks, op'neth the Box
    And what's within discloseth;
That whoso will may take his fill,
    And gain where no man loseth.

Light in Darkness,
  Sick mens Health,
Strength in Weakness,
  Poor mens Wealth.
In Confinement,
  Liberty,
In Sollitude,
  Good Company.
Joy in Sorrow,
  Life in Deaths,
Heavenly Crowns for
  Thorny Wreaths.

Are presented to thy view,
  In the Poems that ensue.

If my Trials had been thine,
  These would Cheer thee more then Wine.

Light in Darkness

Light in Darkness followeth next,
Which holds forth Comfort from the Text,
To such as are in mind perplext,
And with Temptations strangely vext.

Song I

1

Thus far in generall
About Afflictions,
Wherewith the Lord will exercise
All whom he owns for sons.
Now of particular Ailes
And Exercises great
(Such as most commonly befall)
We purpose to entreat.

2

The Spirit of a man
Prov. 18:14.   Will many Griefs sustain:
But who can bear a wounded Sp'rit?
This is the greatest pain.
First then for Spiritual Griefs,
Temptations, and distresses,
Wherewith the Devil keepeth down
And some good Souls depresses.

3

Isa. 50:10,11.   There is a child of Darkness
That walketh in the light,
That thinks his ill state very good
And therein takes delight.
There is a child of Light
whose state is very good,
Yet walks in sadness, in the night,
Till this be understood.

4

    Thick Clouds sometimes arise   25
And darken the noon-day:
    A Mist may blind Believers eyes,
They cannot see their way;
    Although they walk in light,
Satan so undermines   30
    Their Comfort, that they see no Light
Which round about them shines.

5

    Sometimes they doubtful are
Concerning their estates:
    Sometimes conclude against themselves   35
That they are Reprobates.
    Such things may Saints befall;
Yet are they never left
    Of God, nor of his awful fear
Are utterly bereft.   40

6

Jon. 2:4.   They dare not wickedly
Away from God depart,
Ps. 88:1, 2, 3, &c.   But after his sweet presence mourn,
And seek him with their Heart.
Isa. 42:3.   Such bruised trembling Reeds   45
Christ will in no wise break:
Isa. 51:1,3.   But in the most accepted time
Will comfort to them speak.

7

    He will into a flame
Blow up their little spark,   50
    And make his face on them to shine
Isa. 57:15, 16.   That now are in the dark.
    For he will not cast off,
Nor evermore forsake
    Those that relie on him for grace,   55
And him their portion make.

8

Come, poor distressed Souls,
And hear your Grievances:
Learn how you may with Spiritual Arms
   Temptations force repress.   60
Hear what the Flesh suggests
For your discouragement:
Learn what the Spirit may reply
   Soul-sinkings to prevent.

Song II

Being a Dialogue wherein the Speakers are
Spirit *and* Flesh.

Spirit.   1

Ps. 42:5, 11.   My Soul what aileth thee
Thus heavily to droop,
And under thine Affliction
   Dejectedly to stoop?
   Art thou the onely man   5
   That hath Affliction seen?
And have not better men then thou
   As much afflicted been?

2

   Hast thou no part in God?
   Or doth he cease to love thee?   10
If neither this, nor that be so,
   What can so greatly move thee?
Flesh. I heretofore did hope
   My sins were pardoned
Through God's free-grace, that all my debts   15
   were wholly cancelled:

3

  That Christ had satisfy'd
  For me, and clear'd the score;
That God was therefore reconcil'd
  And would be wroth no more:
Yet now he hides his face
  And on me seems to frown;
He will not hear my suit for grace,
  But wounds and casts me down.

4

  He writeth bitter things,
Job 13:26. And makes me to possess
My sins of youth: to mind he brings
  My faults and trespasses.
Will God cast off from ay?
Ps. 77:7, 8. And Anger still retain?
Will he depart ev'n quite away,
  And not return again?

Spirit.   5

  Where Christ once sets his love
John 13:1 He loveth to the end,
And nothing can him change or move
  From being still our Friend.
God cannot cease to love,
  Where once he did begin:
Although he may with stripes reprove
  And chasten thee for sin.

6

  Be humbled for thy falls,
Jer. 3:12. My Soul, and turn to God,
Who from thy wandrings thee recalls
  By this his gentle Rod.
Prov. 3:11, 12. Attend unto his voice,
  Return to him that smites
For good; who every child corrects
  In whom his Soul delights.

7

 Fathers may chide and whip
  Their Children till they smart: 50
 But whil'st their hand inflicteth stripes,
  They pitty with their heart.
 They cast not off a Child,
  Although they angry be:
 Nor doth thy Heav'nly Father mild 55
  Reject and cast off thee.

Song III

Another Dialogue or Combate between the
Flesh *and* Spirit.

Flesh.   1

 Oh but I greatly fear,
  My sufferings are not such
 As Childrens Nurture use to be,
  But that they differ much.
 They are too great and long, 5
  I fear, to stand with love:
 Such everwhehning strokes, methinks,
  Do rather hatred prove.

2

 Were I a child of God
  He would more gently deal: 10
 Nor would he always use the Rod,
  But sometimes help and heal.
 But I am day by day
  Afflicted very sore:
 My sufferings have been many years, 15
  And still are growing more.

	Spirit. 3	
	God doth more gently deal	
	Then thou considerest well:	
Lam. 3:22, 23.	For had he us'd extremities	
	Thou hadst been now in Hell.	20
	He is not so severe	
	As thou imaginest;	
	For some, that were to him most dear,	
	Have been much more distrest.	

4

Gen. 27:43, 44	*Jacob* from *Esau's* rage	25
compared with	To *Padan-Aram* sent,	
Gen. 31.	The toyl and pain of twenty years	
	Hard service underwent;	
	Oft being circumvented	
	By *Laban's* subtile feats:	30
	But he was fain to be contented	
	For he knew no deceits.	

5

Gen. 32:6, 7.	Thou know'st what sorrows great	
	He after passed through,	
Gen. 34:2, 30.	One trouble hardly over-blown	35
	Before he met a new.	
Gen. 35:19, 22.	*Moses* brought up a Prince,	
	From *Egypt* Banished,	
Exod. 2:15; 3:2.	Lived in Exile forty years,	
	And laboured for his bread.	40

6

Gen. 27:28.	*Joseph* an innocent,	
	Through Bretherens cruel hate,	
	Was sold to strangers, and so brought	
	Into a servile state.	
	No sooner gains he favour	45
	I'th' eyes of *Potiphar*:	
Gen. 39:17.	But is accused of that Crime,	
	Which he did most abhor.	

                            7
                    His Master is incens'd,
Gen. 39:19, 20.   The innocent is shut,   50
                    Into a Dungeon dark, his hands
Ps. 105:18.   And feet in fetters put.
                    And though the Lord was pleas'd
                    This rigour to abate
                    After some time; yet dwelt he long   55
                    In this Imprisoned state.

                            8
Exod. 1:14.   The Church was sore opprest
                    In *Egypt* many a day,
                    And made like Slaves with rigour too,
Exod. 2:23.   To serve in brick and clay.   60
                    And though they cry'd to God
                    With groans and many tears:
                    Yet were they in this Bondage held
                    Above an hundred years.

                            9
Read Job   What thinkest thou of *Job*   65
1st & 2nd Chapters. And his great Sufferings?
                    Do not thy griefs, compar'd with his,
                    Seem light and little things?
                    So dismal was his case,
                    So strange his sorrows all,   70
                    As Wise ones thought could unto none:
Job 4:7   But wicked men befall.

compared with   10
Job 42:7, 8.   But God befools them for it,
                    And lets them understand
                    That *Job* was such an upright man,   75
                    As none was in the Land:
                    That notwithstanding all
                    That he had undergone
                    For a long time, yet was he still
                    His most beloved one.   80

11

  David a man of God,
   One after God's own Heart,
  In his long lasting Banishment
   Of sorrows had his part.
  Deprived of God's House,   85
1 *Sam.* 26:1, 18, 19.   Hunted from place to place:
  With restless feet and weary steps
   Forc'd up and down to trace.

12

  Flying to save his life,
   In Caves and Forrests hiding,   90
1 *Sam.* 27:6.   Until at length in *Ziklag*-Town,
   He found some safe abiding.
1 *Sam.* 30:3, 6.   E're long his Town is burnt,
   His Wives are Captive taken:
  His Souldiers speak of stoning him,   95
   He seems of all forsaken.

13

  Had *David* said God hates me,
   In this his greatest need:
  When as all other Comforts Fail'd
   He had been poor indeed.   100
  But in his deep distress,
   And over-bearing grief,
  He comforted himself in God,
   And from him found relief.

14

Ps. 88.   *Heman* from youthful years,   105
   Was ready for to die,
  Distracted with amazing fears,
   He cries continuallie.
  Complaining that the Lord,
   His face away did hide,   110
  And made his wrath pass over him:
   And cast his Soul aside.

15

    Yet *Heman* was a Saint,
      And calls the Lord his God:
Ps. 88:1.   God of his Health, 'midst all complaints: 115
      And lashes of the Rod.
    Take courage then my Soul,
      And put away thy fear:
    Thy sufferings well may stand with love,
      Although they greater were.   120

16

    And as for length of Time,
      Examples do thee show,
    That divers Saints have Sufferers been:
      A longer time then thou.
    So that it well appears,   125
      That altereth not the case,
    (Of mans short life the longest Time:
      Is but a little space).

17

    For what are twenty years,
      Unto Eternity?   130
    Eternal Rest will make amends
      For all this Misery.
    When Time shall pass away,
      Like an untimely Birth,
    These Transient Griefs shall be forgot: 135
      Or though upon with mirth.

Song IV

A Dialogue wherein the Speakers are
Distressed Conscience and
Rectified Judgment.

Consc.   1

Ps. 38:3, 4.

'Tis not Affliction barely
That doth my Soul distress:
But rather multitude of sins
And mine own wickedness.
Nor is it former faults   5
That now are brought to mind,
So much, as swarms of present sins
And hateful Lusts I find.

2

Had ever any one
So vile a heart as mine?   10
So barren under all God's pains
Nurture and discipline?
The Saints of God have found
Affliction to sever
Their souls from sin; but I find mine   15
More boisterous now than ever.

3

Ezek. 24:13.

This makes me greatly fear
And question mine estate;
Lest I be nothing else but dross

Jer. 6:28, 29, 30.

And silver reprobate,   20
That is not purify'd
By passing through the fire,
Fit to be trampled under foot
And trodden in the mire.

Judgment.   4

    Conscience, this is a Time
    Wherein thou are benighted,
And seest not things as formerly,
    Because thou art dim-sighted.
    Now therefore haste to some
    Thy doubts that answer may:
Or for the present hark to me,
    And hear what I shall say.

Job 33:25. (line 30)

5

    While Physick is at work,
    Ill Humours are disturb'd:
So while Chastisements are at work,
    Corruptions may be stirr'd.
    They do but shew what was
    Within the heart before:
They may discover hidden Lusts,
    They do not make them more.

6

Prov. 3:11, 12.   God hath ordain'd the Rod
    To do his Children good;
And this the Saints in God's due time
    Have felt and understood:
    Not alwayes presently,
Job 3.   And while the smart is on:
Ps. 77:2, 3, 4, 7.   For some of them have then cry'd out,
    As if they were undone.

7

Heb. 12:11.   No chast'ning joyous is,
    But seems at present hard:
Yet brings forth fruits of Righteousness,
    And sweet Peace afterward.
    Therefore my sinful Soul,
    And doubting Conscience,
Hope well for after-fruit; and don't
    Judge all by present sense.

8

  Gods Physick is at work
  To purge Corruption out:
And this in time he will effect,
  Believe and do not doubt.   60
  He first discovereth sin,
  Shews thee what wanting is,
Makes thee to feel thy need of help,
  And mourn for what's amiss.

9

  This is some hopeful fruit,   65
  And do not this despise,
Job 42:6. For God is making thee more vile
  And base in thine own eyes.
  Builders may be at work
  Before thou see a Stone: 70
God may be working good for thee,
  Though thou discernest none.

Consc.   10

Isa. 63:27. Oh but my heart is hard,
  Much like the Adamant:
It cannot weep, nor mourn for sin, 75
  Nor pour out its complaint.
  It cannot kindly melt,
  Though daily sins abound
In thought, affection, word, and deed,
  which Conscience prick and wound. 80

Judgm.   11

  There may be tenderness
Compare Where hardness most is felt:
Isa. 63:17 And notwithstanding want of Tears
with chap. 64:6, 7, 8. The heart may truly melt.
  All are not broken-hearted   85
  That store of Tears can weep:
And some that have them now, may have
  Humiliation deep.

12

Ps. 51:2, 3, 4, 7, 10.

Isa. 1:16, 17, 18.

Jer. 31:18, 19.

He that bewails his sins
Because they God offend,
That truly hates them, Pardon begs,
Endeavours to amend:
That flies to Christ for grace
To mortifie his Lust,
That mourns because he mourns no more;
This man repents I trust.

90

95

13

Doth not my Soul do thus
(Speak Conscience) day by day?
I know that thou wilt speak the truth:
Thou canst not this gainsay.
Well then be comforted,
And doubt not of thy state:
But still endeavour every sin
More thorowly to hate.

100

14

Eph. 3:18, 19.

Ps. 119:135, 136.

1 *John* 4:19.

And labour for to taste
The sweetness of Christ's Love:
Nothing can melt the heart like this
Sweet Sun-shine from above.
This can the Rock dissolve,
And make the waters flow
Out of the hardest flinty Heart,
Where never good did grow.

105

110

Song V

A Dialogue between the
Flesh *and* Spirit.

Flesh.   1

    But oh methinks the Lord
      Is angry with my Prayers,
    The more I cry to him for help
      The worse it with me fares.
    The more I sue for grace
      And beg for some relief:
    The more he lets me be distrest,
      And doubled is my grief.

    2

    I fear he reckoneth
      My Prayers to me for sin,
    And rather is displeas'd therewith
      Then takes delight therein.
    If God reject my Prayer,
      I fear he me rejects,
    For how can he despise their Prayer
      Whose persons he respects?

Spirit.   3

Ps. 80:4.   Against his People's Prayers
      The Lord sometimes may smoke,
Ps. 66:18.   When some sin unrepented of
      His anger doth provoke.
    If *David* sin regard
Lam. 3:40.   God will not hear his Prayer:
    To search for, find out, mourn for sin,
      My Soul make this thy care.

4

Josh. 7:13, 14.	God puts thee upon search,	25
	Would have thee diligent	
Jer. 3:4, 13, 14, 17.	To find out what offensive is	
	And to be Penitent.	
Jer. 3:19, 20.	Be thou displeas'd with sin,	
	And he'll be pleas'd with thee:	30
	He'll turn to thee his face, if thou	
	Turn from iniquitie.	

5

	Some-Times the Lord delayes,	
Matt. 15:23, 24, 25.	And makes us long to wait,	
	For other ends; as for to make	35
	Us more importunate;	
	To try our Self-denial,	
	Our Faith, Love, Patience.	
	Sometimes to make his Power shine forth	
	In our deliverance.	40

6

	He lets our troubles grow	
Exod. 14 & 15	Unto the greater height,	
chapters.	That his Salvation might appear	
	More glorious in our sight.	
	For these, and other more,	45
	Such great and gracious Ends	
	The Lord defers to hear our prayer,	
	For he no hurt intends.	

7

Gen. 18:19.	Our Prayers are sometimes heard,	
	Not just unto our mind,	50
	Yet heard they are, and answered	
	In some far better kind.	
2 *Cor.* 12:8, 9.	God may deny to grant	
	That thing that we request,	
	Yet answer in a better thing,	55
	For he knows what is best.	

8

  Be silent then frail Flesh,
  Thou savourest not these things:
Thy wisdom doth but vex my Soul;
  Leave off thy Reasonings.   60
  Satan by Serpents mouth
Gen. 3:1.   Mankind did undermine:
And I perceive he now assayes
  To ruine me by thine.

Song VI

Another Combate between the
Flesh *and* Spirit.

Flesh.   1

  Soul thou hast cause to fear
  Thy Faith will not hold out:
And that it is but ccunterfeit
  Thou do'st so often doubt.
  See what a mighty power   5
  Of Unbelief prevails
From time to time! and how thine heart
  And Faith thee often fails.

Spirit.   2

  Oh sly and sinful flesh!
  Thou art a treacherous Thief,   10
That robs me of my Faith, and then
  Condemns for Unbelief.
  They're thy suggestions vile
  (That do'st with Hell comply)
That make me doubt, who otherwise   15
  On Christ alone rely.

3

John 1:12.	Whole Christ with all my heart
Acts 8:37.	I earnestly Embrace;
1 *Cor.* 1:30.	And for my whole Salvation I
	Relie upon his grace: 20
Phil. 3:9, 10.	Renouncing all my own
	Both Righteousness, and Sin;
Heb. 12:14.	Endeav'ring Holiness, as well
	As Happiness to win.

4

	And blessed by the Lord, 25
	Who will compleat my Faith,
Phil. 1:6.	Weak though it be, as he the same
	At first begotten hath:
	Mean while he it supports;
1 *Pet.* 1:5.	And as himself doth tell, 30
Matt. 16:18.	It never shall be vanquished
	By all the force of Hell.

Song VII

Satanical injections foul
Shall not undo thy godly Soul.
That them bewails, resists, and hates,
Nor need such question their estates.

1

I may not here neglect
Another case to mind,
Wherewith some precious Souls to be
Full sore agriev'd I find:
A case calamitous, 5
Beyond the help of man;
For out of Satans deadly gripe
Christ only rescue can.

2

Blasphemous hellish thoughts
Into his mind are cast 10
Concerning God; which make him quake,
And stand like one agast.
Imaginations black,
And Fancies filthy foul
Are darted in with violence, 15
Which stab him to the Soul.

3

Which way soe're he turns
His Understanding's ey,
Think what he will, these fancies vile
Do meet him presently. 20
Poor Soul he them resists
And struggleth as for life:
But yet he cannot keep them out
By all his care and strife.

4

The more he with them strives, 25
The more they wound and vex him:
The more he dreads and feareth them,
The worse they do perplex him.
And when he meditates
Or prayes to God for grace, 30
Then most of all such horrid thoughts
Do stare him in the face.

5

This makes him dread to pray,
Or read, or meditate,
Because such thoughts mix with his prayers, 35
As God he knows doth hate.
For all these Blasphemies
And thoughts that Hell suggests,
He judgeth them his own hearts sins
Although he them detests. 40

6

Experience daily shews
It may befall a Saint
To be thus dogg'd with Hell's black Hounds
Until he almost faint.
And barely this to know, 45
That ever any were
Thus exercis'd that feared God,
Lam. 2:13. May mitigate thy fear.

7

It yields us some support
To know we're not alone, 50
But that through such a dismal way
Some have before us gone.
But for to come more near,
And speak unto thy grief
What in a few lines may be spoke, 55
The answer is in brief:

8

  Such thoughts how vile soever
  And full of Blasphemy,
Rom. 7:19, 20. They are no further our own sins
   Then we with them comply. 60
  They are the Devils sins,
  And his suggestions foul,
  Not thine who mournest under them
   And hat'st them with they soul.

9

  Be not discouraged; 65
  God will not them impute
  To thee, but unto him who doth
   Those poisoned Arrows shoot.
  But, oh thou wilt complain,
  My heart is tinder-like 70
  As prone and ready to take fire,
Rom. 2:23, 24.   As Satan is to strike.

10

  Well, let it humble thee
  To feel a treacherous part:
  A sinful Self; a wicked Flesh 75
   Remaining in my heart.
  Yet for thy comfort know,
  Thou hast not lost the field,
  So long as thou do'st sin resist,
   And striveth not to yield. 80

11

Ps. 119:113. Are wicked thoughts thy load
  And heavy burden still,
  From which thou longest to be freed
Rom. 7:17, 23, 24, 25.   As from the greatest ill?
  The Lord is nearer thee 85
  Then thou art well aware:
Ps. 91:3. He keeps thee that thou art not caught
   By Satans deadly snare.

12

Yea though Temptations strong
May thee sometimes surprise; 90
Ps. 32:5. If by Repentance from thy falls
God helps thee to arise;
Fear not, all turns to gain;
For God is purify'd,
And loseth nothing, but its dross, 95
By being often try'd.

13

Luke 22:31. Christ hath the Devil fast,
And holds him in a Chain,
And that he may not swallow thee
He doth him still restrain. 100
Rom. 16:20. He can no longer vex thee
Then Christ shall him permit
Who will in season take him off,
When he shall see most fit.

Song VIII

1

And now for such as feel
These hellish Buffettings,
And anguish of these sudden darts,
Which are the Serpents stings;
I shall a word or two 5
Or Counsel here annex:
God make them useful unto some
Whom Satan doth perplex.

2

Exod. 20:9.	Follow they Calling close. Love not to be alone; Save only when by secret Prayer,	10
Eccles. 4:9, 10, 11, 12.	Thou makes to God thy moan. Omit not secret Prayer, Nor other means neglect:	
Matt. 6:5.	The Tempter hath thee where he would, If once he that effect.	15

3

Hos. 13:9.	Thy help is in the Lord; From him it must be sought:	
Ezek. 36:37.	Use thou the Means, and wait his time, Who lingers not for nought. Thy Prayers are poor and vile; Yet do not them foregoe: For what were that, but for to give Thy weapon to thy Foe!	20

4

2 Cor. 12:8.	Cry mightily to God	25
Ps. 56:3.	When other Helpers fail: Relie upon him stedfastly, When terrours thee assail. The more the Devil strives (For this is all his scope)	30
1 Thess. 5:8.	To rob thee of they Spiritual Arms,	
Heb. 10:35.	The faster hold thy hope.	

5

Rom. 7:24, 25.	Bewail the sin that cleaves Unto thine holy things,	
1 John 2:1, 2.	And look unto the Blood of Christ Which acceptation brings.	35
Matt. 8:26.	Be not too much dismay'd, Nor 'stonished with fear: But unto Christ who is thy strength Labour to keep more near.	40

6

Matt. 14:30.   Distracting horrid Fear
The Soul of strength deprives,
Draws in these thoughts, and to the Devil
A great advantage gives.
James 5:16.   Adventure not to smother   45
Temptations in thy brest:
Keep not the Devil's counsel, if
Thou do'st the same detest.

7

Make out for help in time;
2 Cor. 11:3.   Lest by some subtile wile,   50
Or hidden craft to thee unknown,
The Serpent thee beguile.
Temptations are like poyson,
Provide an Antidote:
'Tis easier mischief to prevent,   55
Then cure it when 'tis got.

8

Jer. 4:14.   Recall not wicket thoughts
Of them to take a view
(No not to make thee loath them more)
Lest thou this folly rue: 60
But thrust them out of doors,
And strongly say them nay;
James 4:7.   And if thou canst not rid them so,
Flee thou, and run away.

9

Be not thou like the Sheep,   65
That, being in a maze,
Instead of running from the Woolf
Stand still and at him gaze:
Till having one devour'd
He come to worry more,   70
And then they run, but stand again
Still gazing as before.

10

        Bemoan thy self to God;
        In general them confess:
Ps. 119:113.   But if thou think them o're again   75
        They will thee more distress.
        Let every Christian man
Gen. 6:5.   Unto his thoughts take heed:
Prov. 24:9.   For God can whip thee with thy thoughts,
Ps. 81:12.   Until he make thee bleed.   80

11

Give not thy mind to think
Of vain or evil things,
As thou desirest to escape
These hellish Buffettings.
Thus I have briefly given   85
My Counsel in this case.
The Lord direct thee what is good
To follow and embrace.

Reader, I give thee here
Two Songs in other Meetre:
I hope they will not make a jarre,
But close up all the sweeter.

Song IX

1

	Lord from the deeps I cry'd to thee,
Ps. 130:1, 2, 3.	My voice Lord do thou hear;
	Unto my supplications voice
	Let be attent thine ear.
	Lord who should stand? if thou O Lord 5
	Should'st mark iniquitie:
	But with thee there forgiveness is
	That feared thou may'st be.

2

Ps. 65:3.	Works of iniquity prevail
	Against me sore do they: 10
	But as for our Transgressions
Mic. 7:18.	Thou shalt them purge away.
	For who's a God like unto thee
	Pard'ning iniquity?
	And the transgression of his folk 15
	That freely passeth by?

3

Ps. 130:5, 6.	I for the Lord wait, my soul waits;
	And I hope in his Word.
	Then morning watchers watch for morn,
	My soul more for the Lord. 20
	Let Israel for Jehovah stay,
	In waiting hopefully:
	Because that with Jehovah there
	Is kind benignity.

4

Jon. 2:2.	I to the Lord from my distress 25 Did cry, and he gave ear: Out of Hells belly I did cry, And he my voice did hear.
Ps. 49:5.	Why therefore should I be afraid In days that evil be? 30 When as my heels iniquity About shall compass me.

5

Ps. 42:11.	My soul, O wherefore dost thou bow Thy self down heavily? And wherefore in me makest thou 35 A stir tumultuously? Hope thou in God, because I shall With praise him yet advance, Who is my God, he also is Health of my Countenance. 40

6

Isa. 26:3, 4.	Upon the Lord for evermore See that your selves you stay; For there is in Jehovah store Of strength that lasts for ay. In peace, in peace thou wilt him keep, 45 Whose mind is staid on thee; Because that in thy self, O Lord, His trust repose doth he.

7

Isa. 50:10.	Though such as truly fear the Lord, And's Servants voice obey, 50 Walk in the dark, and have no light: Themselves yet let them stay, With confidence upon their God, And in the Lord's Name trust.
Isa. 50:11.	But such as walk by their own fire, 55 Lye down in sorrow must.

Song X

*A Dialogue or Discourse between
the* Believing Soul *and her* Savior.

Soul.	Oh Christ my grief is such,	
	Because I love not much;	
	As addeth to my sore,	
	Because I grieve no more.	
	Give me a broken heart,	5
	That may both bleed and smart,	
	That I so often stray,	
	That I no more obey.	
	Oh make me love thee dearly,	
	And trust in thee sincerely:	10
	And help me well to prove	
	Mine interest in thy Love.	
	That God Omnipotent	
	Is freely well content	
	To cancel all my debts,	15
	And all my sins forgets.	
	O Christ let me be thine,	
	And be thou wholly mine:	
	Let me be thine entire;	
	Be thou mine I desire.	20
Sav.	Ah poor distressed Soul	
	So sad and sorrowful,	
	That weakly dost believe	
	And wouldst more strength receive;	
	Behold at thy request	25
	I'm here full ready prest	
	To save and succour thee;	
Matt. 3:28, 29.	Fear not to come to me.	
	Thou didst mine aid implore,	
	And now it's at thy door.	30
	I am thy Surgeon,	
Mal. 4:2.	Do not thine Healer shun.	

	Do'st with thine heart embrace	
John 1:12.	Both me and all my grace?	
Matt. 13:44.	Canst me thy Treasure make,	35
	And for thy Portion take?	
Ps. 119:94.	Do'st thou thy self resign,	
	And yieldest to be mine?	
Matt. 11:29.	Would'st thou as willinglie	
	Be rul'd as sav'd by me?	40
John 6:37, 40.	Then I my self entire	
	Do yield to thy desire.	
	Believe and do not doubt	
	I will not cast thee out.	
	I am and will be thine;	45
	And all this Wealth of mine	
Eph. 1:5, 6, 7.	Dear purchased by me	
	I freely give to thee.	
Ps. 5:12.	Light, pardon, joy and peace,	
	Eternal life and ease,	50
Ps. 150.	With full Redemption,	
	Shall be thy portion.	
John 20:17.	Also my Father mild	
	Thy Father will be styl'd:	
John 14:16, 17.	My Spirit the Comforter	55
	Shall be thy Strengthener.	
Ezek. 36:26, 27.	He shall thy Will renew	
	And by degrees subdue	
	Thy Lusts, and all thy foes	
	That Holiness oppose.	60
	He will to thee impart	
	And humble broken heart,	
	Increase of Spiritual strength,	
	And victory at length.	
Ps. 27:14.	Doubt not poor soul; Be strong	65
	For me that waitest long:	
John 14:27.	And fear not to believe	
Ps. 37:3, 4, 5.	That I may peace thee give.	

	Upon me wholly roll	
	The Burden of thy Soul:	70
	Thy self upon me stay,	
	And then rejoyce for ay.	
Soul.	Is this my Saviour's voice	
	That bids me to rejoyce?	
	To me, vile wretch this word	75
	Directest thou, dear Lord!	

Will God be reconcil'd
To one that is so vil'd?
Wilt thou thy self bestow
On me so base and low? 80

Shall I now live for ay
That went so long astray?
Wilt thou such grace out-stretch
Unto a sinful wretch?

O Gracious Grace indeed! 85
Shown in a time of need.
O God of Grace, *All Grace!*
How pleasant is thy face!

Ps. 116:1, 2, 12. To God what shall I render?
Who me vouchsafes to tender 90
In this my low estate,
Which was so desolate.

Had I a thousand hands
To do what he commands:
Ten thousand Hearts to love him, 95
To fear him, and improve him,

As many Lives t'xpose
And for his sake to lose:
Yet could I never do him
The service that I ow him. 100

Eph. 3:18, 19. Thy Love doth all surmount,
And is beyond account:
I never can express,
Sufficient thankfulness.

	Yet help me to endeavour	105
	To honour thee for ever;	
	Thee onely to desire,	
2 *Cor.* 5:14, 15.	Love, Reverence, and Admire:	
Ps. 73:25.	Thee let me ever serve,	
	And never from thee swerve:	110
	Let this sweet face of thine	
	Upon me allways shine.	
	Let no sin interpose	
	To hide, or make me lose	
	Thy Countenances light,	115
	Which on me shines so bright.	

Sick mens Health

For sick men to be well,
For those that are in pain
To find some ease, recover strength,
And to wax whole again
(By Means or else without) 5
This is no Novelty:
But to be sick and well at once,
This is a Mystery:

And for our Sicknesses
To be a Salve to heal 10
Our deadly Sores, a soveraign Balm
For to procure our weal;
This is a Paradox
Hard to be understood:
But these discourses following 15
Explain, and make it good.

I shall not intermeddle
With the Physicians Art:
Nor Medicines prescribe, which may
Relieve thy Body's smart. 20
But what may help thee bear
Thine outward Misery
With Patience, as becomes a Saint,
And to get good thereby.

Meditation I

1

 Of all Afflictions that
  The outward man oppress,
Job 2:4, 5. None are more grievous to endure
  Then Pains and Sicknesses;
 Especially if great,   5
  And long continuing:
 Oh what vexation to the Flesh,
  And Anguish do they bring.

2

 Yet may such anguish great
  Befal a Child of God: 10
Heb. 12:6, 7. Not from an Enemie's wrath, but from
  His gentle Father's Rod.
 God chastiseth his in love
  Ev'n when he seems severe,
 Exempting not from smarting stripes   15
  Those whom he counts most dear.

3

Job 2:7, 8. Most Patient holy *Job*
  Was broken out all o're
 With painful boils from head to foot
  Loathsome, and grievous sore.   20
 What strange Extremities
  Befel this precious Saint
Job 2:12, 13. His Friends astonishment declares,
  So doth his own complaint.

4

	His Visage was so marr'd	25
	Familiars knew him not.	
Job 30:17, 18, 27, 30.	His stiffened Garment girt him like	
	The Collar of his Coat.	
	With running of his Sores:	
	His bowels boil'd within:	30
Job 19:20.	His bones were burnt with fervent heat	
	And clave unto his Skin.	

5

His bones were pierc'd with pain;
His sinews took no rest:
Besides the many other woes   35
Wherewith he was opprest.
He could attain no ease
Nor respite, not a little;
No not so long as till he might
Job 7:19.   Have swallowed down his Spittle.   40

6

Isa. 38:1, 12.   Religious *Hezekiah*
Whose Zeal for God excell'd,
(In whose defence the Lord of Hosts
Had proud *Sennacherib* quell'd)
With Sickness great and sore   45
Was sharply visited,
And in the middest of his dayes
Was numbred with the dead.

7

He poureth out complaints
Isa. 38:3, 14.   And cries to God above,   50
He like a Swallow chattereth
And mourneth as a Dove.
But when the Lord him hears,
And doth Salvation give,
He then can see, and also say,   55
Isa. 38:16.   That by such things men live.

8

John 11:3, 14.

Good *Lazarus* may be sick,
Though Christ's beloved Friend:
Yea of his Sickness he may die,
And to the grave descend.   60

Luke 16:20, 21, 22.

Poor *Lazarus* the Beggar
Laid at the Rich mans doores
To beg relief, he may be sick
And also full of sores:

9

He may through Sickness die,   65
Or through distressing want;
And yet be carried unto Heaven
And crowned for a Saint.
So then 'tis no new thing
The Saints of God to see   70
Under Diseases, Sickness, Pain,
And sore extremitie.

Meditation II

1

Rom. 15:4.

And now my Soul go to,
For thine instruction
What canst thou learn, when thou art told

Lam. 2:13.

What Saints have undergone?
Soul. I see I have too long   5
Me with my self compar'd,
And by much poreing on my self
Have been too much ensnar'd.

2

  I thought my own condition
  Sometimes more sad then any;   10
But now I see I have not felt
  One half so much as many.
  These Saints forementioned,
  It plainly doth appear,
Have suffered more in one Months time, 15
  Then I have in a year.

3

  Nay when I ponder well
  What *Job* did once endure:
My Pains and mine Infirmities
  Are but Flea-bitings sure.   20
  The Lord was just I know,
  In all that them befell:
Both just and gracious toward me
  I may account him well.

4

Job 11:6.   He hath punish'd me   25
  So much as I deserve,
That from his just Commandements
  So much and often swerve.
  And should he still afflict me
  Much more then yet he hath: 30
Lam. 3:22, 39. He will not wrong me, who deserve,
  His everlasting Wrath.

5

  And howsoe're the Lord
  Be pleas'd with me to deal;
Although he never in this world   35
  Should me release or heal;
Matt. 26:39. O let my Will submit
  To his that is most just;
Lam. 3:29. Let me not murmure, but abase
  My self unto the dust.   40

6

1 *Thess.* 5:18.   Lord make me thankful too
            For all that gentleness
            Which in thy Chastenings towards me
            Thou daily do'st express.
            For Mercy 'tis that I   45
            Who more, much more transgress,
            Then many of God's precious Saints,
            And yet afflicted less.

Meditation III

1

            Though Christ were never sick,
Ps. 22:14, 15, 16.   Yet sure he under-went
            Such piercing bitter pains; as were
            More then equivalent:
1 *Cor.* 15:55, 56, 57.   And by his Sufferings   5
            He took away the sting
            Of all our Sufferings, Sickness, Pain,
            And every evil thing.

2

            Yea he them sanctify'd
Ps. 23:4 & 119:71.   By virtue of his Blood,   10
            That they might as effectual Means
            Promote our Spiritual Good.
Job 33:19-31.   For he knew how to make
            Trouble the way to Peace,
Job 36:8, 9, 10, 11.   Sickness the way to soundest Health,   15
            And Pain the way to Ease.

3

  Some men have Bodies sound,
  But Souls most deadly sick:
 Blinds Eyes, hard Hearts, stiff Wills
3 *John* 2.   'Gainst all Commands that kick. 20
  Some men have thriving Souls,
  Though Bodies not in Health:
 And God doth make their Bodies Ailes
  Promote their Spirit's wealth.

4

  'Tis better to be sick, 25
  And have thy Soul wax whole:
 Then in a Body hail and strong
  To have a sickly Soul.
  For through Soul-sicknesses
  Thou do'st dishonour God: 30
 Who may be honoured when thou bear
  Submissively his Rod.

5

  Diseases bodily
  May help thee to do well:
 But Soul diseases, if not cur'd, 35
  Will carry thee to Hell.
  Our Bodies may sometimes
  Need Physick, more then Food.
 So may our Souls need Sicknesses
  And Pains, to do them good. 40

6

  Our Bodies Sicknesses
  Are Physick for the Soul,
 Corrected by a skilful hand
  That can its force controll:
  Who will so moderate, 45
  And qualified the same,
 That is shall do no hurt, but good;
  Oh blessed be his Name!

7

By these he doth prevent
Much hurt that might be got; 50
Preserves us from Infectious Air
As by an Antidote.
'Gainst Constitution sins
Whereto our Nature bends,
And those whereto our Calling leads, 55
Hereby he us defends.

8

Isa. 1:25. By these he purgeth out
Job 34:31, 32. Bad Humours, namely Pride,
Self-love, Impatience, Worldliness, 60
And many more beside.
Heb. 12:10, 11. By these he doth our Wills
Unto his Will subdue:
And makes us Peace, with Holiness,
And heavenly things pursue.

9

By these he quickeneth us 65
Our duty to attend,
Job 42:5, 6. Makes sin more bitter, teacheth us
To mind our latter end.
By these he rend'reth us
More vile in our own eyes, 70
And helpeth us more heartily
His favour for to prize.

10

Makes Christ more precious to us
And Earthly things more vain;
By these he doth from too much love 75
Rom. 8:23. Of present things us wean:
Makes us to think of home,
And long for Heavenly Rest,
Whilst here we feel our selves to be
With endless griefs opprest. 80

	11	
2 *Cor.* 4:26, 28.	As th' outward man decayes	
	And is consum'd away,	
	The inward man thus gathereth strength	
	And vigour every day.	
	Who would not Phisick take	85
	Such Health for to procure?	
	And that their Souls such gains might make	
	A little smart endure?	

Meditation IV

A Dialogue wherein the Speakers are
Fear *and* Faith.

Fear.   1

    But what if Sickness bring
      Extremity of Pain?
How shall I then have Patience, or
      Good thoughts of God maintain?
    I know Extremities   5
      Are grievous for to bear:
And, which more grievous is, *I* shall
      Dishonour God I fear.

Faith.   2

    Dread not Extremities
      My Soul, thou need'st not fear it,   10
But if God please to lay more Pain,
      He'l give more strength to bear it.

Ps. 37:24.   Such is his Faithfulness
      He will no Burthen throw
Lam. 63:9. Upon thy Back, but what himself   15
      Will help thee undergo.

3

Thy Strength is very small,
Thy Patience that is less;
Thy Foes are strong, the World, the Devil,
And thine own wickedness. 20
Thou canst but little bear,
As well as little do:
But th' Everlasting Arms can bear
Deut. 33:27.   Thee and thy Burthen too.

4

If those Almighty Arms, 25
That made the World, infold thee:
No matter what the Pressure be;
Ps. 55:22.   Doubtless they will uphold thee.
His Spirit helps us bear
Rom. 8:26.   Our greatest Miseries, 30
And takes our Burthens heavier end
In our Extremities.

5

If that our Pains increase,
2 *Cor.* 1:5.   And grow upon us sore:
He makes our Comforts to abound, 35
1 *Cor.* 10:13.   And Spiritual Joyes much more.
For God most faithful is,
That lets not his be try'd
Beyond their strength; but them supports,
That they may it abide. 40

6

1 *Sam.* 25:22   When left unto our selves,
compared with   Small Trials vex us sore:
2 *Sam.* 16:10, 11.   And greater ones are better born,
When God assists us more.
In lesser straits, God's help 45
We are less apt to mind:
In greater straits we seek him more,
And more assistance find.

                    7
                Hence then Extremities
                Which makes us for to roll   50
Ps. 37:5.   Upon God's Power and Faithfulness
Ps. 55:22.   The Burthen of our Soul:
                Which force us out of Self
Deut. 33:26, 27. And unto Heaven send us;
                They do but drive us to our Strength,   55
                For God will succour lend us.

            Fear.   8
                But what if God withhold
                His Countenances light
                In time of great Extremity,
                    And leave me in the night: 60
                If God forsake me then,
                    Alas, my Faith will fail:
                And Satan watching for a prey,
                    Will over me prevail.

            Faith.   9
                His countenances light   65
                If God from us withdraw,
                In Sickness, and with fear of wrath
                    Be pleased us to aw:
1 Pet. 1:6.   It's but if there be need,
                    And 'tis but for a while;   70
Isa. 54:7, 8.   When th' end is once attain'd, his frown
                    Is turned to a smile.

                    10
Jer. 33:20, 26. The Sun can sooner cease
                To shine out of the Sky:
                Then Christ can cease to favour thee,   75
Rom. 8:35, 37, 38, 39. That do'st on him rely.
                This Earth that stands so firm,
                    Shall from her Center move:
                Sooner then God Unchangeable
                    Will take away his Love.   80

11

               Nay he will thee support
Cant. 1:6.   And strengthen with his grace:
               And while the one hand thee corrects
Heb. 13:5.   The other will embrace.
               He will not thee forsake,   85
Job 23:10.   Nor leave thee in the mire:
               Yea he will bring thy Soul like Gold
               More bright out of the fire.

12

               Soul, wherefore should'st thou then
               Dread Sicknesses, or Pain?   90
Rom. 8:28.   Which in the upshot hurt no Saint,
               But alwayes turn to gain.
               Lord, help me to rejoyce
               When I am chastened,
Rom. 8:29.   That thou art now conforming me   95
               To Christ my blessed Head.

Hos. 14:9.   *Whoso is wise, and doth*
               These things consider well,
               Shall know God's ways to be most right,
               And forth his praises tell.

Strength in Weakness

That weak ones may grow strong
We very often see:
But Strength in Weakness to behold,
This is a Noveltie.

To see a Weak man Strong, 5
And strongest when most Weak;
To see the Strong through Weakness fall
And all their bones to break:
This is a Mystery
A Christian Paradox; 10
But this ensuing little Key
The Cabinet unlocks.

Song I

1

    Men's Strength meer Weakness is,
      As frail as *Venice* Glass:
    And all his Excellency like
Isa. 40:67.   The flower upon the grass.
    Adam in Paradise,   5
      And in his perfect state,
Gen. 3:6.   When left of God unto himself,
      Could soon degenerate.

2

    He that was strong at first
      Immediately grew weak;   10
    And let the stock of Grace run out,
      Like vessels that do leak.
Rom. 5:6, 12, 14.   Hence we are all made weak,
      And neither have Free-will
    To chuse, nor Power to do what's good,   15
      But only what is ill.

3

    But God, the God of Grace,
      His Blessed Son imploy'd
John 3:17.   And sent to ransome and restore
      What Adam had destroy'd.   20
    He having us Redeem'd
      And Ransom'd with his Blood,
Rev. 1:5, 6.   And also purchased for us
      All grace and saving good.

4

Eph. 2:5, 6, 10.	Restoreth us to life,	25
	Createth us anew,	
	Enableth us to do what's good	
	And evil to eschew.	
John 15:4, 5.	But still he keeps the Stock	
	Of grace in his own hand,	30
	And hath not left it unto us	
	To be at our command.	

5

Phil. 4:13.	The strongest Saints have need	
	Of daily fresh supplies;	
	And Christ will teach them where their strength	35
	And all their power lies.	
	Unless the Sun do shine,	
	Soon vanisheth the Beam:	
	Unless the Fountain feed it still,	
	Soon dry'd up is the Stream.	40

6

Hence if the strongest Saints
   Begin to grow secure,
Neglect their watch, trust in themselves;
   Christ will not this endure.
   He leaves them to themselves,   45
     And lets them trie their strength:
They fall and feel their weaknesses
   Unto their cost at length.

7

2 Sam. 11:2, 3, 4.	Thus *David* sadly fell;	
	And who more strong then *David*?	50
	Or who more graciously himself	
	In all his straits behaved?	
	David, while weak, was strong,	
	And kept his hands most pure:	
	But in his strength he grew most weak	55
	By being too secure.	

8

Luke 22:33, 56, 57,   *Peter* was confident
58, 60.
    And thought he had much strength
To follow Christ through thick and thin:
    But what came on't at length?   60
    He thought his Love so great,
    He could with Christ have dy'd:
But ah frail man! e're morning light
    He Christ three times deny'd.

Obj.   9

    Some haply here will say;   65
    If Saints of such renown
Have been so foil'd, and to the ground
    In time of Trial thrown;
    What will become of me,
    That am so weak and frail!   70
How shall I stand, when violent
    Temptations me assail?

Sol.   10

    Though God sometimes permit
    The strongest Saints to fall,
To stain the glory of all Flesh,   75
    And to awaken all:
    Yet let not weak ones faint,
    Nor be discouraged,
Who feel their wants and weaknesses,
    And flee to Christ their Head.   80

11

Isa. 40:29, 30.   For Christ hath strength enough:
    Do thou on him depend,
And he will make thee stand in storms,
    And hold out to the end.
    For in our weakness great   85
    Christ's strength doth more appear:
We never are so safe, as when
    We get to him most near.

12

    When sense of our own wants,
    And manifold defects,   90
Drives us to Christ our only strength;
    Then he the weak protects.
    Hence we are never stronger,
    Then when we are most weak
Because we then most heartily   95
    Christ's help and succour seek.

13

2 Cor. 12:5, 7, 9, 10, 11.   Thus *Paul* that great Apostle,
    when I am weak, saith he,
Then am I strong; because the strength
    Of Christ then rests on me.   100
    Therefore I rather chuse
    In weaknesses to glory,
Then of my Revelations great
    To tell an ample story.

Song II

1

    And now for want of strength
    And weakness Bodily,
I could say much; For few, I think,
    Have felt it more then I.
    I have been many years   5
    So impotent and weak
As none are able to conceive
    That onely hear me speak.

2

 And when I find most strength
 And thereupon assay   10
To serve the Lord with all my heart
 In the most publick way;
 Just when I should set forth
 Such feebleness assails me
That I am like a man half dead,   15
 All strength and vigour fails me.

3

 I go to God and tell him,
 Thou Lord hast strength, I want it
To do thee service therewithal,
 In faithfulness O grant it.   20
 Thou putt'st me now on service,
 And strength in me there's none:
Therefore on thee the God of strength
 I will depend alone.

4

 Mine eyes are wholly thus   25
 Unto the God of strength:
I cast my self upon his Power,
 Who succours me at length,
 And in the time of need
 Doth such assistance give,   30
That those who hear me scarce know how
 My weakness to believe.

5

 But this is certain truth,
 My strength again is gone,
And languishings return, as soon   35
 As e're the work is done.
 And every such attempt,
 In this my weak estate,
My bodily Ails for divers weeks
 Doth much exasperate.   40

6

By every little doing
I suffer very much:
Yet at God's hand I neither dare,
Nor have I cause to grutch.
Hath not the Potter power 45
To frame out of the clay
One vessel for to serve him thus,
Others another way.

7

But I have said enough,
2 *Cor.* 12:9. All tending to depress 50
The Creature, and for to advance
Jer. 9:23, 24. God's Power and Faithfulness.
For sure his power shines forth
In our Infirmity;
1 *Cor.* 1:31. That whoso glorieth, glory may 55
In God alone most High.

Song III

A Dialogue wherein the Speakers are
Troubled Conscience *and* Rectified Judgment.

Troub. Consc. 1

Oh, but my weakness brings
Unserviceableness,
And takes me off from Christ's sweet works:
Who can this grief express?
When as the Body fails 5
The Soul, and hindereth it
In all its motions, like a clog;
I am for nothing fit.

  Rect. Judgm.   2
  If Christ disable thee
  From doing as before,   10
  He calls thee to some other work
  That he approveth more.
  Passive Obedience
  More hard then Active is:
  And Christ will own and honour that,   15
  Who owns and crowneth this.

      3

1 *Pet.* 4:12, 13, 14.   Thou still art serving Christ,
  Though in another way:
  And he thy Service will accept
  And crown another day.   20
Col. 1:24.   They Suffering is his work,
  As well as Doing was:
  Thy service in a suffering way
  Christ rather chosen has.

      4

1 *Kings* 17:1, 3, 4, 5.   If Christ hath call'd thee off,   25
  After a short assay,
  From Publick Service; cease dispute,
  And cheerfully obey.
  Masters are pleased best,
  When as their will is done,   30
  Although a nobler work be left
  To do a meaner one.

      5

  If he be pleas'd to make it
  Thy business to sit still:
  Thou pleasest him the best, by meek   35
  Submission to his Will.
  God hath no need of us,
  Nor any work of ours:
  Yet for the deed he takes our will,
  Where he denieth power.   40

6

 Although the work be small
 Thou canst for him effect:
2 *Cor.* 8:12. Yet if there be a willing mind
 He doth the same expect:
 For not by th' outward bulk   45
 Of what we do fulfill,
 God doth esteem our services;
 But by the Doers will.

7

 For this he will reward thee
 As richly at the last: 50
 As if thou able wert to do
 More work than e're thou wast.
 Thou hast a gentle Master,
 That sets no cruel task:
 But when he doth abate thy strength   55
 He doth less service ask.

8

 Do what thou canst, my Soul;
 For God no more expects:
Luke 12:48. Where much he gives, he looks for much:
 Where less, he less accepts.   60
 But make not this a cloak,
 Vile Flesh, for Slothfulness:
Deut. 10:12. God will be serv'd with all our might,
 Be 't more, or be it less.

Consc.   9

 Ah me! what shall I say?   65
 This word my Soul doth prick
 In twenty places all at once,
 And wounds it to the quick.
 Will God be served then
Ps. 130:3. With all our wit and might?   70
 Alas! how shall I answer him,
 Or stand before his sight?

Judgm. 10

  Mourn thou for thy neglects,
1 *John* 1:9. Thy self to Christ betake,
  Who will thee cleanse from thy defects, 75
  And thee more fruitful make.
  Endeavour to amend,
  And be more diligent:
  For God will pardon all their sins
Jer. 3:13, 22. Who seriously repent. 80

  Christian, *though thou art weak,*
  Yet thy Redeemer's strong:
  Who under weakness thee supports,
  And will set free e're long.

Song IV

1

Isa. 40:27. Why say'st thou *Jacob*, and,
  O *Israel* spoken hast,
  My way is hidden from the Lord,
  My judgment from him past?
Isa. 40:28. Hast thou not known nor heard, 5
  Th' Eternal God, the Lord
  Who hath the Ends of all the Earth
  Created by his Word.

2

  He never waxeth faint,
  No wearied is he: 10
  His understanding is so deep
  It cannot searched be.
  He giveth strength unto
Isa. 40:29. The faint and feeble wight:
  And he bestows increase of strength 15
  On such as have no might.

3

Isa. 40:30. The youth shall faint and tire,
  And young men wholly fall:
Isa. 40:31. But those that wait upon the Lord
  Their strength recover shall. 20
  They shall mount up with wings
  Like Eagles; run shall they
  And not be weary: they shall walk
  And shall not faint away.

Poor mens Wealth

To talk of Poor mens Wealth,
Or Rich mens Poverty,
Seems to the World an Old Wives Tale,
Or Idle foolery:
But whoso reads our Lines, 5
If God but give him eyes,
Shall see that these things are no Tales,
But Spiritual Mysteries.

Meditation I

1

	What means this Paradox?	
	How can the Rich be poor?	
	Or Poor men Rich? What is their Wealth?	
	Or where is all their store?	
Rev. 2.	I know thy Poverty,	5
	Saith Christ, yet thou art Rich,	
	To *Smyrna's* undefiled Church:	
	Thou seest there may be such.	

2

	But to *Laodicea*;	
	Thou say'st that I am rich,	10
Rev. 3:17, 18.	But thou art naked, blind and poor,	
	A miserable wretch.	
	I counsel thee to buy	
	Eye-salve that thou may'st see,	
	Of me; try'd Gold to make thee rich,	15
	White Robes to cover thee.	

3

	The beggar *Lazarus*	
Luke 16:20, 22.	Laid at the Rich man's doore,	
	To beg relief, all Ulcerous,	
	And full of running sores;	20
	When once his body dies	
	With many griefs opprest:	
	His Soul by Angels carried is	
	Unto that Heavenly Rest.	

4

    The Riotous Epicure, 25
That feasted every day,
That cloath'd himself with Purple, and
    Most gorgeous array:

Luke 16:23.   He dy'd and went to Hell,
    Suff'ring Eternal Pain. 30
What thinkest thou my Soul? which was
    The richer of these twain?

5

He was a Rich Poor man,
    Whose Poverty prepar'd him
for Heav'n: But he a Poor Rich man 35
    Whose Worldly Wealth ensnar'd him.
That man is Poor indeed
    Both when he lives and dies,
That hath some Treasure here on Earth,
    But none above the Skies. 40

6

Luke 12:18, 20, 21.   He that enlarg'd his Barns
    To treasure up his store,
Was fetch'd away to Hell that night,
    And died worse then poor.
And so is every man, 45
    That being worldly-wise
Provides for th' outward man, but doth
    The Heavenly wealth despise.

7

All Poor men are not Rich
    ('Twere happy if they were) 50
But such as Christ enriched hath,
    And unto God brought near.
All Rich men are not Poor
    (That were a woful case)
But such as have no part in Christ, 55
    Nor any saving grace.

8

  Let not the poorest Saint
  Despond; for thou art rich:
Matt. 9:33. Nor richest Worldling bless himself;
  For thou may'st be a wretch. 60
Luke 16:9. But let both Rich and Poor
Luke 12:33. Endeavour to make sure
  Of Heavenly Treasure, Spiritual Wealth.
  This only will endure.

9

  If others will be fools 65
  And no true wisdom learn:
  Yet what belongs unto my peace,
  Lord, help me to discern.
  To have my portion here
  Oh never let me chuse, 70
Ps. 17:4. Not for the sake of trifling Toyes
  Eternal Joyes refuse.

10

  My Soul craves better things
  Then this World can afford:
  Thou art the Portion that I chuse, 75
Ps. 73:25, 26. Give me thy self, O Lord.
  I shall be richer then,
  Then if I were possest
  Of all the Riches, that are found
  Both in the East and West. 80

Meditation II

1

The World doth value men
According to their Wealth,
Without enquiring how 'tis got,
    By Honesty, or Stealth.
What such a man is worth
They commonly declare
By telling what his yearly Rents
    Or his Possessions are.

2

But God doth more esteem
Mens Virtues then Estates;
And if they have small Grace, or none,
    Accordingly them rates.
When *Belshazzar* weigh'd
With *Babel* at his back,
Although he were an Emperour
    He found him weight to lack.

Dan. 5:27.

3

I'le not envie the Rich,
Nor will I sleight the Poor:
But what God prizeth more then wealth,
    That I will value more.
For Poor men may be Rich,
And Rich men may be Poor;
If those have Heavenly wealth, and these
    Have none but Earthly store.

4

For Riches profit not
When as the day of Wrath
Is come; But Gospel-Righteousness
    Delivereth from Death.
The Upright man is better,
(Though in a Sheep-skin clad
And fed with Indian Bread and water)
    Then those whom wealth makes mad.

Prov. 11:4.

Prov. 12:26.

                                5
James 2:2, 3.   Though Riches in the World
                     Do make men honourable;
                     Though Poverty do bring contempt,   35
                     And render despicable:
                     Yet God oft-times bestows
                     True Faith with Saving Grace,
Matt. 11:25.   And Heavenly Glory upon those,
                     Whom men account most base.   40

                                6
1 *Cor.* 1:27, 28.   Weak, foolish, mean, obscure,
                     And such as men despise,
                     Such are the Persons and the things
                     Whereon God sets his eyes.
                     Of such he maketh Sons,   45
                     Yea more then Sons, his Heirs
James 2:5.   And Fellow-heirs with Christ that so
                     The Kingdom may be theirs.

Meditation III

A Dialogue, the Speakers being
Faith *and* Unbelief.

Unbelief.   1
Thou speakest sleighty now
Of all these outward things:
But what, when Poverty thee wounds
  With all her Pois'ned Stings?
What if thy Weaknesses   5
  Bring on distressing wants?
How wilt thou then behave thy self?
  Or live without complaints?

Faith. 2

    Perhaps I may not live
        Those future months to see:
And then 'twere folly to take thought
        For what shall never be.
    But if the Lord see fit
        That I on Earth abide
A longer time, he can and will
        Fit sustenance provide.

Matt. 6:26-34. (line 15)

3

If I have meat and drink,
    Though neither of the best,
And cloathes that will but keep me warm
    I shall not be distrest.
Mean things give me content;
    For God can mean things bless,
More then their overflowing Cups
    That greatest things possess.

1 Tim. 6:8.
Ps. 37:16.

4

Those that abound in wealth
    May lose it in a night;
And be despoil'd of all they have
    Before the morning light;
And if they have no God
    To help them in their need,
It matters not what once they were,
    They'l then be poor indeed.

5

But he that hath the Lord
    Engag'd by Covenant
To stand his Friend at every turn,
    That man can never want.
My Soul be thankful then;
    Thou has a better lot,
Although thy substance be but small,
    Then worldly men have got.

Ps. 23:1.
Ps. 10:5, 6.

6

 Thou has a gracious God
 Who never will forsake thee,
But here on Earth he'll do thee good,
Heb. 13:5.   And then to Heaven take thee.
 A blessed Portion He   45
Ps. 73:24.   To all that on him trust:
Whose Souls and Bodies he will feed;
 But he'll not feed their Lust.

7

 Our Saviour teacheth us
 For daily bread to pray;   50
Matt. 6:11.   Not for a twelve months Bread at once,
 But for each present day:
 That so we might on God
 From time to time depend,
Believing that our present help   55
 Will help us to the End.

8

 Of present things, my Soul,
 What present need requires
1 *Tim.* 6:8, 9. Thou dost possess: here stay thy thoughts
 And bridle thy desires.   60
Matt. 6:25-34. Beware lest future things
 Thy careful mind distract:
For carking care can nothing else
 But guiltiness contract.

9

 Good reason hath the man   65
Rev. 21:7.   To be content with small things,
Who when he is at lowest ebb,
Gen. 33:11.   Yet still possesseth all things.
I have all saith Jacob. For God is All in all
Through Christs his gracious Son,   70
James 1:17. The Ocean whence all streams proceed
 And into which they run.

10

Rom. 11:36.	He is a living Spring,	
	A Fountain never dry:	
	Though water in the Pitcher fail,	75
	The Fountain can supply.	
	That man is not i'th' dark,	
Ps. 84:11.	That still enjoyes the Sun:	
	Although his Fire be quite gone out,	
	And Candle ends be done.	80

Meditation IV

1

	O Man of little faith!	
	Behold the winged Fowls,	
Matt. 6:26.	The Ravens, Crows, and Cormorants	
	The Kites, the Hawks, the Owls,	
	Also the numerous Doves	5
	Whose flocks make dark the Air:	
	And tell me who for all this Crew	
	Doth kindly food prepare.	

2

	The Heavenly Father's wise	
	And wondrous Providence	10
Ps. 147:9.	Gives unto all these Multitudes	
	Their daily sustenance.	
Luke 12:24.	Doth God take care of Fowls	
	And hear the Ravens cry?	
	And can he see his Saints in want	15
	And not their wants supply?	

3

Rom. 8:32.   He that did not withhold
                         From death his onely Son,
                         But gave him up, that we through him
                         Might gain Salvation: 20
                         He that hath given us
                         An interest in his Blood,
                         Will not deny us lesser things
                         That may promote our good.

4

                         He that hath called us   25
                         To his Inheritance,
1 *Pet.* 1:4.   And unto royal dignity
Luke 12:32.   Intendeth to advance:
Matt. 13:43.   He that will make us shine
Matt. 7:9, 10, 11.   In glory like our Head,   30
                         Will not put on his Childeren
                         With stones instead of Bread.

5

                         For Meat and Drink and Clothes
                         What need the Child take care
                         That hath a Father Kind and Rich   35
                         To tender his welfare?
Isa. 49:15.   Thy Father is more kind
                         Then Earthly Fathers be:
Ps. 147:5.   Amongst them all there's none so wise
Ps. 24:1.   Nor none so rich as He.   40

6

                         If Kind, he wants not will;
                         If Rich, he wants not power:
                         If Wise, he knows what's best to give,
                         And when's the fittest hour.
Matt. 6:32.   He knows what be thy want,   45
                         Before thou them declare:
Isa. 65:24.   And oft bestows before thou ask
                         The things that needful are.

7

      He hath thy wants prevented,
      Rather than wants supply'd: 50
      And not without great cause thy Suit
      At other times deny'd.
      He knows what things will most
      Unto thy weal conduce:
      And when such things as may do good   55
      Will be of greatest use.

8

      Thou oft hast try'd his Love,
Luke 22:35.   And found his readiness
      To give thee succour and supplies,
      Whenever in distress.   60
2 *Cor.* 1:10.   Let past Experiences
      Make thee in him confide:
Ps. 34:9, 10.   Who will for all that in him trust
      Most seas'nably provide.

9

      Thou wantest thankfulness: 65
      This calleth for complaint
      Against thy self: of other things
      Thou hast no present want.
1 *Cor.* 1:30.   Oh get a thankful Heart;
Matt. 7:7, 8, 11.   Christ can this want supply: 70
      And if thou seek it seriously,
      Will not thy suit deny.

Meditation V

1

Matt. 15:26, 27.
    This Meditation
Mine heart hath comforted;
That he who feeds the Dogs with crumbs,
    Will give his Children Bread.
By Bread I mean both that
    Which our frail Body feeds,
And also that which doth relieve
    Our Spiritual wants and needs.

2

John 6:27, 51, 55.
    That's Bread of Life indeed,
    Which never doth decay:
Which maketh those who thereon feed
    To live and thrive for ay.
John 11:25, 26.
    This Bread makes dead men live;
    And let, none living dy,
But feeds them to Eternal Life;
    This is a Mystery.

3

Such Bread Christ Jesus gives,
    His own dear Flesh and Blood,
Wherewith he nourisheth our Souls.
    Oh this is wondrous food!
He that the greater gives
    Will not the less deny:
Rom. 8:32.
1 *Tim.* 4:8.
    But when our Bodies stand in need,
    He will their wants supply.

4

Again, when I behold
    What great things God bestows
On Turks and Pagans (Infidels)
    And such as live like those.
I certainly conclude
    He hath some better Treasure
To give his Saints, then Worldly-wealth,
    Honour, or Carnal Pleasure.

5

For will not God deal better
With Servants, then with Foes?
With Children, then with Enemies
And such as Christ oppose?
Hath not Christ purchased
Far better things for Saints,
Then common bounty here affords
To faithless Miscreants?

6

The *Turkish* Empire vast,
What is it? but a Bone
That by the Master of the House
Unto the Dogs is thrown?
The Gold Mines of the West,
And Riches of the East,
Are often-times possest by one
That lives and dies a Beast.

7

Ps. 31:19.   If God bestow such gifts
    On bloody bruitish men:
1 *Cor.* 2:9.   Oh what great things hath he in store
    For his dear Childeren!
    No mortal eye hath seen,
    No Ear did ever hear,
    Nor Heart conceive, what Christ prepares
    For such as do him fear.

8

Phil. 3:8.   Earth's Treasures are but dung,
Amos 2:7.   And carnal Pleasures base,
    Unto those Joyes the Saints enjoy
    Before Christ's Royal face.
    The Richest Robes are Rags,
    And contemptible geer,
Mark 9:3.   Unto those bright and shining Robes
    The Saints in Glory wear.

9

	The stateliest Palaces,	65
2 Cor. 5:1-9.	If we should them compare	
	With those Celestial Mansions,	
	More vile then Hog-sties are.	
	What now we have in hope,	70
	We shall have in fruition,	
	When all ungodly men at once	
	Are drowned in Perdition.	

10

My Soul, rejoyce in God,
Who will enrich thee more
Then those, that of all Earthly wealth   75
    Cant. 2:16.   Possess the greatest store.
If thou be Christ's then He,
And all he hath is thine.
Oh feast thy self with these sweet thoughts
And with them sup and dine.   80

In Confinement Liberty

What may this Riddle mean?
Confined and yet free!
In Bands, yet Loose! A Prisoner,
And Yet at Libertee?
'Tis but a Notion sure;
No, No, It's very true,
And that these Pages following
Will prove and plainly shew.

Song I

1

    Most men live Libertie,
    And covet Elbow-room
To have their Wills, to serve their Lusts,
    And up and down to rome.
Rom 8:6, 7, 8.   God's Wayes they count a Prison,   5
    His Precepts and Commands
A heavy Yoke; his Threatenings
    Like Fetters and strong Bands.

2

Ps. 2:3.   Come let us break their Bands
    And cast their cords from us: 10
Let's give the Reins unto our Lusts,
    And not be Bridled thus.
John 8:34.   This Liberty of theirs
    The greatest Bondage is:
Rom. 6:16.   For he's a Bondslave unto Sin   15
    That loves to do amiss.

3

Eph. 2:2.   He is a Prisoner
    Unto his mortal Foe,
Who leads him bound with Cords of sin
    Unto Eternal woe.   20
    Such Prisoners may enjoy,
    External Libertie,
And being under no Restraint
    They run to Hell more free.

4

  Ah woful Liberty! 25
To such as it abuse;
Which leads them to Captivity,
Who their own Bondage chuse.
Prov. 5:22. I rather had be bound
With Fetters made of Brass, 30
Then to enjoy my Liberty
And be at such a pass.

5

Job 36:8, 9, 10. God bindeth some in Chains,
And in Afflictions Cords,
And by these Bands, unto their Souls 35
More Libertie affords.
Who would not be in thrall,
Soul-Liberty to gain,
Rather than Sins and Satan's thrall,
And Captive to remain? 40

6

  Manasseh was a slave
2 *Chron.* 33:10, 11, 12, To Sin and never free;
13, 15. Until his Foes had carried him
Into Captivitie:
But being bound in Chains, 45
He calls to mind his sins,
Humbleth himself, and to bewail
His former life begins.

7

  His Prison was a place
Of greatest Libertie: 50
For from the bondage of his sins
It helpt to set him free.
As Liberty abus'd
Procur'd his Misery:
So Bonds him humble and prepar'd 55
For blessed Liberty.

8

Jon. 1. While *Jonah's* stubborn will
Did over him prevail
It brought him down into the Deeps
And Belly of the Whale. 60
Jon. 2:10. That fearful Prison house
Him to Repentance brought,
And then for Body and for Soul
The Lord Salvation wrought.

9

Jer. 24:5, 6, 7. The Basket of good Figs 65
To *Babylon* were sent
In mercy that they might be freed
From sorer punishment.
That being humbled there
Under God's mighty hand, 70
He might return them back again
Into their Native Land.

10

Thus some that are in Bonds
By Bondage, get more free:
Others are fetter'd with their sins 75
That walk at Libertee.
His own Iniquity
Prov. 5:20. The wicked man shall take:
His sins like Cords, shall hold him fast,
And Satan's Prisoner make. 80

Song II

1

Though Liberty it self
Is greatly to be sought;
And they are happy that know how
To use it as they ought;
Especially whose hearts
Esteem and highly prize
And likewise carefully improve
Their Spiritual Liberties.

2

Yet when the Lord is pleas'd
Such freedom to deny,
He can another Freedome give
Ev'n in Captivity.
When he our Will subdues,
And helps us be content
With his dispose, there's Libertie
Even in Imprisonment.

3

Rom. 8:7, 8.

Ps. 119:45, 47.

2 *Cor.* 10:5.

Ps. 119:32.

Man's unsubdued Will
Is a most heavy Chain:
That man may walk at Liberty
That can this freedom gain.
When as the Will is brought
Into Captivity
Unto the holy Will of God;
This is sweet Liberty.

4

Phil. 4:11, 12, 13.

Let but the Will be broke;
Its Tyranny undone,
And other Bands that us restrain
Will quickly be as none.
For then the Soul applies
It self to get that good
Thereby, which God intends, and Christ
Hath purchas'd with his Blood.

5

Rom. 8:28.
Job 33:27;
36:8, 9, 10.

And God that can bring good
Out of the greatest ill,
If that we seek him seriously,
His Promise will fulfill.
He will unfetter us,
And set our Souls more free,
Ev'n by restraining Bands, from sin
And Satan's Tyranny.

35

40

6

Matt. 19:29.

2 *Cor.* 4:17, 18.

He'l wean us from the world,
And all things here below;
And better things instead of these
He will on us bestow.
He'l set our hearts upon
The things that are above:
And give us more and more to taste
The sweetness of his Love.

45

7

2 *Cor.* 5:14.

1 *John* 5:3.

He will enlarge our Souls
To run his Precepts way:
The love of Christ shall us restrain
Most gladly to obey.
And his Commandements
They shall delightful be.
Thus he can make Restraint a means
Of greatest Libertie.

50

55

8

Hos. 2:6, 7, 14.

God hedges up with thorns
The Path of Wanderers,
That have of Creature-comforts been
Too eager Followers,
Stops their pursuit, them brings
Into a Wilderness,
That thereunto their humble Souls
He may more Love express.

60

Song III

1

The Saints have never been
To meet with God more free,
Then when they have been most depriv'd
Of outward Libertee.
When Banished, Confined,
Impris'nd they have been,
They have God's Presence more enjoy'd
And more his Glory seen.

2

When *Jacob* fled from home
Because of *Esau's* spight,
And lay abroad i'th' open Aire,
Upon the Earth all night,
He saw that wondrous Ladder,
Whose top to Heaven raught,
Which Jesus Christ God-man, and our
Salvation by him taught.

Gen. 28:11, 12, 13.

3

Moses i'th' Wilderness,
During his Banishment,
Meets with the God of *Israel*,
And is to *Israel* sent
To carry welcome news
Of their deliverance,
And that the Lord would lead them forth
To their Inheritance.

Exod. 3:1, 2, 4-10.

4

Daniel i'th' Lions Den
Had Angels company.
And when those three were in the Fire,
The Son of God stood by.
John in his *Patmos*-Isle
Most glorious Visions had,
And Revelations of such things
As make God's *Sion* glad.

Dan. 6:22.

Dan. 3:23.

Rev. 1:9, 10, &c.

5

Acts 16:25, 26. While *Paul* and *Silas* sing
Together in the Stocks,
The Lord an Earthquake sends, and all   35
The Prison-doors unlocks.
Sundry sweet Visions
Had *Paul* in his Restraint:
Acts 23:11; 27:24. The Lord appearing to confirm
And cheer his Suffering Saint.   40

6

The time would fail to tell
Examples of this kind:
These are enough to prove, that Saints
May God in Prison find.
Where God is most enjoy'd,   45
There's sweetest Liberty:
But many have enjoy'd him most
In their Captivity.

7

Lord, let me more enjoy
Thy Presence in Restraint: 50
And then of wanting Liberty
I need not make complaint.
My Soul bring out of Prison,
That I thy Name may praise:
Ps. 142:7. Oh set my feet at liberty   55
To walk in Wisdom's wayes.

In Solitude Good Company

To be alone sometimes
And want no Company
Whilst men are Musing; this you'l say
Is no great Rarity.
But when we are alone 5
To have Good Company,
The best that ever man enjoy'd,
This is a Mystery.

How such a thing can be,
Although Religion teach it, 10
And many can discourse thereof,
Yet Nature cannot reach it.

Song I

1

    Man's Nature sociable
    Delights in Company,
Ps. 102:6, 7.   Declines and dreadeth Solitude,
    And loves Society.
    Hence to be stript of Friends 5
    And to be left alone,
Must needs be grievous in it self,
    A sore Affliction.

2

    But bitter though it be,
    God's presence can allay, 10
The bitterness of Sollitude
    And take it quite away.
    Our Saviour tells the twelve
    You all desert me will,
John 16:32.   Yet I am not alone, because 15
    The Father's with me still.

3

    And as he was with Christ
    So is he nigh to all
(For Christ his sake) that call on him,
    In truth that on him call. 20
    And he hath promised
Ps. 145:18.   To be with his always,
And that he never will forsake
Josh. 1:5.   Nor leave them all their dayes.

4

  That when they pass through fire   25
  Or water, he'll be there:
  The fire it shall not burn, nor floods
Lam. 43:2.   Them drown, 'cause he is near.
  He dwells i'th' burning Bush.
  To see the fire so blaze,   30
Exod. 8:2, 3.   And yet the Bush keep unconsum'd,
  Good *Moses* did amaze.

5

  Affliction, through a fire,
  God's Saints cannot devour;
  Because the Lord dwells in the Bush,   35
  And keeps it by his Power.
  The Lord is present still,
  And maketh his aboad
  With all true Saints; such Company
  Hath every Child of God.   40

6

  If any man me love
John 14:23.   He will my words obey;
  My father loves him: we will come
  And with him make our stay.
  The holy Spirit of Truth,   45
  That sweetest Comforter,
John 14:16.   He will for ever dwell with those
  That true Believers are.

7

  Oh glorious Priviledge
  Of such as God do fear!   50
Ps. 27:10.   Though other Friends forsake them, yet
  The Lord is always near.
  Christ holds them in his hand,
John 10:28, 29.   And none shall pluck them out:
  The Father, who is more than all,   55
  Them holds; they need not doubt.

8

    They dwell in Solitude,
    Are in a lonely case,
That have no int'rest in this God,
    Nor comfort from his Grace.   60
    For such poor souls as these,
    My heart could even bleed,
For when their Creature-comforts fail,
    They're left alone indeed.

9

    I can remember still   65
    That dismal Solitude,
The horrour of that Lonesomness,
    (And state of Widowhood)
    Wherein my Soul was once,
Prov. 15:29.   From God estranged farre: 70
That was a wilderness indeed:
    Such only Lonesome are.

10

    But he is not alone,
    That hath the Trinity,
The Father, Son, and Holy-Ghost,   75
    To keep him Company:
Isa. 61:3.   Such comforters as These,
    Can chear the Desolate,
Zeph. 3:14, 17.   And make them sing for joy who sit
    In solitary state.   80

11

Ps. 41:3.   When such a man is sick,
    The Lord will make his Bed;
Deut. 33:27.   And when he languisheth, his Arms
    Are underneath his head.
    And when he sits alone,   85
    The Lord will with him talk:
Or if he wander in the Woods
    His God will with him walk.

12

Ps. 3:5.	And when he lieth down
Ps. 4:8.	He may securely sleep: 90
	Because the Lord in his own Arms
	Will him most safely keep.
	He may repose himself
Ps. 91:1, 4, 5.	Under th' Almighty shade:
	And in the time of danger great 95
	He need not be afraid.

13

God watcheth over him
For good, and not for ill:
When he lies sleeping in his Bed,
The Lord is with him still. 100
And when he doth awake,
He may with God converse,
Ps. 139:18. Make known to him his wants, and all
His hearts desires rehearse.

14

Ps. 102:13. Who Truly pities him 105
Who can his wants supply,
Ps. 34:6, 7, 10. Support him in and bring him out
Of all his Misery.
Of Christ's redeemed one
This is the happy case, 110
1 *John* 1:3. To such high Fellowship as this
We are advanc'd through Grace.

15

Speak then all you that reade:
Can that man be alone,
That hath his God so near, to whom 115
He may his wants make known.
Ps. 73:75. Had ever any man
A better Friend then this?
Lord may I but enjoy thee more,
I others less shall miss. 120

16

Ps. 15:16, 17, 18.
O turn to me thy face,
And on me mercy show,
For I am in a lonely case
Afflicted poor also.
Mine heart straits be enlarg'd 125
Bring me out of distress,
My pain and my affliction see,
And all my sins release.

Song II

1

And now for such as are
Of dearest Friends bereft,
That in a Solitary state
Most desolate are left.
Oh might I speak a word 5
That might allay your grief,
Instruct you how to bear your Cross,
Or lend you some relief.

2

Suppose a Friend had lent thee,
A Stock at thy desire, 10
To make thy best improvement of,
Till he should it require.
Would'st think thy Friend unkinde,
For taking of his own,
When as in lending it at all 15
Great Courtesie was shown.

3

                Thy Wife, or Child, or Friend,
                They were but Blessings lent thee:
Ps. 24:1.   They were the Lords both first and last;
                And doth not this content thee?   20
Matt. 20:15.   May not the Lord require,
                When he sees fit, his own?
Job 1:21.   Thou may'st be thankful unto him
                They were no sooner gone.

4

                Hast thou a part in God?   25
                Canst him thy Father call?
John 20:17.   Assure thy self thou hast a Friend
                That doth surmount them all.
Ps. 27:10;   This Friend doth still remain,
102:17.   When other Friends are gone: 30
                Therefore thou needest not to mourn
                As if thou wert undone.

5

                But if thou hast not got
                Assurance of this Friend:
                Acquaint thy self with him in time   35
Job 22:21.   Who lives and loves to th' end.
                He is a better Friend
John 13:1.   Then Father, Mother, Wife,
                Or any other dearest Friend
                Thou hadst in all thy life.   40

6

                Let but Christ Jesus come
                And dwell within thy Heart,
Isa. 57:15.   And he will chear thee wondrously,
                And mitigate thy smart.
Ps. 68:5.   He will a Father be,   45
                Unto the Fatherless,
                A Husband to the Widow sad,
                A Judge in her distress.

7

Rev. 3:20. Behold! he stands and knocks,
 Haste, open speedily, 50
 And he'll come in and thou shalt sup,
 With him, and he with thee.
Ps. 21:7, 9. Lift up your Heads ye Gates,
 Ye Doors that last for ay
 Be ye lift up, that enter in 55
 The King of Glory may.

8

That Soul may change her chear:
 And be no longer sorry,
That entertaineth such a Guest
 Even the King of Glory. 60
Thou canst not be alone,
 Nor want Society:
When God the Father, Son and Spirit,
 Shall be thy Company.

This following song was penn'd
Eight years agone at least:
I hope it may be useful here
As any of the rest.

Song III

A Dialogue between the Flesh *and* Spirit

Flesh. 1

    Lord any Cross but this
       I'le be content to bear
    But oh I cannot part with one
       Whom I esteem so dear.
Sp. Shall mortal man presume
       His Maker to instruct?
    Or teach Jehovah in what Paths
       He shall his Soul conduct?

Job 40:2. (marginal)

2

    Unto the Lofty One
       Becomes it thee to say,
    I will not go to Heaven, Lord,
       In such a rugged way?
Fl. Alas! what means the Lord
       To chasten me so sore?
    I thought my load was great enough;
       And yet he layes on more.

Isa. 57:15. (marginal)

Spirit. 3

    God doth no more inflict
       Then he doth needful see:
    To need more load where was so much
       Should greatly humble thee.
    Had gentler Means prevail'd
       To make thee turn to God:
    'Tis like there would have been no need
       Of this more smarting Rod.

1 Pet. 1:6. (marginal)
Lev. 26:21. (marginal)

Flesh. 4

    What then? am I more vile
        Then all the world beside?
    That none but I in such a sort,
        That none but I am try'd.
Sp. 'Twere good thou wert more vile,
        At least in thine own eyes:
    Another's faults excuse not thine;
        Thy sin for vengeance cryes.

Flesh. 5

    But oh my loss is such
        As none have had but I.
    Did ever any feel the like
        To my Calamity?
    If every Circumstance
        Of mine Affliction
    Be weighed well; in such a Path
        I think no man hath gone.

Spirit. 6

    Thou may'st be much deceiv'd
        To think thy case more sad,
    And thine afflictions heavier
        Then ever any had.
    What if the way be such
        As never foot did tread?
    Some must go foremost, why not thou,
        As well as others lead.

7

    What if through uncouth wayes
        God make thee long to trace?
    If yet at least he bring thee safe
        Unto a resting place.
    Shalt thou not have good cause
        His mercy to adore?
    And to extoll and magnifie,
        His Name for evermore?

Side notes: Job 40:4.   Jer. 2:6, 7.

8

      Are not thy sins much more
Job 11:6.   Then all thy sufferings,
      And dost thou not deserve from God
      Ten times more bitter things?
      Small reason hath the man   60
      To murmure at the Cross,
Lam. 3:22, 39. Whom God might justly punish with
      Eternal Pain and Loss.

9

      Be silent then frail Flesh: 65
      Impatience hold thy Tongue
      And murmure not against the Lord
Job 34:10, 17. As if he did thee wrong.
      Justice can do no wrong,
      Nor mercy cruel be,   70
      Wisdom sees this condition
      To be the best for thee.

10

Rom. 8:28.   Love ordereth all for good
      Power hath undertaken
Ps. 41:3.   To give thee strength, and Truth hath said   75
Heb. 13:5.   Thou shalt not be forsaken:
      Take courage then my Soul,
      And moderate thy fears
Rev. 7:17.   For God himself who causeth grief
      Will wipe away thy tears.   80

11

1 *Pet.* 5:6.   Under his mighty hand
      Do though thy self abase,
Hos. 6:1, 2.   Return to him with all thine heart
      And sue to him for grace.
      Thy Darkness into Light   85
      He speedily will turn,
Isa. 57:15.   Who after-mercies hath in store
      To comfort them that mourn.

Joy in Sorrow

Can Joy and Sorrow Meet
That are so opposite?
The one so Bitter, th' other Sweet?
What, can such Foes unite?
What! meet in one small Heart! 5
And lovingly agree!
Joyn hands and strengthen one another!
Doubtless it cannot be.

Exod. 7:12.   *As* Aaron's Serpent-Rod
Rods of th' Inchanters swallow'd: 10
So godly Sorrow eateth up,
That Sorrow that's unhallow'd.
It worldly Sorrow kills:
But helpeth Spiritual Joy.
These two will strengthen one another, 15
And not each other 'stroy.

Isa. 61:3.   *The deepest godly Sorrow*
Spring-Tides of Joy brings in.
The more a soul can Joy in God,
The more he mourns for sin. 20

This Grief the Channel is
In which Joy loves to run,
And Joy the Channel deeper plowe
Then when 'twas first begun.
If any Nicodemus   25
Say How can these things be?
As Philip *to* Nathaniel *said,*
So I *say, come and see.*

Song I

1

Unto this General Head
We need not much to say.
For all that went before doth tend
Our Sorrows to allay.
Yet forasmuch as Grief
From various causes springs
Nor it is possible to name,
Each thing that Sorrow Brings.

2

Wee'll spend a few leaves more
Concerning Grief, th' Effect
That so we may apply a Salve
And no man's sore neglect.
If then thou art a Saint
That languisheth in Grief,
God hath provided Cordials
To yield thy soul relief.

3

Thou must these Cordials know
And how to take and use them
Beware thou do not in a pett,
Neglect, much less refuse them.
God would not have us Blocks
That nothing lay to heart,
Nor would he have us mourn like those,
In Christ that have no part.

4

	Perhaps thou hast displeas'd him,	25
	And therefore art in pain,	
1 *John* 1:7, 9.	But Jesus Christ will soon appease him,	
	If thou return again.	
	He is thy Father still,	
	And doth not cease to love thee,	30
	Although he scourge thee for thy faults	
	Or for thy sins reprove thee.	

5

Art thou in heaviness,
For some great outward loss?
Of choicest Comforts, dearest Friends,   35
Or for some other Cross?
Jer. 5:3.   'Tis fit that when God smites,
Thou shouldest feel the smart,
But let afflictions Bitterness,
Make thee lay sin to heart.   40

6

If this Affliction be
An evil bitter thing:
Jer. 2:19.   Oh what a bitter thing is sin,
That doth Affliction bring?
More evil is the Cause   45
Then the Effect can be:
Job 11:6.   For God doth punish less by far
Then thine iniquitie.

7

It is a bitter thing
To be in Heaviness?   50
What is it then to grieve the Lord,
Amos 2:13.   And with my sins to press?
To wrong a loving Father?
Deut. 32:6.   Provoke a gracious God
Lam. 3:33.   (Who takes no pleasure in our smart)   55
To whip me with his Rod?

8

	Convert thy Sorrow's stream
	Into the Channel right:
	And chiefly mourn because thou hast
Ps. 51:4.	Done evil in his sight.
2 Cor. 7:9, 10.	Thus into godly sorrow
	Thy worldly sorrow turn,
Jer. 31:18, 19, 20.	And God will turn away his wrath
	When thus he sees thee mourn.

9

As oftentimes we see
In some acute disease,
To cut a Vein and let him blood
Will give him present ease.
Right so doth godly Sorrow
The bleeding of the Heart
Asswage the most heart-killing Grief,
and wondrous ease impart.

10

	Empty Bad humours out;
	First cool and cleanse the Blood,
	And then a Cordial will revive
	And do the man more good.
Isa. 57:15.	So when thou humbled art,
	And purged from thy sin,
	The Lord himself will comfort thee,
	And Cordials sweet give in.

11

Luke 7:47, 50.	The deeper that the plow
	Of true Repentance goes,
	The richer Crop of spiritual joy
	And holiness there grows.
	The greater Spiritual joy,
	The Lord to us imparts,
Ezek. 3:31.	The more again it humbleth us,
	And breaks our stony hearts.

Song II

1

Hearken what God doth speak
To such as mourn aright,
That under his Afflicting hand
Are broken and contrite.
Matt. 5:4.   Blessed are those that mourn;   5
They shall be comforted:
As first in Sorrow, so in Joy
They shall be like their Head.

2

Thus saith the lofty One,
Isa. 57:15, 16.   Th' Eternal, Holy Lord;   10
I dwell in humble contrite Hearts,
That tremble at my Word:
Their Spirits to revive,
And greatly them to chear;
For I'le not always angry be,   15
With such as do me fear.

3

Yea Christ anointed is
To binde the broken heart;
Isa. 61:1, 2, 3.   To comfort such as mourn aright
And to relieve their smart.
Thou need'st not doubt, but that   20
Most seas'nably he will
In pity and in faithfulness
His office well fulfil.

4

	Hee'll heal thy broken heart	25
Ps. 146:8.	And up thy wounds will binde:	
	He will raise up the bowed down:	
	He to the Just is kinde.	
	Hee'll not cast off for ay:	
Lam. 3:31, 32.	But though grief cause he should,	30
	Yet will he have compassion	
	In's Mercies manifold.	

5

	Though Sorrow may abide	
Ps. 30:5.	And tarry for a night:	
	Comfort will come at break of day,	35
	And Joy at Morning light.	
	For Christ doth his support,	
	And comfort in distress:	
John 14:18.	He will not leave them Orphan-like,	
	All sad and comfortless.	40

6

John 14:16, 17.	Another comforter	
	He promiseth to leave,	
	His holy Spirit, whom the world	
	Knows not, nor can receive.	
	He shall abide with them,	45
	And them most Joyfull make:	
	And this their joy no mortal man,	
John 16:22.	Nor Dev'l shall from them take.	

7

Rom. 5:3.	In Tribulations great	
	He teacheth them to glory:	50
	And under Sufferings to rejoyce,	
	Which use to make them sorry.	
	When as their outward case	
1 *Pet.* 1:8.	Is most calamitous:	
	He can give joy unspeakable;	55
	And also glorious.	

8

But what they here enjoy
Is but a little taste,
Unto the Harvest of that joy
They shall receive at last.
Rom. 8:27.   These are but the first-fruits, 60
Joy's fulness is before
Ps. 16:11.   God's face and eke at his right hand
Are pleasures evermore.

Song III

1

This World's the Vale of Tears;
Ps. 23:4.   We must not look to be,
Whilst we are cloth'd with sinful flesh,
From griefs and sorrows free.
Here Grief and Joy take turns, 5
Hereafter Grief shall cease;
Isa. 35:10.   And in the room thereof shall come
Eternal Joy and peace.

2

If for a little moment
Isa. 54:7, 8.   God seem to frown upon thee, 10
With Everlasting kindnesses,
He will have mercy on thee.
Our time of suff'ring here
Is but a little while,
And then his frown, that makes thee sad, 15
Will turn into a smile.

3

        Thy Tears are like good Seed
        Sown in a Fruitful Field:
        They are not lost, but shall in time
        A joyful Harvest yield.   20
Ps. 126:5, 6.   Who sow in tears shall reap
        In joy: who go and mourn
        Bearing choice seed, shall sure with joy
        Bringing their sheaves return.

4

        In midst of Sorrows great   25
        Let this thy grief allay,
Rev. 7:17.   That God will turn thy tears to joy
        And mirth another day.
        The more thy Sorrows here
        And Sufferings have bin: 30
        The greater joy and Happiness
        Hereafter thou shalt win.

5

        'Tis better now to mourn
        And to rejoyce hereafter:
        Then for to wail eternally   35
        For sinful mirth and laughter.
Rev. 18:7.   Short sinful Pleasures have
        Long-lasting endless pains:
2 *Cor.* 4:17.   Short and light suff'rings have long joyes
        And everlasting gains.   40

6

        Eternal Happiness
        Will make amends for all.
2 *Cor.* 4:18.   While Faith beholds what joy's to come,
        It counts all suff'ring small.
        If drops of Heav'nly Pleasure   45
        Be sweet unto thy taste:
Ps. 36:8, 9.   How sweet will steams and rivers be,
        Where drink thy fill thou mayst?

7

               Thy future joy so great
                 And Ocean-like shall be: 50

Matt. 25:21.   That thou must enter into it,
                 It cannot enter thee.
               Oh what a joy is that
1 *Cor.* 2:9.   That Thought cannot conceive!
                 That mortal Tongue cannot express,   55
                 Nor Heart of man believe!

8

        The greatest present Griefs,
        That thee so much annoy,
Will soon be swallowed in that Sea
        Of Everlasting joy.   60
        'Twill then a Pleasure be,
        To think of what is past:
And greatly adde unto thy joy
        To mind how sad thou wast.

Song IV

Solamen miseris socios habuisse doloris
Christum cum sanctis-- *

1

        It is an ease in Grief
        to have Co-partners
It yields some comfort and relief
        T'have Fellow-sufferers.
        Especially to have   5
        Such as our case bemoan,
As lay to heart our sorrows, and
        Under our Burden groan:

2

Eph. 4:4, 5, 6.	The saints all make one body	
	Have Union with one Head,	10
	Are acted by one spirit, and	
	By him are quickened.	
Heb. 13:3.	Hence then they cannot chuse,	
	But feel each others smart,	
	Their Burden bear, Lament their case,	15
	And in their woes take part.	

*"It is a comfort to unhappy people to have had allies in grief: Christ with holy things--"

3

 They cannot chuse but mourn
  With such as mourners be:
Rom. 12:15. And be afflicted too with those
  Whom they afflicted see. 20
John 11:16. Christ gives them tender hearts,
  Therefore they fellow-feel:
 They pitty, pray for, comfort them,
  And seek each others weal.

4

 This is a Comfort then 25
  To Saints in misery,
 To have such sweet Companions
  Of their Calamity.
 That when they are in sorrow
  They sorrow not alone: 30
 But meet with some that heartily
  Their Miseries bemoan.

5

 O let it never be
  That Saints should Saints infest,
James 3:15. And add unto each others grief, 35
  That are with grief opprest.
 This wisdom from above
  Comes not, but from beneath:
 And ill becometh those in whom
  The Spirit of Love doth breath. 40

6

 That Spirit of Love and Peace,
  Who dwells in all the Saints,
 Unite our hearts, appease our strife,
2 Cor. 13:11. Cease quarrels and complaints:
Job 6:14. Help us to pity more, 45
  And pray for one another,
Phil. 2:1, 2, 3. To strive who shall in love outstrip
  And go beyond his brother.

7

	This were a blessed strife;	
Eph. 4:16.	Thus ought we all to strive:	50
	Were this our strife; how would it make	
	Souls, Towns, and Churches thrive.	
	As many shoulders make	
	A heavy Burden light:	
	So might our Burdens lightened be,	55
	Were but our Spirits right.	

8

	Well, Friends may pity us	
	And at our Sorrows grieve;	
	They cannot alwayes help: But Christ	
	Can pity and relieve.	
	This is the main support,	60
	And comfort of the Saints,	
Ps. 103:13.	That Jesus Christ them pittieth when	
	They pour out their complaints.	

9

Ps. 38:11.	Friends sometimes stand aloof,	65
	And Bretheren may forget us,	
	Of strangers be unto our Griefs,	
Ps. 136:23.	The World at naught may set us:	
	But Jesus Christ regards us	
John 14:18.	Ev'n in our low estate:	70
	He minds us well, and leaves us not	
	Forlorn and desolate.	

10

Heb. 2:17, 18;	Our gracious, great High-Priest	
4:15.	Is such an One as can	
	From his Experience pitty us	75
	With bowels of a Man.	
Isa. 63:9.	Afflicted been he has	
	In their Affliction;	
	And therefore their Affliction was	
	As if it had been none.	80

11

Though far above all Griefs
In Glory Christ remains:
Yet of the Sorrows of his Saints
A feeling he retains.
Ps. 56:8.   He tells our wanderings,   85
And bottleth all our tears,
Is well acquainted with our griefs,
And writeth down our fears.

12

He knows thy Sicknesses;
He feeleth all thy smart: 90
Thy sufferings are his sufferings,
And reach his tender heart.
And if he know and feel
All that doth thee agrieve:
Isa. 40:1, 2, 29, 31.   He will with choicest Cordials   95
Thy fainting Soul relieve.

13

Col. 1:24.   If these thy Sufferings
He reckon to be his:
John 14:3.   He'll shortly put an end thereto,
And take thy Soul to Bliss.
Christ will not suffer long: 100
For he's not perfected,
1 *Cor.* 15:49.   Till all his Members be made like
In Glory to their Head.

Song V

1

Thus far we have apply'd
Our Speech to mournful Saints,
To chear them under all their Griefs,
And silence their Complaints.
But all men are not Saints
Whom Sorrow doth oppress:
Some may be in a heavy case,
Yet far from Holiness.

2

Hos. 7:14.

Some Hearts are almost broke
With Carnal Sorrows force;
That godly Sorrow never touch'd
With any true remorse.
What shall we say to these
That may some ease impart?
What Soveraign Medicine shall we use
To mitigate their smart?

3

Pour Souls! I pity you,
And do your case bemoan:
But peace to you I may not speak,
For God himself speaks none.

Isa. 57:20, 21.

There is no peace saith God,
To th' wicked when distrest,
But they are like the Troubled Sea,
Which boils and cannot rest.

4

Oh that the Lord himself,
Who now doth thee chastise,
And makes thee sad, would waken thee,
And open thy blind eyes!
That God would help thee grieve,
For what should grieve thee most!

Jer. 3:13, 21.

That thou a wretched sinner art,
That thou thy God hast lost.

5

    Thou hast not him to go to,
      When sorrows thee agrieve.
Lam. 1:16.   The Comforter is far away,   35
      That should thy Soul relieve.
    Thou hast offended God,
      And grieved him full sore,
Zech. 12:10.   And now he grieveth thee; let this,
      Grieve and ashame thee more.   40

6

    Could'st thou but lay to heart,
      Thy sinful woful state,
    It quickly would thine other griefs
      Asswage and mitigate.
    Oh get thy worldly grief   45
      Turned to Godly sorrow,
    Mourn for thy sins, and put not off
      Repentance till to morrow.

7

Hos. 14:2, 3, 4.   Oh turn from every sin,
      To God with all thine heart,   50
    And make thy peace with him through Christ,
Acts 10:43.   In Christ, Oh get a part.
    If sorrow bring thee home,
Job 33:23, 24, 30.   To God in Christ believe
    It will the happiest grieving be,   55
      That ever thou didst grieve.

8

Hos. 6:1, 2.   For God that wounded thee,
      Thy Soul will also heal:
Isa. 1:16, 17, 18.   And unto thee his gracious love,
      In Christ he will reveal.   60
    Oh therefore haste to Christ!
      That so thou may'st not mourn,
    Like unto them that have no hope,
      Because they never turn.

Life in Deaths

What Mystery is this
To seek for Life in Death,
The great Destroyer of the Sons
Of Adam *and of* Seth?
Can Death *beget sweet Life?* 5
Can such an Honey-comb,
So sweet and precious, come forth
Of Death's devouring Womb?

Yes: Christ hath broke the Teeth
And ta'ne away the Sting 10
Of Cruel Death; that Death is now
Become another thing.
It is a Messenger
Sent for to fetch us home
Unto our Father's Royal House, 15
Whither all Saints must come.

It is a Bridge whereby
We pass to Heavenly Rest,
Out of the Sorrows of this World
Wherewith we are opprest. 20
But I'le not here detain thee:
Read on, and thou shalt see
Both many Deaths in one short Life,
And Life in Deaths to be.

Song I

1

This World's a Wilderness
To God's afflicted Saints:
A place of Dangers, Fears, and Foes;
A place of Woes and Wants.
This Life's a very Death, 5
At least a dying life:
For this is Death in Life, to find
Sin in our Hearts so rife.

2

Rom. 17:23.   That we not only are
Encompassed with Foes: 10
But have a treacherous Part within
That doth with Satan close.
That's ready to seduce
And lead us into Evil,
And on sudden to betray 15
Our souls unto the Devil.

3

We pestered are with Sin,
So long as here we live,
Which makes us cry, From this vile death
Rom. 17:24.   Who will deliverance give. 20
Bodies of Sin and Death,
We carry to and fro,
And carry must unto our grief,
Whil'st we are here below.

4

Rom. 17:23.   We find a Law of sin,   25
 Within our Members dwelling,
 Which is against God's holy law.
 (Chose by our mind) rebelling.
 So that we cannot do
 The good things that we would,   30
 And oftentimes we do those things
 Which leave undone we should.

5

 For though we mourn for sin
 And watch, and strive and fight,
 Yet is our weakness often foil'd,   35
 By Satan's subtile sleight.
 This is a heaviness,
 A Death unto the Saints,
Rom. 7:18, 19.   Whereof the best while here on Earth,
 Make sorrowful complaints.   40

6

 Oh what a glorious thing,
 In all true Christians eyes
Rom. 7:24.   Would full deliverance be from sin,
 They would this freedom prize.
 More then the richest mines   45
 Or most resplendent Gems,
 They would prefer it far before,
 Scepters and Diadems.

7

Ps. 19:9, 10, 12.   It would be richer Gains
 Then Honour, pleasure, Wealth;   50
Ps. 119:5, 71, 72.   It would be sweeter to their Souls,
 Then Libertie or Health.
 Yea Temp'ral life it self,
 Might not herewith compare,
 Which is more worth then all things else   55
 Which most esteemed are.

8

Who would not then be willing,
When Christ him calleth hence,
To lay aside this sinful Flesh,
Cause of so much offence? 60
What Saint that hateth sin,
Can love his life so well
As for the sake thereof to chuse
In sinful Flesh to dwell?

Song II

1

Heb. 12:23.	This then is Life in Death,
	That Death will set us free
1 *John* 3:2.	From Sin, which is our spiritual Death,
	And greatest miserie.
	We shall no more be griev'd 5
Rev. 21:27.	With minds that are so vain.
	Of Pride, or Sloth, or Worldiness,
	We shall no more complain.

2

	Our Ignorance shall cease
1 *Cor.* 13:10, 12.	So shall our Unbelief, 10
	Our passions shall no longer be
	A cause of daily grief.
	Against God's providence
	Our hearts no more shall swell,
	Nor these our unsubdued wills 15
	Against his Will rebell.

3

    Our Senses shall no longer
      Be in-lets unto sin.
Nor shall there be an home-bred Thief,
      To let his Comrades in.   20
    God, whom we here offend,
      And injure every day
In thought, word, deed, we shall no more
      Offend him then for ay.

4

    During this mortal life   25
      We walk in midst of snares,
And we are apt to be surpriz'd
      And caught at unawares.
Luke 22:31.   Our subtile enemy
      Us every hour besets,   30
Seeks to allure us by his baits
      Into his deadly nets.

5

    He like a roaring Lion
1 *Pet.* 5:8.   Runs hunting for his prey,
Gen. 3:1, 2, &c. And like a subtile Serpent he   35
      Lies watching night and day:
    Lets no advantage slip,
      Whereby he may annoy us,
Draw us to sin, disturb our peace:
      Distress if not destroy us.   40

6

    Death is the Red Sea, which
      When once we are got through,
Exod. 14:13, 28, 29. *Pharoah* (the Divel) with his Host,
      Can us no more pursue.
    God will this sea divide   45
      And make it us inclose,
Like walls, letting us pass through safe;
      And then drown all our foes.

7

Th' Egyptians cannot follow
   Unto the other side,   50
They shall be drowned in the Sea,
   O'rewhelmed with the Tide.
The Tempter shall no more
   A wicked thought suggest,
Nor once entice to any thing   55
   That God and wee detest.

8

Temptations unto sin
   (Which vex us here so sore,
Although they do not master us,)
   Shall trouble us then no more.   60
Then shall our joyful souls,
   Eternal praises sing,
For this their full deliverance
   To that immortal King.

Song III

1

              Whil'st we are here on Earth
                 We're dying every day:
1 *Cor.* 15:31.   Each day brings some new woe or grief
                 Whilst we are cloth'd with Clay.
Matt. 6:34.   We dwell in midst of Deaths   5
                 And Death amidst us dwells,
              As too too well appeareth by
                 These daily doleful Knells.

2

  Now one dear Friend departs,
  E're long another goes: 10
Whose turn comes next, or mine, or thine,
  Or whose, God only knows.
Acts 20:37, 38.   Thus we are oft constrain'd
  The pains of Death to 'bide:
2 Cor. 12:29. For Death doth often wound our Heart   15
  Through one or other's side.

3

  Pains, Losses, Sicknesses,
  Temptations, Sorrows, Sin,
All these are daily deaths from which
  We can no Freedom win,   20
  Until we die our last:
  One death will end them all,
And set our Souls at liberty,
  Which here are held in Thrall.

4

  The pains of Life together   25
  Amount to no small pain:
Rom. 8:22, 23. Who would not one Pain more endure
  And get free from all pain?
Job 14:14.   But we must stay God's time,
  And wait till he shall call,   30
And then one Death will set us free
  From Pains and Sorrows all.

5

Rev. 21:4.   Then once for all we die,
  That die we may no more,
2 Cor. 5:1. But live in bliss Eternally   35
  The face of God before.
Rev. 14:13.   Death is of life the Gate,
  It is the Door whereby
We enter shall into a state
  Of immortality.   40

6

  This then our comfort is,
  This is our Life in Death,
To know our Soul shall be in bliss,
  When Death hath stopt our breath.
1 Cor. 15:43.   And that this body vile   45
  That now is laid in Dust,
Phil. 3:21.   And turn'd to earth within a while
  Be rais'd in Glory must.

7

  So soon as Death hath clos'd
  Our mortal bodie's eyes,   50
Luke 16:22.   Our soul shall mount with greatest speed
  Above the Starry Skies.
  Born upon Angel's wings
  Unto that heavenly rest,
Matt. 25:46.   Whereof Eternal happiness,   55
  She shall be full possest.

8

1 Cor. 15:55, 56.   O Death where is thy sting,
  Thy Victory O Grave?
How art thou conquered, and made
  Our servant, yea our slave.   60
  Thanks be to God who giveth us,
  Through Christ the Victory
That we may live to praise his name,
  For this Eternally.

Heavenly Crowns for Thorny Wreaths

Song I

1

Matt. 27:29, 30.
When Christ was crown'd with Thorns,
And smitten with a Reed
Upon the Thorns, to wound his Head
And for to make him bleed;
The world did little think   5
This was the King of Glory:
So when we speak of Crowns for Thorns,
They think it's but a story.

2

But as our Lord doth now
His Crown of Glory wear;   10
Who for our sake did wear those Thorns,
And such abuses bear;
So shall th' Afflicted Saints
That suffer for his sake
E're long be Crowned like their Head,   15
And of his Joyes partake.

3

Those that for doing well,
For keeping Christ's Commands,
For bearing witness to his Truth
Suffer Reproach or Bands,   20
Rev. 7:14, 15, 16, 17. Or any other Pain
To keep their Conscience pure;
Such of a glorious Recompence
And rich Reward are sure.

4

  Those that are persecuted   25
  Because of Righteousness,
  Are Blessed ones, saith Christ, for they
Matt. 5:10, 11, 12.   Heav'ns Kingdom shall possess.
  And Blest are ye whom men
  Revile and persecute,   30
  To whom for my sake heinous Crimes
  They wrongfully impute.

5

  Rejoyce and be ye glad
  Hereat exceedingly;
  Because there is a great Reward   35
  Laid up for you on high.
  For thus they persecuted
  The Prophets that of old
  Reprov'd their sins, and faithfully
  God's Counsel to them told.   40

6

Mark 10:29, 30.   Who Father, Mother, Wife,
  For love of Christ forsakes
  Or of his houses, Lands, Estate,
  For him small reckoning makes,
  Shall here an hundred fold   45
  With persecutions gain;
  And in the world that is to come
  Eternal Life obtain.

7

2 *Tim.* 2:11, 12.   If in a suff'ring state
  Of Christ we followers be   50
  We shall be unto him conform'd
  In Royal dignitie.
Matt. 19:28.   Those that have stuck to Christ
  In Tribulations great
  Shall reign with Christ, and sit with him   55
  Upon his Judgment seat.

8

  But those that suffer pain
   Foul Errours to defend,
  That for vile Fancies of their own
   Dread not their lives to spend   60
  Such do in vain suppose
   They suffer for Christ's sake.
  'Tis not the Suff'ring but the cause
   That doth a Martyr make.

Song II

1

  That Eminent Apostle
   And holy Martyr *Paul*,
  That laboured more for Jesus Christ,
   And suffered more than All,
  When as his race was run   5
   And life almost laid down
2 *Tim.* 4:8.   For Christ. Henceforth, saith he, there is
   Laid up for me a Crown,

2

  Which Christ that Righteous Judge
   Shall give to me above: 10
  And unto all as well as me,
   That his Appearing love.
  Christ Jesus at that day
   Will all Believers own:
Matt. 25:34, 35.   And all their faithful Services   15
   And patient Sufferings crown.

3

  Not only such as have
  For Jesus shed their Blood;
John 8:31, 32. But all that have embrac'd the Truth
  And firm therein have stood. 20
Matt. 11:29. All that have meekly born
  Christ's Yoke because 'twas his
  Shall be rewarded, and shall share
  In Everlasting Bliss.

4

  Although some Stars outshine 25
1 *Cor.* 15:41. The rest in Glory bright:
  Yet every Star i'th' Firmament
  Is full of glorious light.
  So every vessel then
  Shall full of Glory be, 30
  Though some are of a larger size,
  Some of a less degree.

5

  Our Lord will call to mind
  The meanest services
Matt. 19:42. That any man with upright heart 35
  Hath done for one of his:
  So that a Cup of Water
  Tender'd unto a Saint
  For love of Christ, shall not reward
  Nor accpetation want. 40

6

Heb. 6:10 Much less will Christ forget
compared with Their love and labour sure
Heb. 10:32, 323. That take great pains, and for his sake
  Afflictions long endure.
  He that will smallest things 45
  So graciously regard,
  Will not far greater things neglect
  And leave without reward.

7

Acts 9:4, 5.	As in his suffering saints	
	Christ suffereth now; so he	50
2 *Thess.* 1:10.	In all his glorified saints	
	Will glorified be.	
	Their sufferings now are his,	
	Their Glory will be his:	
	Christ should his Glory lose, if saints	55
	Should future Glory miss.	

8

Isa. 53:4, 5, &c.	Christ's precious sufferings,	
	And whole Obedience,	
Gal. 3:13, 14.	Have purchased for us this Crown	
	And glorious Recompence.	60
Rev. 1:5, 6.	He dy'd that we might live,	
	Wore Thorns that we might reign	
	The end of his own sufferings	
	Christ, doubtless will obtain.	

9

	As surely then as He	65
	Reproach and Shame endur'd,	
	And by his Sufferings hath for us	
	A glorious Crown procur'd;	
	As sure as we him follow	
	In patient suffering here;	70
2 *Tim.* 2:11, 12.	So certainly this glorious Crown	
	We shall hereafter wear.	

Song III

1

	How great this Glory is	
	Nor mortal tongue can tell:	
Isa. 64:4.	But that it far exceeds our thoughts	
	And words we know full well.	
Rom. 5:10.	'Tis that which Christ's own Blood	5
	Hath purchas'd and acquir'd:	
2 Thess. 1:10.	'Tis that which God will then bestow	
	That he may be admir'd.	

2

Isa. 55:8.	God's ways are not like ours,	
	Nor are his thoughts like our:	10
Eph. 1:6, 14.	For he will glorifie his Grace	
	And magnifie his Power,	
Rev. 5:12.	Yea and his Wisdom too	
	By glorifying us,	
	And therefore Christ will make his saints	15
	Exceeding glorious.	

3

	That glory must be great	
	And of surpassing fame	
Isa. 55:13.	Which God bestows to get himself	
	An Everlasting Name.	20
Rom. 9:23.	They shall be crown'd indeed	
	With Glory at that day,	
	When as the richness of their Crown	
	God's Glory must display.	

4

Isa. 62:3.	When every saint shall be	25
	A Diamond in Christ's Crown:	
	They must be glorious saints indeed,	
	To set forth his Renown.	
Dan. 13:3.	The saints shall shine like suns	
	Array'd with glorious light,	30
Matt. 13:43.	That thro' their lustre Christs own Beams	
	May shine more clear and bright.	

5

O glorious rich Free-grace!
And Everlasting Love,
That God's own heart unto these thoughts
Before all time did move!
O wondrous Condescension
Eph. 3:18, 19.   Of God's most gracious Son!
And matchless Love of Jesus Christ
Beyond comparison!

6

Who for our sake was pleas'd
Phil. 2:5, 7, 8.   Under a mean outside,
Under the Garment of frail Flesh
His Majesty to hide:
Who wore a Crown of Thorns,
Who shed his dearest Blood,
Who bare his Fathers Wrath for us
Isa. 53:5.   To purchase saving Good,

7

That he might us Redeem
Rev. 5:9, 10.   From endless Misery,
Rom. 5:17, 18, 19, &c.   And by his sufferings us advance
To Heavenly Dignity.
He was content to be
Abus'd, Reproach'd and scorn'd,
That we might be advanced, crown'd,
And gloriously adorn'd.

8

That such as have deserv'd
God's vengeance for to bear
Eternally, should Royal Robes
And Crowns of Glory wear?
Saints can you think of this
And not this Grace admire?
And do not you that are no saints
To share therein desire?

                    9

	Which is the better choice?	65
Deut. 30:17.	With Christ in Bliss to dwell,	
	Or for to roar eternally	
	Amidst the flames of Hell?	
Compare Mark 9:43, 44	What? are you in a doubt	
with Phil. 1:23.	Which of the twain to chuse?	70
	Well, chuse to burn, if that be best:	
	Chuse Hell, and Heaven refuse.	

                    10

This were a fearful choice.
What then? Will you be wise?
Oh be so; get a part in Christ: 75
Him love, him seek, him prize.
Matt. 11:28, 29.   Receive him with his Cross;
His Yoke with meekness bear:
Rom. 5:17.   And then Free-Grace will give you Crowns
Of Glory for to wear.   80

Song IV

                    1

Behold what matchless Love
The God of Heaven shows,
1 *John* 3:1, 2.   To those on whom Eternal Life
And Glory he bestows!
If now God calls them Sons;   5
How glorious shall they be,
When being made like Christ, they shall
Him in his Glory see?

2

  Their Body frail and vile,
   That's in Corruption sown,   10
  Shall then be raised up again
   In Incorruption.
  This Mortal must be cloth'd
   With Immortality:
  And then shall Death be swallowed up 15
   In perfect Victory.

3

1 Cor. 15:42, 43, 44.

  It is at present sown
   A Body Natural:
  But shall arise again e're long
   A Body Spiritual.   20
  We now need many helps
   Our vigour to maintain,
  As Meat, Drink, Sleep: but shall need none
   After we rise again.

4

  It's now in weakness sown;   25
   But shall be rais'd in power:
  Sown in Dishonour: but shall rise
   In Glory at that hour.
  It shall be wholly freed
   From all Infirmities,   30
  And be most active, hale, and strong
   When once it doth arise.

5

  Though subject to Reproach
   Whil'st living; and when dead
  Must needs be carried out of sight, 35

Gen. 23:4.

   And quickly buried:
  Yet Christ shall raise it up

Phil. 3:21.

   With Beauty shining bright,
  More lovely then the Morning fair,
   With Heavenly Glory dight.   40

6

  And if the Body shew
  So beautiful and fair:
  How shall the Soul be beautify'd
  And shine beyond compare?
Rev. 21:11, 18, 19. Adorn'd with costly Robes, 45
  More precious far then Gold,
  Of Christ's unspotted Righteousness
Rev. 19. Most lovely to behold.

7

  When as God's blessed Image
  That was defac'd by Sin 50
  Is perfectly restor'd again
  And ever dwells therein.
1 John 3:2. When as it shall behold
  God's Glory shining bright,
2 Cor. 3. And be transform'd and glorious made 55
  By that most glorious sight.

8

  When like a Glass it shall
  Receive those glorious Rayes,
  And back again reflect the same
  To God's Eternal Praise. 60
  When in the Sea of Bliss
  It constantly shall move:
  And be for ever ravish'd with
  The sweetness of his Love.

9

Exod. 34:29, 30. If *Moses* face did shine 65
  By being forty daies,
  I'th' Mount: how shall their faces shine,
  That dwell with God alwayes;
  Moses his Back-parts saw
  But they shall see his face, 70
  And to their joy unspeakable
  Enjoy the God of grace.

10

      Oh happy, happy Souls
        That in God's bosome rest!
      That of the fountain of all bliss   75
        Already are possest!
      Your Labour's at an end
        Your seed in tears was sown,
2 *Tim.* 4:7, 8.   But now you reap a joyful Crop,
        And wear a Glorious Crown.   80

11

      We that are still below
        Have much work yet undone,
1 *Tim.* 6:12.   A War to wage, sharp thorns to wear,
        A painful race to run.
1 *Cor.* 9:24, 25.   Lord help us so to run,   85
        As that we may obtain:
      That when this life is at an end
        We may in Glory reign.

Song V

1

Heb. 12:12.   Our Saviour, for the joy
        That was before him set,
      Endur'd the Cross, despis'd the shame,
        And paid for all our debt.
      And as himself did eye   5
        The future glorious 'state:
      So would we have the thoughts thereof
        Our souls to animate.

2

To him that hath begun
And will compleat our Faith, 10
We are commanded for to look;
Who thus despised hath
The Ignominious shame
For that most glorious joy;
And having suffered is set down 15
At God's right hand on high.

3

And though some Gospellers
Call this an Hireling Spirit:
Yet more of such a Sprite, Lord,
Grant that we may inherit. 20
For surely thou didst more
Thy Father's Glory prize,
Then these, that at this rich Reward
Would seem to shut their eyes.

4

Oh but the love of Christ 25
Should wholly us constrain
To do all duties, bear the Cross,
And suffer every Pain.
Compare True; and the love of Christ
Matt. 25:34, 35 In this most strongly moves us, 30
with Titus 3:4, 5, 6, 7. That he'l regard us, and thus reward us
Meerly because he loves us.

5

If Christ hath purchased
A glorious rich Reward
For all his Followers: shall not we 35
This Recompence regard?
If he Rewards propound
To whet our diligence:
Is not our over-looking them
The way to Negligence? 40

6

Heb. 11:24, 25, 26.	Unto this Recompence
	Moses had such respect,
	That all the Glory of the world,
	He could for this reject.
	Esteeming Christ's reproach 45
	More rich then *Egypt's* treasures,
	Chusing affliction with God's church
	Rather then sinful pleasures.

7

	Since then we do expect
2 *Pet.* 3:14.	Such glorious things as these 50
	How ought we to bestir ourselves
	So good a God to please.
	How should the ways of Christ
	Most pleasant to us seem?
Rom. 8:18.	How should this make the heaviest Cross, 55
	Grow light in our esteem.

8

	Oh let the thoughts of this
	Incorruptible Crown,
	Which shall on patient suffering saints
	So frankly be bestown, 60
Heb. 12:1, 2.	Effectually perswade us
	For to amend our pace,
	And with more chearfulness and speed,
	To run our heavenly race.

9

	More readily to do 65
	And willingly to bear
	Whatever Christ shall call us to
	So long as we are here,
	Knowing that all our pains
1 *Cor.* 15:58.	Though worthless, poor, and vile, 70
	Shall such a rich reward obtain
	Within a little while.

10

How many men can wade
Up to the knees in Blood
To win an Earthly kingdom, which 75
Can do them little good,
Which brings them nought but sorrow,
Which cannot satisfie,
Which may be lost before to Morrow
And must be, when they die. 80

11

And shall not we take pains:
1 Cor. 9:14, 25.   To win a heavenly Crown,
Which having once through grace obtain'd
Shall ever be our own?
1 Pet. 4-10.   A glorious massie Crown, 85
A rich Inheritance,
That's undefil'd, that never fades,
Not Subject unto chance.

12

Good Lord increase our Faith:
And help us to believe, 90
That thou wilt such a rich Reward
To all thy Servants give.
2 Cor. 5:14, 15.   And let this love constrain us
To give our selves to thee:
Thou hast us bought and thine we are, 95
Thine let us ever be.

13

Rev. 1:5, 6.   *Now unto him that lov'd us*
And wash'd us from our sins
With his own Blood, and made us Priests
To God, and also Kings; 100
That we might live and reign
The face of God before;
To him be Glory, Honour, Power,
Both now and evermore.

Amen.

Be chearful Suffering Saint,
Let nothing cast thee down:
Our Saviour Christ e're long will turn
Thy Cross into a Crown.

OCCASIONAL VERSE

Latin and English Verses Composed about 1660, during the Early Years of Wigglesworth's Extended Illness

Christe, Parum doleo quia Te non diligo multum:
Quodque Parum doleo, causa Doloris Erit.*

Ira premit, Peccata gravant, afflicto frangit;
    Omnia Sub caelo me quoque destituunt.
Aeger, Inops, Orbus, curarum pondere fessus,
    Corpore Languescens, Deficiens Animo.
Obruor adversis; Succedunt imbribus imbres,
    Meque Simul feriunt, Ventus at unda minax.**

My *Sins* & *Wants* still pain my Heart,
My *Hope* in Christ, relieves my Smart.

---

*   "Christ, I grieve too little, for I do not love you much:
    That I grieve too little, will be a cause of grief."

**   "Anger crushes me, Sins weigh me down, afflictions break me;
    All things under Heaven also abandon me.
    Sick, Helpless, Bereft, weary from the weight of cares,
    Languishing in body, Failing in spirit.
    I am overwhelmed by adversities; Rains follow on rain-storms,
    Wind and threatening wave strike me at the same time.

"When as the wayes of Jesus Christ"

Composed about 1665

1

When as the ways of Jesus Christ
    Are counted too precise,
Not onely by some Babes or fooles,
    But also by the wise:
When men grow weary of the yoke   5
    Of godly discipline,
And seek to burst those golden barres
    Which doe their lusts confine:

2

When some within, and some without,
    Kick down the Churches wall   10
Because the doore is found to be
    Too strait to let in all:
The best can then nought else expect
    But to be turned out,
Or to be trampled under foot   15
    By the unruly rout.

3

When as the foxes and wilde Boares
    Come in to dress the Vine,
The vinyard then is like to yield
    But very little wine.   20
When as the Sheep shall with the woolves
    For carnall ends comply,
If my Conjecture faile mee not
    They'l slaughter get thereby.

4

When Godly men cannot agree,
    But differing mindes bewray,
And by their fell dissensions
    Shall make themselves a prey:
Then O New England is the time
    Of thy sad visitation;
And that is like to be the yeer
    Of Gods fierce indignation.

5

When some shall strive to scrue the rest
    To their own apprehensions
In things where difference might be born,
    Then look for sad contentions.
For those that conscientiously
    From others doe dissent,
Against their consciences to act,
    Will never be content.

6

When of their Shepheards faithfulness
    The sheep suspitious grow
Or slight & undervalue them
    To who they reverence ow:
Or when the Shepheards force the sheep
    Where danger doth appeare,
Then both to Shepheards and to sheep
    Calamity is neere.

7

When Joshua and Zerubbabel
    Are thought for carnall ends
To favour the Samaritans
    By some of their best friends:
When such uncharitable thoughts
    Make many hearts to swell:
God grant them grace to act their part,
    Both warily and well.

Upon the much Lamented Death of that Precious
servant of Christ, Mr. Benjamin Buncker, pastour
of the Church at Maldon, who deceased
on the 3d of ye 12th moneth 1669

Mr Buncker's Character

    He was another Timothie
        That from his very youth
    With holy writt, acquainted was
        And vers't i'th' word of truth.
    Who as he grew to riper yeers   5
        He also grew in Grace:
    And as he drew more neer his End,
        He mended still his Pace.

    He was a true Nathaniel,
        Plain-hearted Israelite,   10
    In whom appear'd sincerity
        And not a guilefull sp'rite,
    Serious in all he went about
        Doing it with his Heart,
    And not content to put off Christ   15
        With the Externall part.

    He was most sound and Orthodox,
        A down-right honest Teacher,
    And of soul-searching needfull Truths
        A zealous, painfull Preacher.   20
    And God his pious Labours hath
        To many hearers blest,
    As by themselves hath publiquely
        Been owned & confest.

He hath in few yeers learned more, 25
 And greater progress made
In Christianity, then some
 That thrice the time have had.
A humble, broken-hearted man
 Still vile in his own eyes 30
That from the feeling of his wants
 Christ's Grace did highly prize.

Still thirsting to obtain more full
 Assurance of God's Love:
And striving to be liker Christ 35
 And to the Saints above.
Although he was endu'ed with Gifts
 And Graces, more then many:
Yet he himself esteemed still
 More poor & vile then any. 40

In fruitless, empty, vain discourse,
 He took no good content:
But when he talk't of Heav'nly things,
 That seem'd his element.
There you might see his heart, & know 45
 What was his greatest Pleasure,
To speak & hear concerning Christ
 Who was his onely Treasure.

His constant self-denying frame,
 To all true saints his love, 50
His meekness, sweetness, Innocence
 And spirit of a Dove,
Let them be graven on our hearts
 And never be forgot.
The name of precious saints shall live, 55
 When wicked mens shall rot.

O Maldon, Maldon thou hast long
    Enjoy'd a day of Grace;
Thou hast a precious man of God
    Possessed in this place: 60
But for thy sin, thou art bereft
    Of what thou did'st possess;
Oh let thy sins afflict thee more
    Then do thy wants thee press.

Great strokes, Great Anger do proclaime,   65
    Great Anger, Greater sins.
We first provoke, before the Lord
    To punish us begins.
Good Lord awaken all our hearts
    By this most solemn stroke   70
To search for, finde out, and forsake
    Our sins that thee provoke.

Awake, awake, secure hard hearts;
    Do you not hear the Bell
That for your Pastours Funerall   75
    Soundeth a dolefull Knell?
You that would never hear not heed
    Th' instructions that he gave,
Me-thinks you should awake & learn
    One lesson at his Grave.   80

Repent, Repent, It's more then time
    The Harvest's well nigh past,
And Summer ended: but thy soul
    Not saved, first nor last.
The Belows they are burnt with fire,   85
    The Instruments are gone,
But still thy Lusts are unconsum'd:
    Read then thy Portion:

If that the founder melts in vain
    (Thy lusts do not decay)   90
God will account thee worthless Dross,
    Fit to be cast away.
Since words could not awaken us,
    God tries what blowes can do:
He strikes us on the head, & makes   95
    Us stagger to and fro.

Much more I might have said, but Time
    Will not the same permit.
Come let us put our mouths in Dust
    And down in Ashes sit.   100
The Lord hath giv'n us Gall to drink,
    And laid us in the Dust:
What shall we say? Behold we're vile,
    But thou, O Lord, art just.

If this, and such like awfull strokes   105
    Do not our hearts awaken,
Doubtless the Gospel will ere long
    Be wholly from us taken.
If we repent, return to God,
    Esteem his Gospell more,   110
Improve it better: then the Lord
    Hath Mercies yet in store.

Upon ye return of my dear friend Mr Foster
with his son out of captivity under ye Moors.

Probably composed in 1673

A Song of Praise to keep in remembrance
the loving kindness of ye Lord.

1

Come hither, hearken unto me,
    All ye that God do fear,
And what he hath done for my soul
    I will to you declare.
I to ye Lord fro my distress   5
    Did cry & he gave ear,
Out of Hell's belly I did cry,
    And he my prayer did hear.

2

I shall not die, but live, and shall
    The works of Jah declare: 10
The Lord did sorely chasten mee
    Yet mee from death did spare.
O set wide open unto mee
    The gates of righteousness.
I will go into them, & will   15
    The praise of Jah confess.

3

    Bless thou the Lord, my soul, & all
        In me, his holy name;
    Bless thou ye Lord, my soul, & all
        His boundless minde the same.   20
    With me together o do yee
        Jehovah magnify!
    And let us all herein agree
        To lift his name on high.

4

    The God hee of Salvation is   25
        That is our God most strong
    And to ye Lord Jehovah doth
        Issues of Death belong.
    The Right-hand of Jehovah is
        Exalted upon high: 30
    The Right-hand of Jehovah is
        A working valiantly.

5

    On Princes poure contempt doth Hee,
        Lays Tyrants in ye dust,
    Who proudly crush the innocent   35
        To satisfy their lust.
    He breaks ye teeth of cruel Beasts
        That raven for ye prey,
    Out of ye Lion's bloody jawes
        Hee plucks ye sheep away.   40

6

    Thou broken hast ye iron Barrs
        And loos'd ye fetters strong,
    Thou rescu'd hast ye poor-opprest
        From all that did them wrong.
    Out of ye Dungeon dark & deep   45
        Thou hast my soul set free;
    So long as I a being have
        My praise shall be of thee.

7

How beautiful Jehovah is
    Oh taste, & see likewise;   50
Oh great is that man's blessedness
    Whose trust on him relies!
Upon ye Lord for evermore
    See that your selves you stay,
For there is with Jehovah store   55
    Of strength that lasts for ay.

8

O love ye Lord all yee his saints,
    The faithful he doth guard,
But he unto proud doers grants
    A plentyfull reward.   60
Because ye Lord ye poor doth hear
    Nor 's prisoners doth despise,
Let Heav'n, earth, sea, him praise, and all
    That moves therein likewise.

Death *Expected and Welcomed*

Composed about 1705

Welcome, Sweet Rest, by me so long Desired,
Who have with Sins and Griefs, so long been tired.
And Welcome, Death, my Fathers Messenger;
Of my Felicity the Hastener.

Welcome, Good Angels, who for me Distrest,
Are come to Guard me to Eternal Rest.
Welcome, O Christ, who hast my Soul Redeemed;
Whose Favour I have more than Life Esteemed.

Oh! Do not now my Sinful Soul forsake,
But to thy self thy Servant Gathering take.
Into thine Hands I recommend my Spirit,
Trusting thro' Thee, Eternal Life to inherit.

A Farewel to the World

Composed about 1705

Now Farewel World, in which is not my Treasure;
I have in thee Enjoy'd but little pleasure.
And now I Leave thee, for a Better Place,
Where Lasting Pleasures are before Christ's Face.

    Farewel, Ye Sons of Men, who do not Savour   5
The Things of God; Who Little Prize his Favour.
Farewel, I way, with your *Fools Paradise*,
Until the King of Terrors you Surprise,
And bring you Trembling to Christ Judgment Seat,
To give Account of your Transgressions Great.   10

    Farewel, *New-England*, which have Long Enjoy'd
The Day of Grace, but hast most vainly toy'd,
And trifled with the Gospels Glorious Light;
Thou mayst Expect a dark *Egyptian* Night.

    Farewel, *Young* Brood and Rising Generation,   15
Wanton and Proud, Ripe for Gods Indignation;
Which neither you, nor others can prevent,
Except in Truth you Speedily Repent.

Farewel, Sweet Saints of God, Christs Little Number:
Beware; lest you, thro' Sloth Securely Slumber.   20
Stand to your Spiritual Arms, and keep your Watch,
Let not your Enemy you napping catch.
Take up your Cross, prepare for Tribulation,
Thro' which doth ly the way unto Salvation.
Love Jesus Christ, with all Sincerity: 25
Eschew Will-Worship and Idolatry.
Farewel again, until we all appear
Before our Lord, a *Well-done*, there to hear.

Farewel, Ye Faithful Servants of the Lord;
Painful Dispensers of His Holy Word;   30
From whose Communion and Society
I once was kept thro' long Infirmity;
This of my Sorrows was an Aggrevation;
But, Christ be Thanked, thro' whose Mediation,
I have at Length obtained Liberty   35
To dwell with Soul-delighting Company,
Where many of our Friends are gone before;
And you shall follow with a many more.
Mean while, stand fast, the Truth of God Maintain,
Suffer for Christ, and Great shall be your Gain.   40

Farewel, My Natural Friends and dear Relations,
Who have my Tryals seen and great Temptations;
You have no Cause to make for me great Moan;
My Death to you is Little Loss or none.
But unto me it is no Little Gain;   45
For Death at once frees me from all my Pain.
Make Christ your greatest Friend, who never dies;
All other Friends are fading Vanities.
Make Him your Light, your Life, your End, your All;
Prepare for Death, be Ready for his call.   50

Farewel, Vile Body Subject to Decay,
Which art with Lingring Sickness worn away.
I have by thee much Pain and Smart Endured;
Great Grief of Mind thou hast to me Procured;
Great Grief of Mind, by being Impotent, 55
And to Christs Work an awkward Instrument.
Thou shalt not henceforth be a clog to me,
Nor shall my Soul a Burden be to thee.
Rest in they Grave, until the Resurrection,
Then shalt thou be Revived in Perfection: 60
Endow'd with Wonderful Agilitie,
Cloathed with Strength, and Immortalitie;
With Shining Brightness, gloriously array'd,
Like to Christs glorious Body, glorious made.
Thus Christ shall thee again to me Restore, 65
Ever to Love with Him, and Part no more.
Mean while my Soul shall Enter into Peace,
Where Fears & Tears, where Sin & Smart shall cease.

APPENDICES

Appendix I

"I *Walk'd and did a little* Mole-hill *view*"

Probably Composed in the Early-1660s; Often Attributed to Wigglesworth

I *Walk'd and did a little* Mole-hill *view*
Full peopled with a most industrious crew
Of busie Ants, *where each one labour'd more*
Than if he were to bring home Indian *Ore*;
Here wrought the Pioneers, *there march'd the* Bands, 5
Here Colonies *went forth to plant new* Lands:
These hasted out, and those supplies brought in,
As if they had some sudden Seige *foreseen*:
Until there came an angry Spade, *and cast*
Country *and* People *to a* Pit *at last.*
                                                                            10

Again, I view'd a Kingdom *in a* Hive,
Where every one did work, *and so all* thrive;
Some go, some come, some war, some watch and ward,
Some make the works, and some the works do guard.
These frame their curious waxen cells, & those 15
Do into them their Nector *drops dispose*:
Until the greedy Gardner *brought his smoke,*
And, for the work, did all the workmen choke.

Lo here, frail Mortals may fit Emblems see
Of their great toil, and greater vanity. 20
They weary out their brain, their strength, their time,
While some to Arts, and some to Honours climb:
They search earths bowels, cross the roring seas,
Mortgage their Souls, and forfeit all their ease,
Grudge night her sleep, & lengthen out the day, 25
To fat these bags, & cram those chests with clay;
They rack and charm each creature to explore
Some latent Quintessence, *not known before*:
Torture and squeez out all its juice and blood,
To try if they can now find out the GOOD 30
Which Solomon *despair'd of, but at last*
On the same shore of Vanity *are cast*;
The spade stops their career of Pride *and* Lust,
And calls them from their Clay *unto their* Dust.
Leave off your Circles, Archimede, *away,* 35
The King *of* Terrour *calls, and will not stay*:
Miser, *kiss all your* Bags, *and then ly down*;
Scholar, *your* Books; Monarch, *yield up your* Crown:
Give way Wealth, Honour, Arts, Thrones; back, make room,
That these pale Souls *may come unto their doom.* 40

Nor shew vain men *the fruit of all that pain,*
Which in the end nothing but Loss *did* gain:
Compute your lives, *and all your* hours *up cast,*
Lo here's the total sum *of all at last.*

I rose up early, sat up late, to know 45
As much as man, as tongues, as books could show;
I toil'd to search all Science *and all* Art,
But died ignorant *of mine own* Heart.
I got great Honour, *and my* Fame *did stream*
As far as doth the Mornings shining Beam; 50
My Name *into a page of* Titles *swell'd,*
My head *a* Crown, *my* hand *a* Scepter *held*:
Ador'd without, but shameful lusts *within*;
Adorn'd with Titles, *but defil'd with* sin.

With anxious thoughts, with saddest cares & cost 55
I gain'd these Lordships, *and this* Soul *I lost*:
My greedy Heir now hovers o're my pelf,
I purchase Land *for him,* Hell *for my self.*
Go on you nobler Brains, *and fill your sight*
As full of Learning *as the Sun's of light*; 60
Expand your Souls to Truth *as wide as Day,*
Know all that Men, *know all that* Angels *say*:
Write shops of Volumns, *and let every* Book
Be fill's with lustre as was Moses *look*:
Yet know, all this is but a better kind 65
Of sublime vanity, *and more refin'd*:
Except a saving knowledge crown the rest,
Devils know more, and yet shall ne'r be blest.

Go on, ambitious Worms, *yet, yet aspire,*
Lay a sure Scene how you may yet rise higher: 70
March forward, Macedonian Horn, *add on*
Gaza *to* Tyre, Indies *to* Babylon;
Make stirrups *of the peoples* backs *and* bones,
Climb up by them to Diadems *and* Thrones:
Thy Crowns *are all but* grass; *thine was the* toil, 75
Thy Captains *come, and they divide the* spoil.
Except one heav'nly Crown crown all the rest,
Devils are Pontentates, and yet not blest.

Go on, base dunghil-souls, *heap gold as mire,*
Sweep silver as the dust, emulate Tyre, 80
Fill every Ware-house, purchase every Field,
Add house to house, Pelion *on* Ossa *build*:
Get Mida's *vote to transubstantiate*
Whate're you please all into golden plate;
Build wider barns, sing requiem *to your heart,* 85
Feel your wealths pleasures only, not their smart.
Except his Riches who for us was poor,
Do sweeten those which Mortals so adore;
Except sublimer wealth crown all the rest,
Devils have nobler Treasures, yet not blest. 90

*Cease then from Vain delights, & set your mind
That solid and enduring* GOOD *to find,
Which sweetens life and death, which will encrease
On an immortal Soul immortal peace;
Which will replenish and advance you higher* 95
Then e're your own ambition could aspire.
Fear your great Maker with a child-like aw,
Believe his Grace, love and obey his Law.
This is the total work of man, *and this
Will crown you here with* Peace, *and there with* Bliss. 100

*Be kind unto your selves, believe and try:
If not, go on, fill up your lusts and die.
Sing peace unto your selves;* 'twill once be known
Whose word shall stand, your Judg's *or your* own.
Crown thee with Rose-buds, *satiate thine eyes,* 105
Glut every sense with her own vanities:
*Melt into pleasures, until that which Lust
Did not before consume, rot into dust:
The* Thrones *are set, the* Books *will strait be read,*
Hell *with her souls, & gravs give up their dead:* 110
Then there will be (and the time is not far)
Fire *on the* Bench, *and* Stubble *at the* Bar.

*O sinners ruminate these thoughts agen,
You have been* Beasts *enough, at last be* Men.
Christ *yet intreats, but if you will not turn,* 115
Where grace will not convert, there fire will burn.

Appendix II

On the following Work, and It's Author.

**Prefatory Lines to the First and Subsequent
Editions of** *The Day of Doom*
By Jonathan Mitchell (1624-1668)

A Verse may find him who a Sermon flies,
Saith *Herbert* well. Great Truths to dress in Meeter;
Becomes a Preacher; who mens Souls doth prize,
That Truth in Sugar roll'd may taste the sweeter.
  No Cost too great, no Care too curious is   5
  To set forth Truth, and win mens Souls to bliss.

In Costly Verse, and most laborious Rymes,
Are dish't up here Truths worthy most regard:
No Toyes, nor Fables (Poets wonted Crimes)
Here be; but things of worth with Wit prepar'd.   10
  Reader, fall too; and if thy tast be good,
  Thou'lt praise the Cook, & say, 'Tis choicest Food.

David's affliction bred us many a *Psalm*;
From Caves, from mouth of Graves that Singer sweet
Oft tun'd his Soul felt Notes: For not in's Calm,   15
But Storms, to write most Psalms God made him meet;
  Affliction turn'd this Pen to Poetry,
  Whose serious strains do here before thee ly.

This Man with many griefs afflicted sore,
Shut up from speaking much in sickly Cave: 20
Thence painful leisure hath to write the more,
And sends thee Counsels from the mouth o'th' Grave.
    One foot i'th' other World long time hath been:
    Read, and thou'lt say, His heart is all therein.

Oh, happy Cave, that's to mount *Nebo* turn'd! 25
Oh, happy Pris'ner that's at liberty
To walk through th' other World! the Bonds are burn'd
(But nothing else) in Furnace fiery.
    Such Fires unfetter Saints, and set more free
    Their unscorch'd Souls for Christ's sweet companie. 30

Cheer on, sweet Soul, although in briny tears
Streept is thy seed, though dying every day;
Thy Sheaves shall joyful be, when Christ appears
To change our death and pain to life for ay.
    The weepers now shall laugh; the jovial laughter, 35
    Of vain ones here, shall turn to tears hereafter.

Judge right, and his restraint is our Reproof;
The Sins of Hearers, Preachers Lips do close,
And make that Tongue to cleave unto its roof,
Which else would check and cheer full freely those 40
    That need. But from this Eater comes some Meat,
    And sweetness good from this affliction great.

In these vast Woods a Christian Poet Sings
(Where whilome Heathen wild were only found)
Of things to come, the last and greatest things, 45
Which in our Ears aloud should ever sound.
    Of Judgment dread, Hell, Heaven, Eternity;
    Reader, think oft, and help thy thoughts hereby.

                                      J. Mitchel.

NOTES ON SOURCES, EDITIONS, AND TEXTS

The notes that follow indicate all emendations made by the present editor in poems based upon printed texts and all emendations and alterations made by Wigglesworth or the present editor in poems based upon existing manuscripts. Any who wish will thus be able to reconstruct the originals upon which the present texts are based.

As indicated above in "A Note on the Present Text of the Poems," the editor has preserved all irregularities and peculiarities of Wigglesworth's style in his transcription from printed texts and manuscripts -- as long as such preservation does not impede clear reading and understanding of the poems. This rule applies to spelling, capitalization, italicization, line indentation, and punctuation within all texts. Within previously printed texts, obvious typographical errors have been noted and corrected in this edition; also, the old-style "f" has been replaced by the modern "s", and no effort has been made to preserve ornamental lettering that sometimes decorated an opening word in a line of verse. Wigglesworth's inconsistent use of "then" and "than" has been preserved, as has his irregular use of the ampersand. The texts of *marginalia* are reproduced here as originally printed; however, biblical citations, initial capitals for opening words, and terminal punctuation with *marginalia*, all of which vary greatly in the originals, have been normalized according to current usage without notice below.

Within texts for which manuscripts are the source, Wigglesworth's superscript letters (as "e" in "y^e" and "r" in "o^r" [for "our"]) have been brought down to the line of text. His abbreviations have been printed in unabbreviated form (thus, "o^r" appears as "our"), but all abbreviations in the original are noticed below. For the conjunction "and", Wigglesworth variously wrote "and", used an ampersand, or used a scrawl flourish that might best be described as "a^d". His "and" and ampersands are preserved throughout; his flourish has been printed as "and" and noticed below. In the descriptions of manuscript alterations, "over" means "in the same space" and "right-hand margin" or "left-hand margin" indicates the location of margin-entries as found on the manuscript page relative to the viewer's position. Because Wigglesworth inconsistently wrote and had printed brackets ([ ]) for parentheses, all pairs of single brackets below ([ ]) are his; pairs of double brackets ([[ ]]) are the editor's. The presence of a caret is always noticed. Throughout, the expression "originally" signals Wigglesworth's or the editor's alterations, with the original as found indicated in single quotation marks. Wigglesworth and subsequent printers of his work neglected line numbers; thus, line numbers below and in the text are the editor's.

Following each heading below is a note on the source and location of each text used in this edition. Bibliographical information in the notes on sources may be verified by reference to Charles Evans, *The American Bibliography: A Chronological Dictionary of All Books, Pamphlets and Periodical Publications Printed in the USA, 1639-1800* (New York: P.

Smith, 1941-57); Roger Bristol, *Supplement to Charles Evans' American Bibliography* (Charlottesville: University Press of Virginia, 1970); O. M. Brack, Jr., "Michael Wigglesworth and the Attribution of 'I Walk'd and Did a Little Mole-Hill view [*sic*],' " *Seventeenth-Century News*, vol. 18, no. 3 (Fall 1970):41-44; Richard Crowder, *No Featherbed to Heaven: A Biography of Michael Wigglesworth, 1631-1705* (East Lansing: Michigan State University Press, 1962); John Ward Dean, "Appendix II: Editions of Wigglesworth's Poems," in *Memoir of Rev. Michael Wigglesworth*, 2nd ed. (Albany, N.Y.: Joel Munsell, 1871), pp. 140-151; Harold S. Jantz, *The First Century of New England Verse* (1943; rpt. New York: Russell & Russell, 1962); Matt B. Jones, "Notes for a Bibliography of Michael Wigglesworth's 'Day of Doom' and 'Meat Out of the Eater,' " *Proceedings of the American Antiquarian Society*, 39 (1929):77-84. On occasion, the present editor has deviated from standard assumptions held by Wigglesworth's bibliographers; those occasions are noted and explained below.

THE DAY OF DOOM, pp. 3-86

Source: The DAY of | DOOM: | OR, | A Poetical Description | OF | The GREAT and LAST | Judgement. | WITH | A *Short DISCOURSE* about | Eternity. | By Michael Wigglesworth, Teacher of the | Church at *Maldon* in *N.E.* | The Fifth Edition, enlarged with | *Scripture* and *Marginal Notes*. | [complete texts of Acts 17:31 and Matt. 24:30] | *Boston*: Printed by *B. Green*, and *J. Allen* | for *Benjamin Eliot*, at his Shop under the | West End of the Town-House. 1701.

Location: In the collections of the American Antiquarian Society, Worcester, Massachusetts, and the Houghton Library, Harvard University.

First printed in a run of 1,800 copies in Cambridge, Massachusetts, in 1662, the first edition of *The Day of Doom* was sold out within a year. A fragmentary copy in the collections of the New England Historic Genealogical Society, Boston, is believed to be the only extant copy of the first edition. Editions were printed in London in 1666, 1673, and 1687 without Wigglesworth's supervision or permission. These omit both "To the Christian Reader" and Jonathan Mitchell's "On the following Work, and It's Author" but include the controversial "I *Walk'd and did a little* Mole-hill *view*," which is printed in Appendix I above and discussed below in the "Notes on Sources, Editions, and Texts." No London edition has ever been considered authoritative; however, except for Brack and Bristol, bibliographers have tended to count the first two London editions as at least one of the four editions to precede the "fifth" American edition (Boston, 1701).

Incorporating evidence reported by Brack and substantiated by independent research, the most sensible account of the authoritative American editions of *The Day of Doom* published during Wigglesworth's life is this. When the first run of 1,800 copies had sold out in 1663, Samuel Green and Marmaduke Johnson, owners of the Cambridge press, probably undertook another printing of the volume late in 1663 or early in 1664. This printing, which one might assume to be a "second edition," was undertaken on their own authority (Wigglesworth was in Bermuda at this time) in an effort to capitalize on the remarkable popularity of the volume. Though no copies are known to exist, this edition is the probable source for the London editions (and, possibly, the misattributed "I *Walk'd and did a little* Mole-hill *view*"). A "third edition" (but not so entitled) was printed in Cambridge under Wigglesworth's supervision in 1666. This edition, of which fragmentary copies are in the collections of the American Antiquarian Society and the Massachusetts Historical Society, was enlarged from the first with scriptural and marginal apparatus. A "fourth edition" has long been assumed by all to have been printed in Cambridge in 1683; however, there is no evidence, fragmentary or otherwise, to verify its publication. Finally, a "fifth edition" (so entitled by Wigglesworth), the source for the present edition, was printed in Boston in 1701 under Wigglesworth's supervision. This edition, enlarged from previous editions with scriptural and marginal apparatus and notes, unquestionably represents the author's final intentions toward the work.

The Day of Doom continued to be a profitable venture for publishers long after Wigglesworth's death in 1705. An English edition was printed at Newcastle upon Tyne in 1711. In America, a "sixth edition" was published in Boston in 1715 under two imprints: "Boston: printed by John Allen for Benjamin Eliot, at his Shop in King-street. 1715" and "Boston: printed by John Allen for N. Boone, at the Sign of the Bible in Cornhill. 1715". A "Seventh Edition enlarged" appeared in 1751 under the imprint "Boston: printed and sold by Thomas Fleet, at the Heart and Crown in Cornhill. 1751." Abridged editions were printed in Norwich, Connecticut, in 1774 and 1777, and these were followed by complete editions printed in Newburyport in 1811, in Boston in 1828, and in New York City in 1867. The edition by the late Kenneth B. Murdock, The Day of Doom (New York: The Spiral Press, 1929), is the last printing of the complete volume. Basing his edition on the fifth edition (Boston, 1701), Murdock printed all poems from the original except for Jonathan Mitchell's introductory lines. Murdock's text, which is the source for most subsequent anthologized versions of "The Day of Doom" and "Vanity of Vanities," is generally faithful to the original, although Wigglesworth's punctuation and ampersand-use are regularized throughout without specific notice.

"To the Christian Reader," pp. 5-8.
line 27   Peru] originally 'Peru.'
      28   forebear;] originally 'forbear.'
      38   conceit,] originally 'conceit.'
      64   (Once and again)] originally '(Once and again)'
      73   Nor speak] not indented in the original

"The Day of Doom," pp. 11-66.
line 4   ay.] originally 'ay'
      17   Like as of old,] originally 'Like as of Gold'
      41   rush] originally 'cush'
      45   (they ... tears)] originally '[they ... tears)'
      58   Word,] originally 'Word.'
      62   see,] originally 'sae,'
      63   believe,] originally 'believe'
      65-66 (whose ... out-face)] originally '[whose ... out-face]'
      71   (fool hardiness)] originally '[fool hardiness]'
      93   (O ... blocks!)] originally '[O ... blocks!]'
      121 might,] originally 'might'
      125 (nor ... pen)] originally '[nor ... pen]'
      167 (To ... sad)] originally '[To ... sad]'
      172 woe,] originally 'woe.'
      195 (Gospel receivers)] originally '[Gospel receivers]'
      229 (sinful Crew)] originally '[sinful Crew]'
      250 were] originally 'where'

263	Ale-house haunters,]	originally 'Ale house-haunters,'
271	not,]	originally 'not'
297	Sheep,]	originally 'Sheep'
318	born,]	originally 'born.'
338	claim,]	originally 'claim'
348	free;]	originally 'free,'
364	me,]	originally 'me.'
372	declare:]	originally 'declare;'
383	bring:]	originally 'bring.'
477	Talents]	originally 'Tslents'
504	store.]	originally 'store,'
516	treasuries.]	originally 'treasuries'
522	hand,]	originally 'hand.'
528	scath.]	originally 'seath.'
532	misery. .]	originally 'misery'
544	these:]	originally 'these.'
566	last,]	originally 'last.'
644	hypocrites (in *marginalia*)]	originally 'hyporites'
664	neglected.]	originally 'neglected,'
684	known.]	originally 'known,'
687	perished,]	originally 'perished;'
699	35 (in *marginalia*)]	originally '55'
724	end.]	originally 'end'
744	offenders.]	originally 'offenders,'
801	wrath,]	originally 'wrath'
804	Believers,]	originally 'Believers'
812	carriages;]	originally 'carriages'
820	contemn.]	originally 'contemn'
901	pleasure,]	originally 'pleasure'
904	wickedness.]	originally 'wickedness,'
941	Judge:]	originally 'Judge;'
956	face.]	originally 'face'
974	studied,]	originally 'studied.'
978	reveals,]	originally 'reveals;'
982	you,]	originally 'you'
986	pleas;]	originally 'pleas'
999	durst]	originally 'dust'
1012	endure:]	originally 'endure.'
1026	me,]	originally 'me.'
1030	rather;]	originally 'rather.'
1124	draw.]	originally 'draw,'
1179	shall]	originally 'shall*', with asterisk keyed to 1 Sam. 2:15 in margin

1196 own.] originally 'own,'
1255 abus'd,] originally 'abus'd'
1305 well,] originally 'well'
1308 shown.] originally 'shown'
1337 he,] originally 'he'
1341 been,] originally 'been'
1342 our,] originally 'our'
1356 pass.] originally 'pass'
1392 reward?] originally 'reward,'
1519 (O ... cheer)] originally '[O ... cheer]'
1633 caitiff-hands,] originally 'caitiff-hands'
1676 endeth.] originally 'endeth'
1718 lins,] originally 'lins.'
1756 end:] originally 'end.'
1790 transcendency,] originally 'transcendency'

"A Short Discourse on Eternity," pp. 67-72.
line 75 (if ... destroy)] originally '[if ... destroy]'
98 propound;] originally 'propound;'
121 love,] originally 'love'
124 Sovereign,] originally 'Sovereign.'
127 (and ... then)] originally '[and ... then]'

"A Postscript unto the Reader," pp. 73-83.
line 34 Doom,] originally 'Doom.'
38 in;] originally 'in,'
40 Faith,] originally 'Faith.'
136 anger,] originally 'anger.'
160 remain;] originally ''remain,'
172 voice,] originally 'voice.'
173 roll'd,] originally 'roll'd'
174 fold;] originally 'fold.'
177 expire,] originally 'expire.'
198 told.] originally 'told,'
228 flesh,] originally 'flesh;'
229 late,] originally 'late.'
230 state:] originally 'state'
285 end,] originally 'end.'
303 say:] originally 'say'
322 shame;] originally 'shame.'
352 best:] originally 'best.'
364 iniquities,] originally 'iniquities;'

NOTES ON SOURCES, EDITIONS, AND TEXTS

    387   appeased,] originally 'appeased.'

"A Song of Emptiness," pp. 83-86.
line 27   gone,] originally 'gone.'
       69   Cares,] originally "Cares;'
       73   rest,] originally 'rest'
       74   Country-Clown,] originally 'Country-clown:'

GOD'S CONTROVERSY WITH NEW-ENGLAND, pp. 87-102

Source: Autograph manuscript.
Location: The collections of the Massachusetts Historical Society, Boston.
Previous publications of *God's Controversy with New-England* include the first printing of the poem, in the *Proceedings of the Massachusetts Historical Society*, 12 (1871-1873):83-93, where it is cited as having been given to the Society in the name of the Rev. Thomas J. Greenwood, and appearances in many anthologies of American literature since then. Anthologized versions of the poem, including the most recent, in Jane Donahue Eberwein, ed., *Early American Poetry* (Madison: University of Wisconsin Press, 1978), pp. 323-338, are often said to be based upon the manuscript or upon another text which was itself carefully derived from the manuscript. However, all publications of the poem inspected by the present editor retain errors and variations consistent with those found by the present editor between the manuscript and the first publication of the poem.

title   CONTROVERSY | 'SY' originally interlined above 'CONTROVER', its position indicated by a caret
line 1   Reader] originally 'Read^{r,}'
      20   Subtitle that follows, "New-England planted, . . . punished.", originally enclosed in a box
      39   forth] originally preceded by a canceled 'fo[[one undecipherable letter]]rth'
      44   following the stanza concluded by this line, the expression 'Over Casting' originally appears flush with the left-hand margin
      54   clay:] colon originally preceded by an uncanceled comma
      61   Heathen] 'a' originally interlined above 'Hethen', its position indicated by a caret
      63   o Lord,] originally followed by uncanceled, repetitive 'of fame' in the right-hand margin
      67   croutching] 't' originally interlined above 'crouching', its position indicated by a caret
      73   fierce and] originally preceded by canceled 'blind'; "and" originally 'a^{d,}'
      75   beasts (or] "(" originally written over a comma, presumably to cancel it
      87   For] "F" originally written over one undecipherable letter
      117   in two groups of four lines each, the eight lines from 117 to 124 are originally written lengthwise in the right-hand margin; their position in the text is indicated by 'Our Governor &c--------', which is inserted below line 116, and by line 125, which is written at the end of the margin-entry as 'Our Temp'rall blessings &c vid. supr.'
      117   Governour] originally 'Governo^{r,}'
      119   and] originally 'a^{d,}'

NOTES ON SOURCES, EDITIONS, AND TEXTS 311

157   the sequence of stanzas from line 157 to line 342 is written in a bold, labored script, presumably to represent the voice with which 'Th' Almighty thundring spake.' (line 156)
162   originally indented flush with lines that precede it
178   harm?] originally 'harm'
186   carcases] originally interlined with a caret above one undecipherable canceled word
216   same?] "?" originally written over a possible comma
234   never] originally preceded by canceled 'else'
250   and cry] "and" originally 'a^{d,}'
279   horrour] originally 'horro^{r,}'
288   and thoughts] "and" originally 'a^{d,}'
310   your] originally 'yo^{r,}'
324   and wicked] originally 'a^{d,}'
328   multitude] originally interlined above canceled 'younger out'
336   and awfull] "and" originally 'a^{d,}'
337   hearken ... your] 'e' originally interlined above 'harken', its position indicated by a caret; "your" originally 'yo^{r,}'
344   High] originally preceded by canceled 'h'
361   our] originally 'o^{r,}'
368   and more] "and" originally 'a^{d,}'
370   place] originally interlined above canceled 'house'
375   One] originally preceded by elevated, canceled 'On'
381   our] originally 'o^{r,}'
382   rod.] originally 'rod'
389   and hearts] "and" originally 'a^{d,}'
390   and anguish] "and" originally 'a^{d,}'
393   our] originally 'o^{r,}'
408   and excess] "and" originally 'a^{d,}'
410   and wantonness] "and" originally 'a^{d,}'
415   threatened] 'e' between 't' and 'n' originally interlined above 'threatened', its position indicated by a caret
431   originally the stanza beginning on line 431 is separated from the stanza that precedes it by a full-page rule and a four-line space
437   and turn] "and" originally 'a^{d,}'
442   and word] "and" originally 'a^{d,}'

MEAT OUT OF THE EATER, pp. 103-275

Source: MEAT | OUT OF THE EATER | OR | MEDITATIONS | Concerning | The Necessity, End, and Usefulness of | AFFLICTIONS | Unto GODs Children. | All tending to Prepare them *For*, and Comfort them *Under* the | *CROSS*. | By Michael Wigglesworth. | The Fourth Edition. | Boston. | Printed by R. P. for *John Usher*. 1689.

Location: In the Thomas Prince Collection at the Boston Public Library.

Completed in 1669, the first edition of *Meat Out of the Eater* was printed at the Cambridge, Massachusetts, press of Samuel Green in 1670; a unique, but mutilated, copy of that edition is preserved in the Beinecke Library at Yale University. No copies of the second or third editions, which are presumed to have been printed sometime between 1670 and 1689 (between the first and fourth editions), are known to exist. Except for the fourth edition cited above, all other printings of *Meat Out of the Eater* are posthumous and are thus of less authority than the fourth. This includes the fifth edition (and so entitled), which was printed in Boston in 1717 by J. Allen for booksellers N. Boone, Nicholas Buttolph, Benjamin Eliot, Thomas Fleet, and Robert Starke, and the sixth edition (and so entitled), which was printed in New London, Connecticut, in 1770 by T. Green for Seth White. Of Wigglesworth's major works, *Meat Out of the Eater* has been the most neglected and is the most inaccessible, there appearing to have been no additional complete editions of the volume between 1770 and the present edition.

"*Tolle Crucem*," Meditation I, pp. 107-109.
line 29 originally not indented flush with the line that precedes it
30 originally not indented flush with line 28
53 originally not indented flush with lines that precede and follow it

"Tolle Crucem," Meditation III, pp. 111-114.
line 2 Love,] originally 'Love' '
24 more.] originally 'more'
46 Aloe,] originally 'Aloe.'
70 over,] originally 'over.'

"Tolle Crucem," Meditation IV, pp. 114-117.
line 14 originally not indented flush with the line that precedes it
60 imitate.] originally 'imitate'
70 originally not indented flush with the line that precedes it
71 originally indented flush with the line that follows it

NOTES ON SOURCES, EDITIONS, AND TEXTS

    78   Gold;] originally 'Gold'
    86   Upbraid,] originally 'Upbraid'

"Tolle Crucem," Meditation V, pp. 118-120.
line 17   stanza 3 originally misnumbered '4'
        73   haste;] originally 'haste,'

"Tolle Crucem," Meditation VI, pp. 121-123.
line 12   assail:] originally 'assail.'
        60   sup.] originally 'sup,'

"Tolle Crucem," Meditation VII, pp. 123-128.
line   4   prosperous:] originally 'prosperous.'
        51   oil,] originally 'oil'
        84   And] originally 'and'
      108   worse.] originally 'worse,'
      129   originally not indented flush with the line that follows it
      137   stanza 18 originally unnumbered
      152   all.] originally 'all'

"Tolle Crucem," Meditation VIII, pp. 128-130.
line   8   originally indented flush with the line that precedes it
        35   Saint,] originally 'Saint'
        47   supports,] originally 'supports'

"Tolle Crucem," Meditation IX, pp. 130-135.
line   8   Was] originally 'was'
        25   wayes,] originally 'wayes.'
        46   him,] originally 'him;'
        88   May] originally 'may'
      126   Sin;] originally 'Sin,'
      127   offend, Self-ease] originally 'offend Self-ease,'
      132   i'th' evil] originally 'i'th evil'
      145   creature] originally 'creatnre'

"Tolle Crucem," Meditation X, pp. 136-137.
line 30   ye,] originally 'ye'
        35   *Kedar's*] originally '*Kedar*'s'

"Tolle Crucem," "A Conclusion Hortatory," pp. 138-142.
line 30   unto] originally 'uhto'
        60   command.] originally ''command,'
        89   originally not indented flush with the line that follows it

      96   mourners.] originally 'mourners,'
     108   appease.] originally 'appease,'

"Light in Darkness," Song I, pp. 146-148.
line 28   way;] originally 'way,'
      39   God,] originally 'God,,'

"Light in Darkness," Song II, pp. 148-150.
line 41   falls,] originally 'falls.'

"Light in Darkness," Song III, pp. 150-154.
line   3   be] originally 'be.'
       5   long,] originally 'long'
       6   fear,] originally 'fear'
       9   Were] originally 'Where'
      31   originally indented flush with lines that precede and follow it
      38   Banished,] originally 'Banished'
     128   space).] originally 'space)'
     136   Or] originally 'Our'

"Light in Darkness," Song IV, pp. 155-158.
line   1   'Tis] originally 'Tis'
      66   despise,] originally 'despise'

"Light in Darkness," Song V, pp. 159-161.
line 14   rejects,] originally 'rejects.'

"Light in Darkness," Song VII, pp. 163-166.
line   1   may] originally 'May'
      10   Into] originally 'into'
      56   brief:] originally 'brief;'
      74   part:] originally 'part'
      97   fast,] originally 'fast.'

"Light in Darkness," Song VIII, pp. 166-169.
line   3   darts,] originally 'darts;'

"Light in Darkness," Song IX, pp. 170-171.
line   7   thee] originally missing, but required by sense and meter
      45   indentations of lines 45 and 46 are originally reversed
      46   mind] originally 'mid'

NOTES ON SOURCES, EDITIONS, AND TEXTS   315

"Light in Darkness," Song X, pp. 172-175.
line 35   make,] originally 'make.'
      40   rul'd] originally 'rul.d'
      60   originally not indented flush with lines that precede it
      62   originally not indented flush with lines that precede and follow it
     110   originally not indented flush with lines that precede and follow it

"Sick mens Health," introductory lines, p. 177.
line 10   heal] originally 'heal.'

"Sick mens Health," Meditation I, pp. 178-180.
line 28   Coat.] originally 'Coat'

"Sick mens Health," Meditation II, pp. 180-182.
line 25   punish'd] originally 'punish d'

"Sick mens Health," Meditation III, pp. 182-185.
line 20   'Gainst] originally 'Gainst'
      52   Antidote.] originally 'Antidote,'
      74   vain;] originally 'vain.'

"Sick mens Health," Meditation IV, pp. 185-188.
line 12   He'l] originally 'He l'

"Strength in Weakness," Song I, pp. 190-193.
line   4   grass.] originally 'grass'

"Strength in Weakness," Song II, pp. 193-195.
line   4   then I.] originally 'then I'

"Strength in Weakness," Song III, pp. 195-198.
line   3   works:] originally 'works'

"Poor mens Wealth," Meditation II, pp. 205-206.
line 13   originally not indented flush with lines that precede and follow it

"Poor mens Wealth," Meditation III, pp. 206-209.
line 30   need,] originally 'need;'
      48   he'll] originally 'he ll'

"Poor mens Wealth," Meditation V, pp. 212-214.
line 50   On] originally 'O'

"In Confinement Liberty," Song I, pp. 216-218.
line   33   Chains,]   originally 'Chains;'

"In Confinement Liberty," Song II, pp. 219-220.
line   25   broke,]   originally 'broke;'

"In Confinement Liberty," Song III, pp. 221-222.
line   12   night,]   originally 'night.'
       34   Stocks,]   originally 'Stocks;'
       56   wayes.]   originally 'wayes'

"In Solitude Good Company," introductory lines, p. 223.
line   10   Religion]   originally 'Reigion'

"In Solitude Good Company," Song I, pp. 224-228.
line   1   Song I originally untitled
       12   away.]   originally 'away'
       14   You all]   originally 'Youall'
       24   dayes.]   originally 'dayes,'
       64   They're]   originally 'Theyr'e'
       71   indeed:]   originally 'indeed.'
       72   are.]   originally 'are:'
       105   originally not indented flush with the line that follows it
       116   known.]   originally 'known,'
       119   thee]   originally 'the'
       120   miss.]   originally 'miss,'

"In Solitude Good Company," Song II, pp. 228-230.
line   13   Would'st]   originally 'Would st'
       44   smart.]   originally 'heart.', but changed to accord with sense
       51   he'll]   originally 'he ll'

"In Solitude Good Company," Song III, pp. 231-233.
line   47   foremost,]   originally 'foremost'
       51   thee]   originally 'the'
       58   sufferings,]   originally 'sufferings'

"Joy in Sorrow," introductory lines, pp. 235-236.
line   24   when ... begun.]   originally 'ween ... begun'

"Joy in Sorrow," Song I, pp. 237-239.
line   4   allay.]   originally 'allay'
       8   Brings,]   originally 'Brings'

NOTES ON SOURCES, EDITIONS, AND TEXTS

    10   th' Effect] originally 'th Effect'
    12   neglect.] originally 'neglect,'
    14   Grief,] originally 'Grief'
    18   them;] originally 'them'
    25   him,] originally 'him.'
    28   again.] originally 'again,'
    33   heaviness,] originally 'heaviness.'
    36   Cross?] originally 'Cross,'
    73   out;] originally 'out'
    74   Blood,] originally 'Blood'
    78   sin,] originally 'sin.'

"Joy in Sorrow," Song II, pp. 240-242.
line   8   Head.] originally 'Head'
    20   smart.] originally 'smart,'
    40   comfortless.] originally 'comfortless,'

"Joy in Sorrow," Song III, pp. 242-244.
line   4   free.] originally 'free,'
    39   suff'rings] originally 'suff rings'

"Joy in Sorrow," Song IV, pp. 244-248.
line   6   bemoan,] originally 'bemoan'
    41   Peace,] originally 'Peace.'
    42   Saints,] originally 'Saints.'
    48   brother.] originally 'brother,'
    81   stanza 11 originally misnumbered '12'

"Joy in Sorrow," Song V, pp. 249-250.
line   12   remorse.] originally 'remorse,'
    16   smart?] originally 'smart.'
    22   th' wicked ... distrest,] originally 'th wicked ... distrest'
    36   relieve.] originally 'relieve,'
    39   thee;] originally 'thee,'
    42   state,] originally 'state'
    51   Christ,] originally 'Christ'

"Life in Deaths," introductory lines, p. 251.
line   2   *Death*,] originally '*Death*'

"Life in Deaths," Song I, pp. 252-254.
line   2   Saints:] originally 'Saints.'

22   fro,]   originally 'fro'
30   would,]   originally 'would'
32   should.]   originally 'should,'
50   Honour, . . . Wealth;]   originally 'Honour . . . Wealth,'

"Life in Deaths," Song II, pp. 254-256.
line   7   Sloth, or Worldiness,]   originally 'Sloth or Worldiness'
       12 grief.]   originally 'grief,'
       43 Host,]   originally 'Host.'
       50 side,]   originally 'side'

"Life in Deaths," Song III, pp. 256-258.
line   17 Losses,]   originally 'Losses'
       27 endure]   originally 'endure.'
       28 pain?]   originally 'pain'
       57 where is]   originally 'whereis'

"Heavenly Crowns for Thorny Wreaths," Song I, pp. 261-263.
line   41 Mother,]   originally 'Mother'
       43 Lands, Estate,]   originally 'Lands Estate'
       44 makes,]   originally 'makes'
       60 spend.]   originally 'spend'
       63 'Tis . . . Suff'ring]   originally 'Tis . . . Suff ring'

"Heavenly Crowns for Thorny Wreaths," Song III, pp. 266-268.
line   21 crown'd]   originally 'crown d'
       44 His]   originally 'Mis'
       54 scord'd,]   originally 'scorn'd'
       55 advanced,]   originally 'advanced'

"Heavenly Crowns for Thorny Wreaths," Song IV, pp. 268-271.
line   67 I'th' Mount . . . shine,]   originally 'I'th Mount . . . shine.'
       79 originally indented flush with lines that precede and follow it
       83 wage,]   originally 'wage'
       85 run,]   originally 'run.'

"Heavenly Crowns for Thorny Wreaths," Song V, pp. 271-275.
line   60 bestown,]   originally 'bestown.'
       61 us]   originally 'us.'
       62 pace,]   originally 'pace.'
       63 speed,]   originally 'speed.'
       72 while.]   originally 'while'

87	fades,]	originally 'fades'
88	chance.]	originally 'chance'
95	are,]	originally 'are'

OCCASIONAL VERSE

Title: Latin and English Verses Composed about 1660, p. 279
Source: Cotton Mather, *A Faithful Man, Described and Rewarded* (Boston: Printed by B. Green, for *Benj. Eliot* . . . , 1705), pp. 42-43.
Location: The Houghton Library, Harvard University.
Extracted from Wigglesworth's "Memorials of Piety, Left behind . . . among his Written Experiences," these verses were used by Mather to "flesh out" Wigglesworth's pious character in the funeral sermon he preached before the poet's Malden congregation. These verses have never been incorporated into editions of Wigglesworth's poetry.

Title: "When as the wayes of Jesus Christ," pp. 280-281
Source: Autograph manuscript in the "Ewer Manuscripts" collection.
Location: The New England Historic Genealogical Society, Boston.
"When as the wayes of Jesus Christ" was first published in *The New-England Historical & Genealogical Register*, 26 (1872):12, by John Ward Dean. At the time of publication, Dean, Wigglesworth's biographer and librarian of the Society, observed, the "handwriting shows that these lines were written at an earlier period than the elegy [on Benjamin Bunker]," which was published in the same issue of the *Register* and is discussed below. Dean did not suggest a date of composition nor did Jantz in his bibliography of Wigglesworth's writings; however, Crowder, in *No Featherbed to Heaven* (p. 284), offered 1665 as an approximate date. The present editor concurs with that estimate, for the tone, content, and style of the poem provide evidence that it is a transitional piece between *God's Controversy with New-England* and several of the meditations and songs collected in *Meat Out of the Eater*.

line 2   precise,] originally 'precise'
     41   Shepheards] 'e' originally interlined above 'Shephards', its position indicated by a caret
     48   neere.] originally 'neere'

Title: "Upon the much Lamented Death of . . . Benjamin Buncker . . . ", pp. 282-285
Source: Autograph manuscript in "Ewer Manuscripts" collection.
Location: The New England Historic Genealogical Society, Boston.
Wigglesworth's elegy on Benjamin Bunker was probably composed shortly after Bunker's death on February 3, 1669/70. It is surprising that the elegy was not published at the time, for Wigglesworth had access to a publisher (*Meat Out of the Eater* was then in press) and Bunker, who was well-liked and had served the Malden congregation as Wigglesworth's associate for nearly six years, was obviously a fit subject for this particular poetic form, which was then becoming

NOTES ON SOURCES, EDITIONS, AND TEXTS   321

increasingly popular.

The elegy was first published in the *Puritan Recorder*, a Congregational newspaper published in Boston, on October 11, 1855. Dean Dudley of Boston provided the transcript for that occasion. Subsequently, a transcript of the elegy was prepared by Aaron Sargent of Somerville, Massachusetts, and published in a Malden newspaper. Finally, in 1872, John Ward Dean printed his own transcript of the elegy together with "When as the wayes of Jesus Christ" (discussed above) in *The New-England Historical & Genealogical Register*, 26 (1872):11-12.

title		Christ,] originally 'Christ'
title		pastour] originally 'pasto^r'
line	4	i'th' word] originally 'ith' word'
	12	sp'rite,] originally 'sp'rite.'
	24	Been] originally 'been'
	33	full] originally 'full:'
	48	Treasure.] originally 'Treasure:'
	62	did'st] 's' originally written over a third 'd', presumably to cancel it; the apostrophe originally inserted above the 's'
	62	possess;] originally misspelled 'possessess'; the second 'ess' is canceled and the semicolon is inserted after the cancelation
	67	provoke,] originally preceded by an asterisk, which is keyed to 'offend' in the left-hand margin
	76	Soundeth] originally 'soundeth'
	81	It's] originally 'Its'
	88	Portion:] originally 'Portion;'
	110	more,] originally 'more'

Title: "Upon ye return of . . . Mr Foster and his son out of captivity . . .", pp. 286-288
Source: *American Historical Record*, 1 (1871):393.

William Foster (d. 1698), a shipmaster out of Charlestown, Massachusetts, and his son, Isaac (c. 1652-1682), were taken captive by the Turks in 1671 and released in 1673. This "Song of Praise" was probably composed shortly after their return to New England in November, 1673. The poem was circulated in manuscript, but despite popular interest in the plight of the Fosters, it was not printed for nearly two centuries. Cotton Mather memorialized the Fosters' fate in his life of John Eliot, *The Triumphs of the Reformed Religion, in America* (Boston, 1691), pp. 44-45, a work that he later incorporated into his *Magnalia Christi Americana*, but he made no reference to Wigglesworth's poem. When the poem was finally published, the text was based on a transcription by John Ward Dean. The original has not been located and is presumed lost.

title		with] originally 'wth'
line	18	name;] originally 'name'
	33	Hee,] originally 'Hee'
	34	dust,] originally 'dust'
	38	prey,] originally 'prey'

46	free;]	originally 'free'
50	likewise;]	originally 'likewise'
54	your ... stay,]	originally 'yor ... stay'
56	that]	originally "y^{t,}
57	saints,]	originally 'saints'
58	guard,]	originally 'guard'
62	despise,]	originally 'despise'

Title: "Death *Expected* and *Welcomed*," p. 289
Source: Cotton Mather, *A Faithful Man, Described and Rewarded* (Boston: Printed by B. Green, for *Benj. Eliot* ... , 1705), p. 45.
Location: The Houghton Library, Harvard University.

As with the Latin and English verses discussed above, "Death *Expected* and *Welcomed*" was extracted by Mather from Wigglesworth's "Memorials of Piety." Unlike the dating of those earlier poems and of "A Farewel to the World" (discussed below), the dating of these twelve lines is difficult to establish with certainty. In tone, for instance, the poem resembles Wigglesworth's occasional dramatic monologues collected in *Meat Out of the Eater*, and, of course, it is not unreasonable to imagine Wigglesworth contemplating death during any of his many years of illness. Nevertheless, this poem and the one that follows it in Mather's work have a ring of mortal finality about them, so it is likely that both were composed during Wigglesworth's last years. Together, they were reprinted in the sixth (Boston, 1715) and subsequent editions of *The Day of Doom*.

Title: "A Farewel to the World," pp. 290-292
Source: Cotton Mather, *A Faithful Man, Described and Rewarded* (Boston: Printed by B. Green, for *Benj. Eliot* ... , 1705), pp. 46-48.
Location: The Houghton Library, Harvard University.

The tone and content of "A Farewel to the World" unquestionably place the composition of the poem during Wigglesworth's last years -- in 1704 or early in 1705. Progressively weakened by a variety of disorders, Wigglesworth finally succumbed to a fever, which began during the last week of May, 1705. This poem, which Mather appropriately thought summarized Wigglesworth's attitude toward the relation between this world and the next, is a poet-teacher's "swan song" for his congregation and his audience and evidences both the vigor and the variety of Wigglesworth's early poetic efforts. With "Death *Expected* and *Welcomed*," it was reprinted in the sixth (Boston, 1715) and subsequent editions of *The Day of Doom*.

NOTES ON SOURCES, EDITIONS, AND TEXTS 323

APPENDIX I

Title: "I *Walk'd and did a little* Mole-hill *view*," pp. 295-298
Source: *The Day of Doom*: Or, A *Description of the Great and Last Judgment* . . . (London: Printed by *W. G.* for *John Sims* . . . , 1673), pp. 68 [misnumbered 70]-71.
Location: The Houghton Library, Harvard University.

Untitled in the original, these 116 lines have been the subject of controversy in recent years. Printed only in the London editions of *The Day of Doom* which were published during Wigglesworth's life, the lines were not incorporated into any known American editions of *The Day of Doom*. It may be that American publishers, lacking any concrete evidence that the poem was Wigglesworth's, chose to ignore the poem in the unauthoritative London editions. More likely, as Brack hypothesizes, the poem did appear in one American edition, the now-lost 1663/64 edition of *The Day of Doom*, which was printed without Wigglesworth's knowledge or permission by his Cambridge publisher and which is itself the source for the London editions. Brack theorizes that when Wigglesworth revised *The Day of Doom* for American publication in 1666, he deleted this poem from the 1663/64 printing, to which it had been supplied by the publisher or a friend of Wigglesworth's, believing that the poem was his. Murdock completely ignored the issue in 1929, printing only the poems by Wigglesworth that appeared in the Boston, 1701, edition. Crowder and Jantz both assume the poem to be Wigglesworth's, though Crowder does recognize that it is quite unlike anything that Wigglesworth ever wrote and, he observed, "much better poetry than almost anything [he] left behind" (*No Featherbed to Heaven*, p. 151). Most recently, Robert Daly entered the debate, writing in *God's Altar: The World and the Flesh in Puritan Poetry* (Berkeley, Los Angles, and London: University of California Press, 1978) that it would be "uncharitable as well as unscholarly to deprive Wigglesworth of what might be his most naturalistic poem" (p. 241*n*). After studying all evidence on all sides, the present editor concurs with the judgment fully expressed and documented by Brack: the poem is almost certainly not Wigglesworth's.

line 12   *one*] originally '*own*'
      18   *workmen*] originally '*morkmen*'
      25   *night*] originally '*nighnt*'
      26   *clay*;] originally '*clay*,'

APPENDIX II

Title: Jonathan Mitchell's "On the following Work, and It's Author," pp. 299-300
Source: The fifth edition of *The Day of Doom* (Boston, 1701), as described above.

Jonathan Mitchell's recommendatory poem appeared in the first and subsequent editions of *The Day of Doom*. Placed between "To the Christian Reader" and "A Prayer unto Christ . . . ", the poem makes explicit reference to two significant aspects of Wigglesworth's work: its sermonic aspect and its origin in the author's desire to teach "plain truth" to his congregation.

NOTES TO INTRODUCTION

¹Biographical information on Michael Wigglesworth presented in both the "Introduction" and "Chronology" has been drawn from several sources. Essential primary sources include: "Autobiography [of Michael Wigglesworth]," in John Ward Dean, *Memoir of Rev. Michael Wigglesworth, Author of The Day of Doom*, 2nd ed. (Albany, N.Y.: Joel Munsell, 1871), pp. 135-39; "[Michael Wigglesworth's] Commonplace Book," in manuscript at the New England Historic Genealogical Society, Boston; *The Diary of Michael Wigglesworth, 1653-1657: The Conscience of a Puritan*, ed. Edmund S. Morgan (1951, 1965; rpt. Gloucester, Mass.: Peter Smith, 1970); and these published letters and memoranda: "Wigglesworth to the Church at Malden, June 19, 1658," in *Proceedings of the Massachusetts Historical Society*, 12 (1871-73): 93-98; "Increase Mather to Michael Wigglesworth, May 8 and May 12, 1679," in *Collections of the Massachusetts Historical Society*, 4th ser., 8 (1868): 94-96; "Wigglesworth to Increase Mather, October 27, 1684," in *Collections of the Massachusetts Historical Society*, 4th ser., 8 (1868): 645; "Wigglesworth to Increase Mather, July 22, 1704," in *Collections of the Massachusetts Historical Society*, 4th ser. 8 (1868): 645-47. Secondary sources, dealing principally with Wigglesworth's biography and with contemporaneous reports of his activities in Malden, include: Deloraine P. Corey, *The History of Malden, Massachusetts, 1633-1785* (Malden: Pub. by the Author, 1899); Richard Crowder, *No Featherbed to Heaven: A Biography of Michael Wigglesworth, 1631-1705* (East Lansing: Michigan State University Press, 1962); John Ward Dean, *Memoir of Rev. Michael Wigglesworth, Author of The Day of Doom*, 2nd ed. (Albany, N.Y.: Joel Munsell, 1871); Cotton Mather, *A Faithful Man, Described and Rewarded* (Boston, 1705); [Cotton Mather,] *The Diary of Cotton Mather*, ed. Worthington Chauncey Ford, 2 vols. (1911-12; rpt. New York: Frederick Ungar Publishing Co., 1957); [Samuel Sewall,] *The Diary of Samuel Sewall, 1674-1729*, ed. M. Halsey Thomas, 2 vols. (New York: Farrar, Straus and Giroux, 1973). For accessible biographical and bibliocritical essays on Wigglesworth, see Ronald A. Bosco, "Michael Wigglesworth," in *American Writers before 1800: A Biographical and Critical Dictionary*, ed. James A. Levernier and Douglas R. Wilmes, 3 vols. (Westport, Conn.: Greenwood Press, 1983), 3:1589-93; John Langdon Sibley, *Biographical Sketches of Graduates of Harvard University . . . 1642-1658* (Cambridge, Mass.: Charles William Sever, 1873), pp. 259-86; and William B. Sprague, *Annals of the American Pulpit; or Commemorative Notices of Distinguished American Clergymen of Various Denominations*, 7 vols. (New York: Robert Carter & Brothers, 1866), 1:143-46.

²Cotton Mather, *A Faithful Man, Described and Rewarded*, p. 48.

³For a complete history of all previous publication of Wigglesworth's poetry, see "Notes on Sources, Editions, and Texts."

⁴Nathaniel Hawthorne's assumption of guilt for the excesses of his Puritan ancestors, who came to the New World armed, as he stated in "The Custom House," with Bible and sword, and his contempt for the repressiveness of Puritan culture are well known to readers of *The Scarlet Letter*, "Ethan Brand," "The May-Pole of Merry Mount," "The Minister's Black Veil," and "Young

Goodman Brown." Emerson held views comparable to Hawthorne's -- and for much the same reasons. From 1721 to 1767, Joseph Emerson (1700-1767), Ralph Waldo's great-grandfather, served in the Malden pulpit once occupied by Wigglesworth. Parson Emerson's sermons, which are noteworthy largely for their plain-spoken threats of fire and brimstone and their perpetuation of Calvinist themes such as the complete depravity of man, and the culture they appealed to were absolutely incompatible with the younger Emerson's idealistic philosophy, "Transcendentalism," and his romantic belief in "self-reliance." Although Ralph Waldo did not write fiction, in his journals he repeatedly execrated the Calvinist bias inherent in American Puritanism as a barbaric influence that destroyed originality and character. See Joel Porte, ed., *Emerson in His Journals* (Cambridge: Harvard University Press, 1982), pp. 77, 82ff.

[5]Samuel Kettell, ed., Specimens of *American Poetry with Critical and Biographical Notices*, 3 vols. (Boston: S. G. Goodrich, 1829), 1:iii.

[6]Rufus Wilmot Griswold, ed., *The Poets and Poetry of America*, 11th ed. (Philadelphia: A. Hart, 1852), pp. xvii, xxviii.

[7]Moses Coit Tyler, *A History of American Literature*, 1607-1765 (1878; rpt. Ithica, N.Y.: Cornell University Press, 1949), pp. 227-29.

[8]*Ibid.*, p. 248.

[9]*Ibid.*, pp. 276-77, 280.

[10]Kenneth B. Murdock, ed., *Handkerchiefs from Paul* (Cambridge: Harvard University Press, 1927), pp. lxii, lxiv.

[11]Kenneth B. Murdock, ed., *The Day of Doom* (New York: The Spiral Press, 1929), p. x.

[12]*Ibid.*, p. viii.

[13]*Ibid.*, p. ix.

[14]*Ibid.*, p. x.

[15]*Ibid.*, pp. x-xi.

[16]F.O. Matthiessen, "Michael Wigglesworth, A Puritan Artist," *New England Quarterly*, I (October 1928): 493-504.

[17]Harold S. Jantz, *The First Century of New England Verse* (1943; rpt. New York: Russell & Russell, 1962), pp. 50-51.

[18]Hyatt H. Waggoner, *American Poets from the Puritans to the Present* (Boston: Houghton Mifflin Co., 1968).

[19]Donald Barlow Stauffer, *A Short History of American Poetry* (New York: E. P. Dutton & Co., 1974), pp. 23-25.

[20]Robert Daly, *God's Altar: The World and the Flesh in Puritan Poetry* (Berkeley: University of California Press, 1978), p. 133.

[21]*Ibid.*, pp. 131-32, 134.

[22]Harrison T. Meserole, ed., *Seventeenth-Century American Poetry* (New York: New York University Press, 1968); Kenneth Silverman, ed., *Colonial American Poetry* (New York: Hafner Publishing Co., 1968).

[23]*Ibid.*, p. 41.

[24]Recently, a number of important articles have appeared which employ this strategy and may well contribute to a revival of scholarship on Wigglesworth; see Jeffrey A. Hammond, " 'Ladders of

Your Own': *The Day of Doom* and the Repudiation of 'Carnal Reason,' " *Early American Literature*, 19, no. 1 (Spring 1984): 42-67, and Alan H. Pope, "Petrus Ramus and Michael Wigglesworth: The Logic of Poetic Structure," in *Puritan Poets and Poetics: Seventeenth-Century American Poetry in Theory and Practice*, ed. Peter White (University Park: Pennsylvania State University Press, 1985), pp. 210-26. In *Puritan Poets and Poetics*, see also the following essays, which incorporate considered discussion of Wigglesworth into their larger contexts: Karen E. Rowe, "Prophetic Visions, Typology and Colonial American Poetry," pp. 47-66, and Ursula Brumm, "Meditative Poetry in New England," pp. 318-36.

[25] For recent, accessible accounts of Puritan covenant theory and of declension, see Harry S. Stout, *The New England Soul: Preaching and Religious Culture in Colonial New England* (New York: Oxford University Press, 1986), and the editors' introductions to *The Puritans in America: A Narrative Anthology*, ed. Alan Heimert and Andrew Delbanco (Cambridge: Harvard University Press, 1985), and *The Puritan Sermon in America, 1630-1750*, ed. Ronald A. Bosco, 4 vols. (New York: Scholars' Facsimiles & Reprints, Inc., 1978).

Although all scholars agree that an understanding of covenant theology is essential to an understanding of the Puritan experience in the New World, scholars are divided with respect to the reality of declension, with some holding the position that declension was an actual, measurable fact of experience in Puritan times and others holding the position that declension was only a rhetorical conviction used primarily by the ministry to keep New Englanders on the straight and narrow path of righteousness. For illuminating discussions by those holding the first position, see Emory Elliott, *Power and the Pulpit in Puritan New England* (Princeton: Princeton University Press, 1975); Perry Miller, *The New England Mind: From Colony to Province* (1953; rpt. Boston: Beacon Press, 1961); Darrett B. Rutman, *Winthrop's Boston: A Portrait of a Puritan Town, 1630-1649* (1965: rpt. New York, 1972). For evidence supportive of the second position, see Robert G. Pope, "New England Versus the New England Mind: The Myth of Declension," *Journal of Social History*, 3 (1969): 95-108, and Philip J. Greven, *The Protestant Temperament: Patterns of Child-Rearing, Religious Experience, and the Self in Early America* (New York: Knopf, 1977). As will be apparent throughout the "Introduction," the present writer takes the position that declension was a very definite reality in Puritan New England and that Wigglesworth's poetry was, in large part, a magisterial attempt to curb the progress of declension among New England's third and fourth generations.

[26] For details of fast and humiliation observances in New England, see Ronald A. Bosco, ed., *The Puritan Sermon in America, 1630-1750*, 1:xxi-l; for the frequency of fast and humiliation observance in New England, see William de Loss Love, "Fast and Thanksgiving Day Calendar," *The Fast and Thanksgiving Days of New England* (Boston: Houghton, Mifflin, 1895), pp. 465-514.

[27] From the *Cambridge Platform* (1648) as quoted in John Ward Dean, *Memoir of Rev. Michael Wigglesworth*, p. 52.

[28] Cotton Mather, *A Faithful Man, Described and Rewarded*, pp. 24-25.

[29] Edmund S. Morgan, ed., *The Diary of Michael Wigglesworth, 1653-1657*, p. 51.

[30] See note 1, above.

A NOTE ON THE PRINTING

This book was printed on a Hewlett Packard LaserJet+ printer using Microsoft Word version 4.0 for word processing. The typeface is Hewlett Packard's version of Times Roman. The design and input were produced by Cathie Gifford, Key Information Processing, Albany, New York.